BIRD
MEDICINE

"Evan Pritchard has put together a wonderful book showing how we mammals have learned and still learn from birds. History, history, history! And future possibilities."

PETE SEEGER, AMERICAN FOLKSINGER

"*Bird Medicine* is wise, informative, folksy, and eminently readable. The narratives are clear and detailed, and Mr. Pritchard, noted scholar and author on Native American cultures, has the credibility to present them, being both a traditional 'insider' and an accredited Western scholar. Even more important, this volume fills a major gap in our knowledge of the natural myths of the Americas. I can see this book becoming required reading for secondary schools all over the country."

E. H. RICK JAROW, PH.D., PROFESSOR OF RELIGIOUS STUDIES
AT VASSAR COLLEGE, FORMER MELLON FELLOW
IN THE HUMANITIES AT COLUMBIA UNIVERSITY, AND
AUTHOR OF *IN SEARCH OF THE SACRED*
AND *CREATING THE WORK YOU LOVE*

"*Bird Medicine* is a beautifully blended culmination of the sacred and the scientific. With content ranging from the ornithological to the philosophical, from the historical to the heartwarming and humorous, *Bird Medicine* delivers a satisfying array that entertains as much as it enlightens."

AMY KROUT-HORN, AUTHOR OF *MY FATHER'S BLOOD*
AND COAUTHOR OF *TRANSCENDENCE*

"Birds have many practical and transformative things to say to us if we will only listen. Evan Pritchard has fashioned a masterwork of insight and inspiration distilling the wisdom of these winged spiritual teachers as interpreted by Native Americans in stories and rituals."

FREDERIC AND MARY ANN BRUSSAT, COAUTHORS OF
SPIRITUAL LITERACY: READING THE SACRED IN EVERYDAY LIFE
AND PUBLISHERS OF SPIRITUALITY & PRACTICE

"Eagles, ravens, hawks, owls, crows, and other birds have always played a crucial role in Native American shamanism. In this remarkable book Evan Pritchard demonstrates why these spiritual traditions consider birds to be sacred, giving numerous historical accounts, personal stories, and traditional legends that illustrate the special place that birds have in the hearts and minds of tribal men and women. Pritchard is a master storyteller; each of his vignettes is a source of wonder and fascination. *Bird Medicine* is a book that his readers will find impossible to forget."

STANLEY KRIPPNER, PH.D., PROFESSOR OF PSYCHOLOGY
AT SAYBROOK UNIVERSITY AND COAUTHOR OF
PERSONAL MYTHOLOGY AND *THE VOICE OF ROLLING THUNDER*

"Evan Pritchard has an instinct for bringing the spirit of the Original Peoples into his scholarship, its fresh breath of wisdom still intact. This book combines bird lore with Native American shamanism in a truly unique way. I celebrate the latest release of a very original thinker."

STEPHEN LARSEN, PH.D., AUTHOR OF *THE SHAMAN'S DOORWAY*
AND COAUTHOR OF *JOSEPH CAMPBELL: A FIRE IN THE MIND*

"In *Bird Medicine*, Evan Pritchard has surpassed his previous books. Not only is his book enjoyable and informative, it is also quite scholarly. Though he is, in his own words, not an ornithologist, he teaches us a great deal about the habits and patterns of many familiar birds."

ELSPETH ODBERT, CERTIFIED SHAMANIC PRACTITIONER AND
AUTHOR OF *OUT OF THE FOREST* AND *GYLANTRA'S LEGACY*

BIRD
MEDICINE

The
Sacred Power
of
Bird Shamanism

EVAN T. PRITCHARD

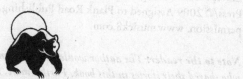

Bear & Company
Rochester, Vermont • Toronto, Canada

Bear & Company
One Park Street
Rochester, Vermont 05767
www.BearandCompanyBooks.com

Bear & Company is a division of Inner Traditions International

Library of Congress Cataloging-in-Publication Data
Pritchard, Evan T., 1955–
  Bird medicine : the sacred power of bird shamanism / Evan T. Pritchard.
    p. cm.
  Includes bibliographical references and index.
    ISBN 978-1-59143-158-9 (pbk.) — ISBN 978-1-59143-825-0 (e-book)
  1. Indians of North America—Religion. 2. Indian mythology—North America.
3. Indian cosmology—North America. 4. Shamanism—North America. 5. Birds—
Folklore. 6. Birds—Mythology. 7. Birds—Symbolic aspects. I. Title.
  E98.R3P94 2013
  299.7—dc23
                                                              2012042200

Printed and bound in the United States

10 9 8 7 6 5 4 3

Text design and layout by Brian Boynton
This book was typeset in Garamond Premier Pro with Spectrum and Swiss as display
typefaces

Excerpt from *Moving Within the Circle* by Bryan Burton © 2008 World Music
Press/© 2009 Assigned to Plank Road Publishing, Inc. All Rights Reserved. Used by
permission. www.musick8.com.

Note to the reader: *The author would like to extend his deepest gratitude to all those
who shared their stories in this book. Furthermore, he invites readers to contact him with
corrections or bird stories or aboriginal teachings they wish to share. Please write to Evan
Pritchard at P.O. Box 140, Salt Point, NY 12578 or evan.pritchard7@gmail.com.*

CONTENTS

ACKNOWLEDGMENTS

I would like to thank deeply everyone who has helped bring this book into being, starting from around New Year's 2010. It was at that time I got the call from a concerned environmental leader asking me on behalf of Native elders to help birds in their struggle to be free from the little-known but disastrous effects of recent technology. This book is one of the by-products of that conversation. I would also like to thank Jon Graham at Inner Traditions for asking to publish this book and to matchmakers Alex and Allyson Grey and Stephen and Robin Larsen for nudging me to say yes. I especially thank all the amazing elders from all over North America who have taken time from their duties to help me with this project. I hope they find it was worthwhile. A special *welalin* (thank you) goes to my big sister, Lynn Pritchard, for being the wind beneath my wings when it comes to birds. I could not have written this without her and the teachings of Grandfather Turtle. I also thank our mother for teaching us to respect birds as our equals, and perhaps our betters. I also thank those that passed on into the spirit world, continuing their help on this book undaunted by the mere detail that we call death: Patrick Pritchard, William Commanda, Shoshana Rothaizer, Blessing Bird, Oannes Pritzker, Roland Mewer, Shirley Tanner, Carol Bruchac, Jake Swamp, and Sagamore Mike, not to mention earlier teachers now gone but somehow present: Twylah Nitsch, Archie Cheechoo, Joseph Campbell, William Mewer, Helen Perley, and others.

My aunt Helen Perley's influence was monumental. How lucky I was to have contact with her and share in her knowledge at such an early age. She was the first one to say to me, "I'm a Mi'kmaq, and that makes you one too. There's nothing you can do about it! You might as well enjoy it!" And I did! I appreciate now the invitation she had just given me, a welcome into a disappearing world that she was struggling mightily to preserve, in all its varying levels of "authenticity." She always thoroughly enjoyed herself throughout all her cultural battles to preserve Maine's Native history; by the time I was hanging around, she had become an icon of all that was right and good about Maine. Her ability as a septuagenarian, and later an octogenarian (and even later a nonagenarian) to translate Bird Medicine effectively to the reporters and photographers that followed around this Mi'kmaq woman of the Miramichi has been one of the major inspirations for this book. The experience of watching her communicate with and heal birds when I was fifteen is one I will always cherish. It has taken me forty years to find a way to thank her. This book is that thank you.

I would like to thank Jan Henriksen for giving us permission to use his snowy egret photo, proving my sister's "tall tale" to be true; David Pritchard for helping me clean my birdcage; Jeanie Levitan of Inner Traditions for her literary vision; Jessica Wimett for her "bluebird" optimism; Peri Ann Swan for hatching such an uplifting cover design; Whitney North Seymour, the distinguished white eagle of avian jurisprudence; Gabriel Seymour for her work on behalf of Native and avian civil rights; Dina Jaeger, the patron saint of all Native American bird activists; Dr. Joseph Bruchac for immediately confirming the scientific and ethnological value of this proposed work, based on his forty years of groundbreaking experience in this field; unsung genius Alan Wells for his amazing photos, whose love of birds speaks louder than words; Moonfire Studios for their tireless work slaving away at graphic design, helping to bring Alan Wells's photos to this edition; award-winning photographer John DeSanto for getting a crow council to pose for him; the Audubon Society of Rockland County, New York;

Drs. Dennis Hastings and Margery Coffey for their important Omaha insights about crows; Dr. Michael Gillen for editing the manuscript in its early stages; Becky Spear for capturing the seagulls of Old Orchard Beach, Maine, on film; and the wild Quaker parrots of Edgewater, New Jersey, for giving new meaning to the words *live free or die*. As there are so many others to thank for their timely and strenuous efforts to benefit all creatures great and small, I will present the rest of the names alphabetically. If I forgot one or two, you know who you are.

Judy Abbott; Ahngwet; Watie Akins; Anamika; Cheryl and David Aranovitch; Greg Artzner; Joseph Attien; Richard Bach; Debbie Bahune; Dr. Alfonso Balmori; Professor Tracy Basile; Dr. Eunice Baumann Nelson; Sam Beeler, Big Toe; Birdy King; Eugene Blackbear Sr.; Dr. Anthony Bledsoe; Lisa Breslov; Nathan Brown; Joan Burroughs; Cora Chandler, Robin Hill-Chandler; Anthony Chiappelloni; J. Alan Clarke, J.D.; Kenneth Cohen; Therese Crowley; Shawna Cutler; Jim C. Davis; Rebecca Davis; Depsimana (Katherine Cheshire); Patricia Dowdell; Mircea Eliade; Etaoqua; Dan Evehema; John Fadden; Ray Fadden; Featherhawk; David Fescier; Alison Evans-Fragale; St. Francis of Assisi; FIDO (Fellowship in the Interest of Dog Owners); Ken Gale; Mahatma Gandhi; Mary Goetze; Golden Coyote; Manna Jo Greene; Bente Hansen; Violet and Melody Hansen; Liz Hartman; Barbel Haynes; Dr. A. Elaine Henwood; Dave Holden; Dr. Charles Holmes; Amy Krout Horn; The Hungry Mouse Research Library; Mary Jackson; Janet Jappen; Paul and Teresa Jennings; Dr. Peggy Jodri; Eleanor Noyes Johnson; Katchongva; Dr. Gisela Kaplan; Dr. Robin Wall Kimmerer; Dr. Martin Luther King Jr.; Alexie Kondratiev; Valeria Kondratiev; Tony Moonhawk and Marcey Langhorn; Stephen, Merlin, and Robin Larsen; Vicky Latta; Terry Leonino; Albert Lightning; Linda Lucas; Manitou Ikwe (Spirit Woman); Vincent Mann; Marist College; "Max"; Simon Mercer; Mirabai Books, Morningstar; "Nathan"; Andy Nixon; Kay Olan; Pace University; Dwayne Perry; Lisa Petagumskum; Joseph Polis; Tina Powell; Rainbow Weaver; Red Hawk Sister; Monique Renaud; Liisa Rissanen; Loriman Rodell; Raymundo Rodriguez;

Rolling Thunder; Running Deer; Madeleine Saiga; Jamie Sams; Santha and Craig; Candy Schill; Linda Schutt; Sequoia; Grandfather Sings Alone; Heather Sole (Eagle Woman); Beverly Spear; Kay Spear; Betsy Stang; Eddy and Bobbie Stevenson; Dark Rain Thom; James Alexander Thom; Henry David Thoreau; Edgar Torres; Romola Trebilcock; Walter "Silent Wolf" Van Dunk; Mercy Van Vlack; Woody Vasquel; Vassar College; "Wanda"; Phyllis Wedding; Harry Wheeler; Raymond Wheeler; White Deer of Autumn (Gabriel Horn); Carol Wickwire; Heather Wiggs; Grandmother Wyakin; Yenyahola; Robin Youngblood; Bob Young Eagle; and all the birds who have dropped by to help.

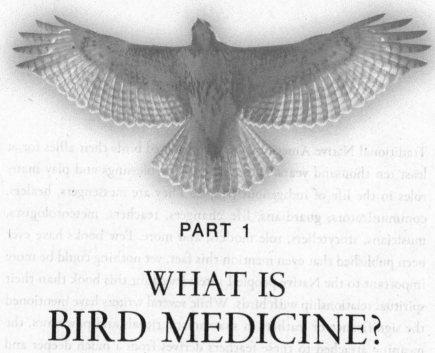

PART 1

WHAT IS
BIRD MEDICINE?

A WHISTLE AND
A WORD TO THE WISE

Traditional Native Americans have considered birds their allies for at least ten thousand years. Birds bring many blessings and play many roles in the life of indigenous people. They are messengers, healers, communicators, guardians, life changers, teachers, meteorologists, musicians, storytellers, role models, and more. Few books have ever been published that even mention this fact, yet nothing could be more important to the Native people I interviewed for this book than their spiritual relationship with birds. While several writers have mentioned the significance of feathers in shamanistic rituals and powwows, the meaning attached to these feathers derives from a much deeper and older tradition, one that is harder to catalogue. That would be the living spiritual tradition surrounding the relationships that Native people today cultivate with living birds. It is a key to understanding Native culture.

I am not an ornithologist, and this is not primarily a study of birds but of people who love birds. It should require no great quantum shift in the paradigm of the reader's mind to acknowledge that countless Native Americans have these beliefs and see birds as messengers, or oracles, to use a European term. Therefore, the fundamental basis of this study is anthropological, and I hope it will be a significant, if long overdue, contribution to this field. We could stop there and simply enjoy these amazing stories as figments of the primitive shamanic mind. John Burroughs, for example, loved birds and was a keen observer of their ways, but he consistently prevented himself, in the name of science, from attributing human intentions and thought processes to birds, and I respect him for that. He truly advanced the universal and objective understanding of these remarkable beings. Birds are rather different from us—their thought processes still a mystery, their emotions alien to ours in many respects. Nonetheless, I would like to ask the reader to put conventional science aside, to forgo the conceit of objectivity, and enter a realm where birds, whether inspired by departed human or divine spirits or their own compassion, are able to reach out to us and communicate with us—for a moment or for a lifetime.

Perhaps we can enter directly into the heart of shamanic experience itself where the barrier between man and beast is removed for a moment in the midst of ritual. I ask you to join me on the other side of anthropology, the wild side where there are no books or laboratories, only direct experience, as seen through the eyes of the numerous Native Americans (and their friends) I queried. I invite the reader to put aside learned skepticism and embrace innate faith instead, a faith that simply acknowledges the possibility that we might in fact still be able to enter into a shared space of divine communication and mutual prayer with birds and coexist as equals with our two-legged relations, as Native American teachings suggest.

Native American elders have taught me that "birds pray at dawn." We can hear their fervent voices as they greet Grandfather Sun rising in the east. It is interesting that when a medicine man named Grandfather Turtle taught me to pray in Mi'kmaq he said that it was good to say, "I am standing here, now, Creator. I am Chipmunk!" (*Neegeh, ga'ami, Geezoolgh! Neen Abachbahametch!*) According to ornithologist Gisela Kaplan, bird vocalizations at dawn seem to say "I am here and I am a [starling, nightingale, or any other species]."[1]* That similarity, to me, is stunning.

Based on the field interviews I conducted with people within the Native community for this book, it is clear that a living, dynamic

---

*Many ornithologists have made similar observations. Konrad Lorenz's book *Here Am I— Where Are You? The Behavior of the Greylag Goose* provides many insights into the communication styles of geese and ducks, both wild and tame, starting with the book's title.

tradition still exists concerning our spiritual relationship with birds. A strong case can be made that successful interspecies communication still does occur between individual birds and individual humans, in this case Native American humans. Beyond this point of agreement stands the wild frontier of numinous mystery.

Is there an actual "language" that birds and Native Americans share at times in order to communicate? Can birds actually communicate telepathically with Native elders? Do they have anything to say? Can they guide us, warn us, teach us, tell us the future? Or are birds simply able to become vessels for a higher power or powers, or departed human spirits, and reach out to us as humans? Can local and cosmic deities cause birds to materialize before the faithful as they pray for help, in answer to their prayers? Can some humans develop the ability to consciously enter into the mind of a bird, inhabit its body, and actually observe things at a distance and send messages to loved ones and, if so, continue this practice after death? Don't answer until you've read the stories that follow.

The interview material recorded here brings up these puzzling questions. It is doubtful that they can be answered using the scientific method. There are four epistemologies or pathways by which we determine our beliefs and values: science, philosophy, religion, and mythopoetics. The latter three may be more helpful in this case. Native American culture has a tradition of careful observation that is scientific in spirit, but it also has a philosophy that emphatically grants equality to all species, though expressed, perhaps, in different ways. It includes various forms of the Red Road, the Native American concept of the right path in life, and of spiritual teachings that embrace the quest for enlightenment (*neoline* in Lenape), the realization that we are all one, that we all (animals included) have a soul, a place on the hoop of life. A wealth of Native stories and songs reinforces these beliefs, carrying within them deeply buried clues of ancient secret teachings about birds that most have forgotten. If, in the manner of the ancient Greeks, Westerners could cease to be solely attached to the pathway we call science and return to philosophy, religion, and mythopoetics, using them in combination with science, we might find verdant acres of common ground with indigenous people and might even come to similar conclusions.

At its roots, Native bird spirituality is shamanistic; it has a distinct similarity to worldwide core shamanism, as understood by Mircea Eliade and Joseph Campbell, and this pathway to understanding is not rational. At its ancient and most powerful root, shamanism involves a return to the animal state and a rejection of much that is human. As Grandfather William Commanda explained to me, "You have to believe in the birds, believe with all your heart. Only then can they show you all they have to share, only then can they change your life." He said these words in an emotional moment after being visited by twenty-five golden-colored doves who came to his window an hour earlier to announce my arrival with a special message.*

Shamans use trance, such as achieved in the shaking tent ceremony, the sun dance, the sweat lodge, the long fast, and in certain nightlong dances. These trance states help the shaman drop the barrier that has grown up between animals and humans in the last five thousand years. When it drops, the medicine person sees what birds see, hears their thoughts, feels as they feel, and understands their concerns. In this open state, according to the shaman's solitary path, they see the past and the future and see what is going on at a distance and in the spirit world. They can even see glimpses of the Creator, "he who dreams us into being." It is then that their words become unimaginably powerful, their thoughts become manifest the instant they think them. They are able to heal others by touch, by word, or by inner travel through spiritual dimensions. They can communicate with the overlighting spirit of an animal or bird and ask for its help. This is the belief that Native American ceremonialism holds. This is not to say that each of the persons I talked to tried to reach this state, but it's not necessary that he or she does so. Native spiritual practice was clearly developed

---

*See "Twelve Birds" on page 226 for the complete story.

over millennia by powerful teachers who had experienced such a state many times—Sweet Medicine, Deganawida, Masa'au, Tecumseh, Seattle, Tamanend, White Buffalo Calf Woman, Sitting Bull, Neoline, Wovoka, Sequoia, to name a few—and the culture is imbued with this holistic type of understanding in which there are no brick walls or cage bars between species. Anyone deeply involved in such a culture will sooner or later stumble into some kind of heart connection or mind link with a living bird or animal.

Depsimana (also known as Katherine Cheshire) medicine helper of the last fully traditional elder of the Hopi, Dan Evehema,* commented, "Birds do it all! They play many roles in Native American society, and the elders have entrusted their vast knowledge—about birds and other traditions—to certain young people, who must now carry this information onward into the digital age."[2] Elaine Henwood, Ph.D., was a friend and student of the charismatic elder Rolling Thunder for several years. As she recollects, he would look for and discuss signs and omens with her every day, and many of them were bird signs. The variety of the species and the intricate nature of the signs involved was, in Elaine's words, "overwhelming to me sometimes."

Henwood said that to Rolling Thunder everything that happened during the day was filled with meaning. He saw no firm barrier between the physical and spiritual worlds, or between what we call science and what the Native Americans call sacred knowledge, except that the Native view is more expansive and explains more of what we experience during our lives here on Earth.

U.S. law recognizes aspects of Native American spirituality as religion and has placed that religion under the protection of the Freedom of Religion acts.† This brings up an interesting point. If birds are an essential part of Native American religion and in fact sacred to that faith,

---

*Evehema is widely considered the last Native American to live totally without dependence on the capitalist system or on the utility grid.

†These rights were first recognized in The American Indian Religious Freedom Act of 1978, then further codified in the 1993 Religoius Freedom Restoration Act.

how do we leave unchallenged the destruction of bird habitats across the continent—not to mention the birds themselves—without protest?

If prayer, communication with the Divine in a ritualized format, constitutes the heart of a religion, and Native Americans pray to the Creator and other divine beings, believing as they pray that a bird may come and give them their answer, then isn't it true that anything that harms that bird or causes it to change its course or even its behavior (as they generally communicate nonverbally) is an obstruction to religious freedom? Some Native Americans, as we shall see, believe that the primary function of birds within ritual practice is to either come as messengers in response to prayer, or to materialize before them for the same purpose. Shouldn't there, at the very least, be areas created where no technological threats to birds would be found for miles around, areas where Native Americans can pursue religious fulfillment in safety? It sounds easy, but it is now harder than you would think.

Certain Cheyenne paintings show how prayers caused living birds to manifest as expressions of higher powers and cosmic forces invited into the ceremony. How can anyone believe such a thing? John the Baptist understood that the white dove that appeared over Jesus's head as the two met at the Jordan River was a materialization of the Holy Spirit in bird form and was therefore the sign that Jesus was the Messiah, the leader of the Jewish people. It was John's recognition of this bird sign that led many people in that time and place to almost immediately accept Jesus as a great teacher.* The Sermon on the Mount that followed attracted a great multitude, and yet it was Jesus's first great lecture. How did that happen? Because of the bird!

Today, the distance between bird and human, not to mention that between spirit and society, is widening. Nissequogue Raymundo Rodriguez says we have forgotten how to become birds and other

---

*Translations differ as to whether it was a dove or like a dove. The King James version of the Bible says "like a dove," as does *The Modern Language Bible;* but *The Living Bible* says "Holy Spirit in the form of a dove," and *The Holy Bible: Revised Standard Edition* says "the Holy Spirit descended as a dove," and in fact, Andrew accepted Jesus as the Messiah almost immediately afterward.

animals. We have forgotten how to dance hawk, dance crane, dance mouse. He told of a man who would attach feathers to his hat and jacket and dance like a crane in front of actual cranes so that they would produce more eggs. He would bounce and weave and strut like a crane and must have gotten the steps right, because people claimed he could get his birds to lay more eggs than any others. "No animal or bird has a human totem. It's we humans who look to them for our power," he says, dramatically. "On the powwow circuit we have more and more social dances, but that's so human. We used to dance birds and animals and become them. The first stage of shape-shifting is to dance the animal. You want a 'power animal'? Go dance!"[3]

When one says bird, the first thing people think of is cage, but by caging a bird we deprive the world, and ourselves, of its healing and its messages. It is mainly wild birds that have the freedom to live, move, and have their being as messengers of spirit. Caged birds don't behave the same way, and yet that is how modern humans prefer their birds, locked up. I heard a story of a smart parrot that broke a splinter off a piece of wood in its cage, then picked the padlock on the cage with the splinter and broke free. The padlock was placed there because he had broken all the previous clips, locks, and handles that had kept him confined in the past.[4] The reader will find many similar stories in the section about parrots. Birds don't love being locked up any more than you or I would. They were born with wings so that they could fly.

The problem modern people have with bird signs is that you can't always turn them on and off like a radio. Sometimes one may go for months without seeing a bird sign. This can be frustrating, but it is probably a sign that everything is fine. One can't pay a bird to deliver a message like a carnival card reader. They hold all the cards and have no need for money. Fasting, the making of offerings, and praying for a bird message from the Creator has worked well for shamanic healers for thousands of years, but few want to fast any more or wait for up to three days for an answer, and birds are getting scarce due to environmental hazards and loss of habitat.

TEK, or Traditional Ecological Knowledge, and TIK, or Traditional Indigenous Knowledge, are terms that have made inroads into the scientific community these last five years due to the pioneering work of Robin W. Kimmerer, Ph.D., and others.* Traditional Bird Medicine (TBM) is an important part of that wisdom. Although not all the material in this book is scientific in every aspect, every aspect of it could prove useful from one or more academic perspectives sooner or later. The roots of sociology, theology, linguistics, musicology, and literature cannot be fully understood without understanding early human tendencies to mold society, song, and religious beliefs in accordance with bird behavior. There is a distinct possibility that Native American mound burials, for example, such as those at Fort Ancient in Ohio, were first built in imitation of birds. One woman swears that she observed a flock of blue jays create a mound burial out of leaves and sticks and other available debris to cover a fallen comrade lying on a public sidewalk. Debbie Bahune, my great aunt Helen's granddaughter and former assistant, has seen a different kind of crow funeral: a large number of crows perched in the surrounding tree branches and circled around the corpse of one of their own, lying in the grass.[5]

TBM is not intended to be a complete system for making all life decisions. To depend on Bird Medicine for decision making is to place yourself at the whim of a little character with very little brains but lots of cranial air space. This is not wise. Few if any Native Americans rely exclusively on bird signs. There are dozens of other types of signs that can stand in the gap: weather, clouds, animals, dreams, plants, trees, casting of stones, casting of cowrie shells, children, planets, patterns on buckskin, images in water, voices, visions, and on and on. Great *sachems,* or chiefs, relied mainly on information their scouts gathered

---

*A scientist of Potowatomi descent and citizenship, Kimmerer is the author of *Gathering Moss: A Natural and Cultural History of Mosses* and many influential magazine articles helping to establish TEK as a "way of knowing." There is also a group of Hawaiian scientists that are making breakthroughs with TEK, notably Jonatha Giddens. Parks Canada has also opened a department of Traditional Ecological Knowledge.

and then used their own logic, convictions, sense of right and wrong, or gut instincts to make decisions. Oracular methods are helpful when conventional information is unavailable. A human can ask for a bird sign, but even after the tobacco (or cornmeal) offering is properly made, it is something that comes at the most unexpected moments and is not under most people's control. Bird messages are almost always "out of the blue," like the birds themselves. I present this information to readers so that when the realization strikes them that they have just received an urgent message from a bird, they will be well informed and better able to interpret the message. These warnings and news bulletins come from a very different world than ours, but they could some day save our lives and steer our futures toward a better pathway, a closer walk with the Great Spirit, in harmony with this garden of earthly delights we have been given.

BIRD ORIGINS AND EARLY INFLUENCES ON HUMANS

Birds, the Real First Nations People

In order to understand the importance of Bird Medicine, it is helpful to realize that birds were here, with their own complex societies and well-established languages, long before humans. This is taught in the wisdom tales of the teaching lodges across North America and by scientists dwelling in cavelike laboratories studying fossils. As early humans were learning how to behave during their earth walks through life, they had only to look up and copy what birds had been doing for millions of years. In fact, most human societies did, and then forgot. That is why Native shamanism has so internalized our relationship with birds that it is seldom spoken of.

According to Gisela Kaplan:

The first bird evolved in the Jurassic period, although most ancient bird species evolved later, in the Cretaceous period. Millions of years separate the appearance of the various species (Feduccia, 1996). For instance, the first known occurrence of some flightless birds, including species of game birds and waterfowl, may have been close to 100 million years ago,* separated from the appearance of parrots by about 10 million years. Owls evolved about 60 million years ago, about 30 to 50 million years earlier than songbirds. Songbirds and most other birds of prey were among the "newcomers," appearing in

---

*These flightless birds apparently evolved from a feathered dinosaur called the dromaeosaur, such as those recently discovered in China from 130 million years ago. (Norell, "The Proof Is in the Plumage," 58.)

the Tertiary period as recently as a mere 5 to 30 million years ago. Albatrosses, which are the largest seabirds on Earth, frigatebirds (with a wingspan of up to eight feet!), penguins, and petrels evolved earlier. Thus, when humans began to evolve about 4 million years ago, the air, the ground, and the waters were already occupied by winged and beaked species.[6]

Songbirds have continued to diverge into widely differing subspecies until 2 million years ago, which suggests that they are one of the few creatures on Earth that evolved at the same time as *Homo sapiens*. They, too, are Johnny-come-latelies to this planet like ourselves. They are our siblings in time.

The earliest known human habitation in what is now Alaska was in the Tanana River Valley: at the Swan Point, Broken Mammoth, and Mead sites archaeologists have found evidence that birds were butchered for food. At Broken Mammoth, we find dietary swan bone collagen dating back to 9500 BCE, denoting human occupation, but no human remains.[7] They also hunted cranes and geese. According to Dr. Charles Holmes, affiliate research professor of anthropology at the University of Alaska and a senior archaeologist now working in the Tanana Valley, who first discovered the site in 1989, "There is evidence for hunting birds at the Swan Point site in Alaska that goes back to around 14,000 years ago (~12,200 radiocarbon years BP). Species include upland game birds (grouse or ptarmigan) and migratory waterfowl (ducks and geese)."[8] In his article "The Beringian and Transitional Periods in Alaska: Technology of the East Beringian Tradition as Viewed from Swan Point," Holmes writes:

> Despite poor organic preservation, it has been possible to identify a few specimens. Data suggest that people harvested upland game birds (grouse/ptarmigan) and waterfowl (ducks and geese) and may have hunted horse and mammoth. Evidence of the latter two species is based on teeth and tusk fragments. Two horse molars were

found between hearth 1b and hearth 2, and one mammoth molar along with numerous molar plates were scattered along the west side of hearth 2. Antler fragments indicate that caribou, elk, or moose could have been hunted as well.[9]

The oldest burial site in Alaska so far, discovered by Ben A. Potter in the summer of 2010 at the Upper Sun River Site above the Tanana River, is the 11,500-year-old cremation of a three-year-old in a house fire pit. Although bones of ptarmigan/grouse, passerine, and unknown types of birds were found in the pit, and although pieces of red ochre suggest burial rituals were performed, no evidence was found of mortuary bird rituals, per se.[10]

Archaeologists have found sites that seem to be of similar antiquity all over the United States, including a ten-thousand-year-old site near Perry, Florida, so the question remains, "Where did Amerindians come from?" However, one can be sure that whenever Native Americans arrived (by boat or on foot) or were created by the hand of Great Mystery here in North America, birds were here first, and these early Native Americans must have known their habits and anatomies intimately.

Scientists agree: most bird species predate *Homo sapiens,* and the Hopi stories corroborate this Western belief nicely but, typically, on a much more sweeping scale. In the story "The Beginning of Life," as told by Katchongva (who lived until 1970), humans had already been living underground for countless generations but wanted to find a new way of life and a better place to live. They had heard thumping noises from above, and wanted to investigate. (Some say they were hearing deer on the surface.) Being more powerful than today's humans, they created three birds, the *kisa* or hawk, the *pavowkaya* or swallow, and the *moochnee,* a type of mockingbird. As described in *Hote Villa: Hopi Shrine of the Covenant; Microcosm of the World:*

They were each created at separate times by magic songs, tobacco smoke and prayers, from dirt and saliva, which was covered by a white cape (or ova). Each was welcomed respectfully and given instructions for his mission, should he succeed. The first two failed to reach the top side of the sky but the third one, Moochnee, came through the opening into this world.

The new world was beautiful. The earth was green and in bloom. The bird observed all his instructions. His sense of wisdom guided him to the being he was instructed to seek. When he found him it was high noon, for the being, Maasauu, The Great Spirit [Guardian of the Great Spirit, as corrected by Dan Evehema, in this same source] was preparing for his noonday meal. Ears of corn lay beside the fire. He flew down and lit on top of his kisi (shady house) and sounded his arrival. Maasauu was not surprised by the visitor; for by his wisdom and sense of smell he already knew someone was coming. Respectfully, he welcomed him and invited him to sit down. The interview was brief and to the point. "Why are you here? Could it be important?" "Yes," said Moochnee, "I was sent here by the underworld people. They wish to come to your land and live with you, for their ways have become corrupted. With your permission they wish to move here with you and start a new life. This is why I have come." Maasauu replied bluntly, but with respect, "They may come."

With this message, the bird returned to the underworld. While he was gone the Kikmongwi and the leaders had continued to pray and wait for his successful return. Upon his return with the good news of the new world and Maasauu's permission for them to come, they were overjoyed.[11]

So as you see, the Hopi tales show us that without birds, we would not be here on the surface of our mother Earth at all. It is the birds that brought us permission to live here from the guardian of the Great Spirit. Without them we would still be in a cave beneath the earth, living in darkness.

If humans and their seemingly benign inventions were to inadvertently wipe out all birds on Earth, it would be the first time in our history that any society was without birds; unimaginable to any of our ancestors. It would open a dark new chapter in history that could only lead to an unhappy ending. Both our inner and outer expressions of spirituality would be changed forever. If we ignore the "canaries in the coal mine" and destroy our environment, we, too, will have to live in environmentally controlled artificial pods beneath the earth. But will it be for the first time? The Hopi say this is our fourth and final chance.

Birds and Burial Rites:
Birds as Embodiments of the Soul

We find that early human burials in the Levant (today's Israel, Syria, Palestine, Lebanon), Cyprus, and in an early North American burial in Texas are united by a focus on birds that is strange to us, but logical given their close proximity to human activity and the sense of awe and wonder they still inspire. I have seen studies of several such burials, each about twelve thousand years old but thousands of miles apart, where a bird was placed in the mouth of the deceased for reasons that are no longer clear. It suggests to me that at the dawn of human civilization, a link was made between the flight of the soul or spirit and the flight of birds. Even today the Mi'kmaq say, "*Och-tchi-tcha-cha-midj ma-djai dech*" (my spirit goes somewhere else). The idea of the soul leaving the body and traveling far away to a loved one, to the Creator, or along the Milky Way are very old concepts within Native culture.

In the book *Birds with Human Souls: A Guide to Bird Symbolism,* by Beryl Rowland, we can find some clues to answering this mystery. It seems that in European art there are many indications that souls are generally depicted as birds. In a painting of the martyrdom of St. Quintin, birds are shown coming out of the mouth of the martyr's severed head as he is dying. In general, birds represent the human soul but never the body as a mammal might. The Bella Coola (a Northern Salishan tribe) see the soul as a bird enclosed in an egg at the nape of the neck. If the shell breaks, the soul will fly away and the man will die. Worldwide, the bird is seen as the embodiment of transcendence, which the shaman achieves often through trance. The author writes, "The shaman owes his power to the belief that he was able to leave his body and fly about the universe like a bird."[12]

The inhabitants of the West Indies in the Caribbean are quite familiar with the idea of spiritual flight and go to great lengths to make the human-avian connection. Eliade writes, "For instance, Laborde reported that the masters 'also rub his (the neophyte's) body with gum and cover it with feathers to make him able to fly and go to the house of the zemeen (spirits).'" Eliade notes that the birdlike costume and other symbols of magical flight are an integral part of Siberian, North American, and Indonesian shamanism.[13]

As many societies believe the soul leaves through the mouth, it can be rightfully suggested that these ancient burials with a bird propped in the mouth of the deceased (or bird bones in mouth bones as we see now) were meant to ritually amplify the prayer that the person's soul would not be trapped on Earth but would transcend to the highest realms.

It is a natural comparison; a belief in winged angels dates back beyond the earliest known cuneiform writings from Sumeria, and wings are a feature that is exclusive to birds, bats, and insects—not humans. Over time, most societies became earthbound and materialistic and turned away from bird spirituality, with exceptions like St. Francis of Assisi and Leonard da Vinci, who, like the legendary Icarus, wanted wings to fly like a bird. But countless traditional Native Americans I have spoken to, and most modern shamans, continue to receive regular communications from "the other two-leggeds."

Why Are Birds Sacred to Native People?

The Mohawk "Giving of Thanks Address" oratory contains a section thanking birds for existing. This is perhaps the most famous and most often-repeated speech in Native American culture. It is significant that birds merit an entire section to themselves. It is a beautiful statement and an important thank you to our feathered counterparts. Different versions can also be found in the late Chief Jake Swamp's *Giving Thanks* children's book and in a small book inspired by him and published by The Tree of Peace Society called *Thanksgiving Address* as well as in an unpublished version in Mohawk with direct translations (which I will refer to later in the book). In it is a prayer of thanks to the birds. In the translation by David Benedict and John Stokes, it reads: "We put our minds together as one and thank all the Birds who move and fly about over our heads. The Creator gave them beautiful songs. Each day they remind us to enjoy and appreciate life. The Eagle was chosen to be their leader. To all the Birds—from the smallest to the largest—we send our joyful greetings and thanks. Now our minds are one."[14] This prayer of thanks clearly indicates the importance of birds to Native Americans. That birds are sacred to Natives is a well-documented fact. But it is an altogether different thing to ask why. Why is a hard question. I presented this hard question to a number of traditional Native Americans to discover why living birds are sacred, and their answers were fascinating. They might even challenge your understanding of what the word *sacred* means.

First I asked Betsy Stang, founder of The Wittenberg Center for Alternative Resources, coproducer of The Cry of the Earth: The Legacy of the First Nations Conference at the United Nations, and someone who has taken on the difficult task of helping traditional Native elders get their voices heard in the media, this question: Are birds an essential part of Native American spirituality? Her answer was quickly forthcoming: Absolutely![15]

I have received a similar answer from every elder, Native American, and scholar to whom I have posed the question. And yet no book has been written specifically on this subject. I hope to fill this gap by gathering wisdom from a wide variety of Native American and scholarly sources on the subject of human-bird interactions.

Eugene Blackbear Sr., a noted Cheyenne arrow priest, says that many birds are sacred, including geese. "We respect our birds!" he says and adds, "People should respect nature, themselves, and their children." He confirmed emphatically that living birds were sacred to the Cheyenne and that eagle feathers play a role in the restoring arrow ceremonies. He said that different nations from the East, West, and Great Plains have differ-ent traditions, but they respect each other, including each other's bird tra-ditions.[16] According to Etaoqua, a Mohican woman, the Mohicans tend not to attribute as much special significance to the eagle as do most other nations but have an affinity to the hawk, which in a way serves to confirm what Blackbear has said: You can't lump all Indians together.

Therese Crowley, talk-show host and editor of *The Alternative Press,* recently wrote, "The Native Americans believe in animal medicine—that we are all extended kin, that creatures carry a message, and that Great Spirit speaks thru the creatures."[17] There are few generalizations that can be made about Native Americans, but I believe that Crowley has grabbed a good one and eaten it whole.

The Earth Does Not Belong to Us

Wampum Belt Carrier and former Grand Chief of the Algonquin (Mamawinini) Nation of Canada, William Commanda, and I worked together for fourteen years, and I learned a lot from him about birds and animals. He was not only a Wisdom Keeper for Algonquian-speaking people (which I will refer to in this book as the Algonkin-ode* [al-**gon**-kin-o-dey] or those of the Algonquin family of nations) of North America but was an environmental leader as well. To say he had a close relationship with birds is a bit of an understatement.† On

---

*The oldest known term for all Algonquian-speaking people as a group is Anishinaa-beg, or "good people." However this term is now used by scholars to refer only to the Odawa, Ojibway (Chippewa), and Algonquin specifically; therefore another term is needed. Algonquin is used in official state and federal publications in the United States and by the Catholic Church for this purpose, but this does not work in Canada, as it would cause confusion with the single nation Algonquin (Mamawinini). Therefore, in this book I will use Algonkin-ode, a word that has no other meaning. *Ode,* "family" or "clan" in Anishinaabe, is the root of *dodem,* which is known to many as *totem. Odey,* a closely related word, means "heart." The term implies not only "the Algonquin fam-ily" (of nations) but "allies of the heart." As I will be referring frequently to both types of Algonquins, I will use Algonquin (Mamawinini) to refer to the single nation and Algonkin-ode to refer to the culture.

†See page 113 to read about his life-changing encounter with a bird.

October 30, 2005, Commanda received an honorary doctorate from the University of Ottawa. In his address at the ceremony presenting the degree, which I attended, he said the following:

[A] deeper strength of my ancestors kept me alive and taught me to work for the two important things they believed in: First, absolute respect for mother earth and the waters, air and fire, and the animal teachers. Today, we see where our collective disrespect for mother earth has brought us—to the destruction of life as we have known it; today we worry daily about natural disasters, cancers and new diseases. My ancestors also taught that we were all related, and so we learned to treat everyone and everything on the earth with respect, generosity, and love—as a relative. As we moved away from those values, exploitation, hatred, violence, and crime poisoned our lives and destroyed our world.[18]

One aspect of the Seven Fires prophecies teachings, as taught by Commanda, is that there are seven prayers that we need to keep continually on our lips as we strive to "light the Eighth Fire." When Commanda spoke at The Cry of the Earth conference at the United Nations in 1993, he outlined these seven and spoke from his heart about the seven prayers.

Seven Fires Prayers

To save water from pollution
To save the Mother Earth
To save the trees and all living things
To save the air that we breathe
To save our children from destroying themselves with
drugs and alcohol
To save all things that live in the waters (fish, ducks,
beavers, otters, etc.)
To save all bird life (small and large)

Here is the transcription of that seventh prayer, as recorded on film and set down on paper by Betsy Stang and Jim C. Davis of the Wittenberg Center of Bearsville, New York.*

To Save All Bird Life (Large and Small)

We pray that our birds may still survive, for they too are suffering due to air pollution and earth damages of wood, berries, and other food supplies that they rely on to survive. The water pollution does not help matters any for our bird relations. They are being poisoned by these types of harm. We as people believe that when our bird relations are extinct, that all life will cease to exist.

Bird Shamanism

Most readers know of the importance of birds in Native American life only through old creation stories, myths, and legends. This is obviously a very important factor, as many of these creation stories are regarded as truth and may have actually happened or, at the very least, present a way of describing what actually happened in ancient times. There is hardly another creature that plays a more important role than the birds. They show up everywhere, in every nation's creation stories. What is the significance of this?

As Kenneth Cohen, author of *Honoring the Medicine,* wrote in a recent letter:

Bird behavior plays a central role in the origin/creation stories of many tribes. The raven is linked with the sun among the Tlingit of Alaska. The eagle teaches early humans how to survive among tribes as diverse as the Hopi and the Ojibwe. The Innu, an Algonquian

---

*Extensive videography from the conference can be found at www.wittenbergcenter .org/id5.html. For additional transcriptions and videos, please write to The Wittenberg Center, 17 Jonet Lane, Bearsville, NY 12409.

people closely related to the Micmaq, Passamaquody, and Cree, revere Canada geese because, in the Cree's creation story, they helped bring the warmth of the South. Geese migrating south to north mean that the snows are melting and it is time to hunt again. When they return south, it is time to store goods for winter. And at the end of a prayer, or in closing a ceremony, instead of saying "Amen," Innu will sometimes exclaim "*Ho ho ho Eshqua.*" *Eshqua* is Innu for goose.[19]

Among the Kickapoo, migratory birds are called Indian birds and are not killed because it is thought that they spend time during their absence in the heavenly regions with Kitzihiat. Apparently, the western scientific notion that some birds fly north in the summer and south in the winter while others stay all year-round is puzzling to the Kickapoo of Mexico. They prefer to believe that some birds can shift to another dimension, while others cannot, just like humans, in accordance with their belief system.[20]

In *Shaman's Doorway,* Stephen Larsen writes, "One of the earliest shamanic trances we know of is found in a deep crypt at Les Trois Frères, a Paleolithic site in France. Here lies a Paleolithic shaman in trance, next to him his staff surmounted by a bird, signifying the flight of the spirit. Poles with birds on them are found in many primitive settings. The totem pole or ritual pole in the shaman's tent indicates this vertical arrangement of universes of the spirit world that may be reached from this one."[21]*

An Anishinabi healer, Manitou Ikwe, who worked closely with William Commanda, once told me, "I always pay attention to birds; they are attuned to spiritual energies, they are our messengers. They don't always give the message the same way, it depends on your relationship with them. Repeated behavior is usually significant. They aren't

---

*Modern shamans north of the Arctic Circle still use the same symbols and still participate in an ancient "cult of the eagle." The shaman appears as a radiant heavenly bird. (See Henry N. Michael, *Studies in Siberian Shamanism,* 129.)

possessed but a spirit can enter a bird for a time being and then leave. Significant birds have appeared inside apartments where no windows are open, also butterflies."[22]

Bird Medicine is a worldwide tradition that finds its most beautiful and sincere expression in Native American culture. Still free of formalism and formulas, without pomp or platitudes, this tradition continues today within Native American culture as a joyous, spontaneous exploration of the bond connecting what we call nature, what we call God, and what we call ourselves. In fact it is the place where the three merge and become one force, one spirit. It is one area of earthly physical reality that is still completely untamed and unharnessed and blissfully unfathomable to the human mind. Bird Medicine, whether it happens in New York City or in the Grand Canyon, is as much a "wild frontier" today as it was in the 1670s when Nicholas Perrot observed with wonder the surprising Bird Medicine practices of the Miami at what is now Green Bay, Wisconsin, on the eve of battle.*

As long as we don't kill the messengers by destroying their habitats, we should be able to rely on receiving these messages from beyond the blue horizon for eons to come. But perhaps that is asking for a miracle beyond what even birds can offer.

---

*Perrot was in what is now Green Bay, Wisconsin, between 1654 and 1670. His "memoir," *Memoir on the Manners, Customs, and Religion of the Savages of North America,* was translated and included in Emma Helen Blair's *The Indian Tribes of the Upper Mississippi Valley and Region of the Great Lakes* and quoted in W. Vernon Kinietz's *Indians of the Western Great Lakes, 1615–1760.* Kinietz states that although well-informed about tribal customs and highly influential among the people, Perrot let personal grievances cloud his writing and was unclear about which tribes or nations he was describing (Kinietz 335).

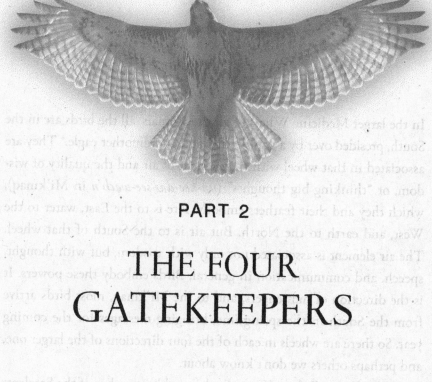

PART 2

THE FOUR GATEKEEPERS

THE BIRDS OF
THE FOUR DIRECTIONS

In the larger Medicine Wheel of all the animals, all the birds are in the South, presided over by a grandfather and grandmother eagle.* They are associated in that wheel with the element of air and the quality of wisdom, or "thinking big thoughts" (*un-kee-das-see-wach'n* in Mi'kmaq), which they and their feathers embody. Fire is to the East, water to the West, and earth to the North. But air is to the South of that wheel. The air element is associated not only with wisdom, but with thought, speech, and communication in general. Birds embody these powers. It is the direction of messengers, and to the Mi'kmaq, most birds arrive from the South in the springtime, bringing messages for the coming year. So there are wheels in each of the four directions of the larger one, and perhaps others we don't know about.

According to Robert Young Eagle, an elder member of the Setalcott Nation of Setauket, New York, one of the thirteen Matouac nations of Long Island, there are four sacred birds that are associated among his people with the four cardinal directions of the Medicine Wheel. These are eagle, hawk, crow, and owl. The eagle is in the North, the hawk is in the East, the raven (or crow) is in the South, and the owl is in the West. According to this teaching, these four powerful gatekeepers look after the other birds.[1]

First is the eagle. It ranges far to the north, to the Arctic Circle and beyond. It migrates from that direction, and not others. Southern eagles do not migrate. The eagle is perched on top of the wheel, as he flies the highest. He is associated with the ancestors, who are also in the

---

*This is according to the current Medicine Wheel teachings of the Mi'kmaq of the Miramichi Valley; others may differ widely.

north. For all of these reasons, the eagle sits in the North of the wheel of master birds.

The hawk is most sacred to the people of the Atlantic coast, where in many places it is more important than the eagle. The golden eagle is rarely seen in the eastern United States. It visits these regions around the first week of November as it flies south from Canada.* The direction of the East is associated with the color red, because the sun is most red when it is rising over the ocean, and this can only be seen on the eastern shore. Red ochre burial rituals were mostly performed in the easternmost arms of the land as they stretch toward the dawn. Therefore, the red-tailed hawk is sacred to the people of Long Island and the people of the East in general because of its red feathers.[2] The Mi'kmaq, who are eastern doorkeepers, pray to the East to learn of their mission in life and receive their instructions, and so it is said they look to the red-tailed hawk and ask, "Where is my life going?" Then they watch to see which direction this majestic hawk is going. (See color insert, plates 5 and 6.)

The raven or crow is the storyteller, the communicator, and the shape-shifter, who transits between the upper and lower worlds of existence. It sees our dark side, our shadow self, but also seeks the light for itself and others. Therefore, raven is in the South.

The owl, or night eagle, is the messenger between the dead and the living, and the West is the direction in which the dead travel on their journey to the spirit world. (See color insert, plate 27.) It is where the sun, moon, and stars go to die. The Delaware (including Munsee and Unami) who lived on the plains after being forced from their homes in New Jersey and New York, would tell stories and sing songs about "riding off into the sunset." The song "I Ride an Old Paint," which implores us to "tie my bones to my saddle, turn our faces to the west," is about a Native American horseback burial ritual where the horse carries the dying person westward toward the spirit world (not so much

---

*For additional information about eagles and hawks, including sites where you can view them, log on to www.hawkmountain.org and check out their "Raptorpedia" section.

fun for the horse). (See my book *Native New Yorkers: The Legacy of the Algonquin People of New York* for more detail.) The owl, as mentioned elsewhere, is the guardian of the portals of the underworld. Therefore, the owl is in the West.

The four gatekeepers, the eagle, hawk, raven, and owl, are not the only birds to which Natives look for signs by any means, but they are all strong birds and can be our protectors in various ways. For this reason, I will present these birds first, before moving on to other birds and their stories.

The following Anishinabi story, "Broken Wing," is no longer in its original form, but it gives us at least evidence that ancient North Americans saw the eagle, hawk, owl, and crow (or raven) as being closely related to each other and explains what their relationship might have been. Certainly, the idea of the eagle as a selfless older brother and teacher to the hawk is a timeless teaching, and depicting the owl as a worthy and respected adversary is right on target. We don't know who the two species who migrated South are, but typically they would have been actual migrant birds. Only eagles that live in the North migrate and only if they run out of food. I took the liberty to make the migrants Heron and Loon, to include them in the story. I have also asked Crow into the story as one of those who stayed north to take care of Gray Eagle.*

Broken Wing

There were six young birds living in a nest, all but one of whom was unable to fly. It so happened that both the parents were shot by hunters on the same day. The young waited impatiently for their parents' return, but when night came, they realized they were now orphans and without food. Meeje-geeg-wona, or the gray eagle, the eldest and the

---

The Sibley Guide to Bird Life and Behavior includes a gray hawk as a smaller relative of the Buteo family. In any case, it is clear that we are not to see these birds literally as brothers, that is from the same mother. These raptors are "brothers" in a broader sense.

only one whose feathers had become stout enough to enable him to leave the nest, assumed the duty of providing food. Unfortunately, after a short time, he broke one of his wings while pouncing upon a swan. It was the season of the year in which they were soon going to need to migrate to a southern climate to pass the winter.

The younger birds went off in search of Meeje-geeg-wona and found him lying there wounded. Meeje-geeg-wona told them to leave him there to die and to go south in search of safety. "No!" they responded. "We will not forsake you! You took care of us, and now we will take care of you! If one of dies, all of us will die together."

They found a hollow tree to spend winter in, placed Meeje-geeg-wona in the hole, and stored up a hoard of food, but hardly enough for all six. So two of the birds went south (the blue heron and the loon). The other three (the crow, the red-tailed hawk, and the pigeon hawk) stayed with the injured older brother.

In time, Meeje-geeg-wona recovered from his wound and repaid their kindness by giving them hunting instructions, based on his greater experience. When spring came, they were all successful in gathering food, except for Peepi-geewi-zains, the pigeon hawk, who was the youngest of all the brothers. Being small and foolish, he would fly in circles and back and forth and always came back with nothing. At last, Meeje-geeg-wona spoke to him and asked him why he was so unlucky.

"It is not because I am small or weak," he said. "I kill ducks and other birds every time, but then when I pass by the great woods, Ko-ko-ko-ho, the white owl, comes out and steals away my food."

"Don't worry, brother," said Meeje-geeg-wona, "I will go out with you tomorrow."

The next day the two went out, and Peepi-geewi-zains soon found a duck and pounced on it and lifted it in its claws. Peepi-geewi-zains began to fly away with it, but immediately, Ko-ko-ko-ho came and tried to grab the duck from his claws. Big brother Meeje-geeg-wona rushed up and grabbed Ko-ko-ko-ho in his talons and flew homeward with him. Peepi-geewi-zains followed behind and was so excited that he flew in Ko-ko-ko-ho's face and began to peck out his large yellow eyes. But Meeje-geeg-wona reproached his younger brother, saying, "Do not be so vengeful! Let us be examples to him and teach him how to be kind to those smaller and weaker than himself!" With this Meeje-geeg-wona showed Ko-ko-ko-ho what kind of herbs to use on his wounds, and then let Ko-ko-ko-ho go.

Just then, the two brother birds (the heron and the loon) returned from their migrations south. The six brothers were reunited. They chose mates and enjoyed a wonderful spring together. From that day on, they always showed respect for the gray eagle, their older brother who taught them so much about life.

This is loosely adapted from an Algonquin story published in Ellen Russell Emerson's *Indian Myths*. It may have been created partially in protest of industrial-revolution ethics, which placed both parents and the eldest son on the production lines, leaving young ones to fend for themselves. It also shows the relationship between the four gatekeepers, which is why I have included it here.[3]

EAGLES

Big Birds and High Fliers

First, we turn to the North, where the eagle is the gatekeeper (see color insert, plates 1, 4, and 30). Many Native Americans have expressed great love for eagles and hawks in particular, among all birds. These two types of birds are considered wise counselors, healers, and strong protectors, are of great purity, and convey messages from the Great Spirit. They are both considered elders. Much of their prestige is based on their abilities as high fliers.

Although the red-tailed hawk is hailed in some Native American stories as the highest flying hawk, the eagles soar yet higher. The golden eagle is mainly seen west of the Mississippi and more rarely in the Appalachians in the United States and is common in Canada and Mexico, where it is honored as the national bird. The bald eagle is seen pretty much everywhere, and both outrank other birds in terms of high-altitude flying.

The golden eagle is larger than the bald eagle, or any bird of prey in North America, and can fly to the highest altitude. While a golden eagle's wingspan normally reaches six feet, some have been found with wingspans of well over seven feet across, and they may reach diving speeds of over 150 miles per hour. With the exception of the peregrine falcon, this is possibly the fastest that any animal can travel on its own steam in the wild. Neither Amtrak's fastest Acela Express train nor a stock car racer on an overland track could outrace a golden eagle's shadow while it is diving. Some of these individuals live over thirty years and can weigh more than fifteen pounds.* For all these reasons and more, the golden eagle is a

---

*This is commonly held information. My descriptions here are based on a dozen mainstream sources, not Native sources. Similar descriptions can be found in any encyclopedia.

symbol for unrivaled power in the United States. The golden eagle is dark brown, without the distinctive white head associated with the bald eagle. It has a ruffled collar of golden-brown feathers called hackles, not unlike a lion's mane, and its wings are lighter in color than its body. The young may feature a white tail with a black border. Golden eagles eat mainly mammals, such as rabbits, marmots, and ground squirrels, but also fish, reptiles, and other birds. They are more likely to eat carrion than the bald eagle, and unlike the bald, will occasionally kill a full-grown deer for fresh meat. Insects are also on their menu.

The territory of a golden eagle pair, if seen as a circle, would most likely stretch over nine and a half miles across. Monogamous, they may stay with one mate for several years or for life. Golden eagles nest in high elevations, including cliffs, trees, or human structures such as electrical poles. They build large nests and may return for several breeding years to the same home. Females lay from one to four eggs. Both parents incubate them for forty to forty-five days. Typically, one or two eaglets survive to fledge in about three months.

It is interesting that the Algonkin-ode of northern Canada hold these eagles in the highest regard spiritually, as messengers of God, and live under the flight path of the golden eagle, while the Algonkin-ode of Long Island and the Eastern Seaboard do not favor the eagle above other raptors, and some don't even regard raptors above other birds such as the goose, as messengers or otherwise. They do not live in the flight path of this monster species of eagles, which can pick up a full-grown fox and deposit it a mile away if it chooses. Might I speculate that there is a connection? It seems that any bird-watching Native American who has seen a golden in action never views eagles the same way again. For some, it is a "religious" experience. Stories of golden eagles snatching human infants and taking them to the nest abound but have never been proven. Let us say they are to be included among tall tales and medicine stories. In the medicine story called "Big Eagle," which I repeated in *Native New Yorkers,* a teenage Munsee is snatched up and taken to an eagle's nest. In the story of the

Ang, the monster bird that the Washo people still tell stories about, a grown man meets a similar fate.*

On Eagles' Wings

The eagle plays a central role in a number of teaching traditions, mainly as a messenger of the Creator. Although a number of birds can fulfill that role from time to time, no other bird can replace the eagle because of its purity of spirit. "The bird that flies the highest sees the farthest" is an old Native American saying, and the eagle is the highest flier of all. The upper limits of the altitude each bird can reach was known to the ancestors, and this was often used as a way of ranking the birds in terms of spiritual vision and purity.

The following story is based on an English tale, in which a linnet, a trickster stowaway bird, gets all the accolades and the eagle gets nothing. In this Native American version, the tricked eagle gets the honor he deserves restored to him, and the English linnet gets nothing. The linnet is not a North American bird and therefore could not be a bird of any power or significance to Native Americans. The story shows the importance many Native Americans place on how high a bird can fly, which is a most significant way of ranking birds, and also how distrustful some nations were of the English. Just as the eagle carried the linnet on its back in the story, Tisquantum and the Wampanoags "carried" the English Puritans on their backs for several winters, helping them to survive, only to be dismissed and then detained on Deer Island in Boston Harbor in 1675, one of the world's first concentration camps.

The Linnet and the Eagle

The birds met together one day to try to see which could fly highest. Some flew up very swiftly but soon became tired and were passed by

---

*A Washo elder gave me this story in its traditional form to share in my book *Native American Stories of the Sacred*. Such stories are meant to instruct and entertain the youth, and not surprisingly, often include birds.

others of stronger wing. The eagle flew beyond them all and was ready to claim the victory, when the gray linnet flew from the eagle's back, where it had perched unperceived, and being fresh and unexhausted succeeded in going the highest. When the birds came down and met in council to award the prize, it was given to the eagle, because that bird had not only gone up nearer to the sun than the other large birds, but it had carried the linnet on its back. Hence the feathers of the eagle are esteemed the most honorable marks for the warrior, as it is not only considered the bravest bird, but also endowed with strength to soar the highest.[4]

The Heart of an Eagle

William Commanda, Algonquin (Mamawinini) elder and wampum belt carrier, said, "Birds are close to the Indian heart. I love them because they have such wisdom. Why are they wise? The highest flying bird is the closest to Creator's ways. When they are close to you, something happens to make things better. Either they bring you goodness, or they warn you. If you truly believe they can help you, the bird knows what you are thinking and can help you in many ways. We have bald eagles across the lake at my reservation, they are huge in size. They don't come that close but they salute us each day as they fly over our heads and it's an honor for us. It's good luck. We use the eagle feather to smudge others and we ask for good tidings. The eagles don't fight, they get along together."[5]

The Omaha Nation lives on the banks of the Missouri River in Nebraska, a major migratory route between Canada and Mexico. It's big sky country, so bird watching is a popular occupation. Eagles can still be seen flying over the Omaha Reservation. The Omaha prefer and give more significance to the sighting of a golden eagle rather than a bald eagle, and as noted earlier, the golden is quite a bit larger.[6]

White Deer of Autumn (Gabriel Horn) is a member of the family of Princess Red Wing, Metacomet, and Nippawanock of the Narragansett Tribe/Wampanoag Nation. He is the author of many books. He was the Native American contributor to the book *The American Eagle,* published in 1988. This book was given to George H. W. Bush by the Chief of Protocol at his inauguration and subsequently to many foreign dignitaries as the Bush administration's official gift of state. He had this to say about the importance of the eagle to Native Americans and the United States:

This is what loving your country is about; you have to show respect to the eagle, our national symbol. The eagle is sacred to possibly all of our tribes and nations in North America. Ben Franklin adopted (or borrowed) the eagle as a symbol of liberty from the Haudenosaunee, or Iroquois. We talk about the American eagle, but the eagle does not have a voice in the affairs of humans except through the words of Native American elders, and people who care. The cell phone towers are harming the eagles, our feathered relatives, our grandfathers. We are intimately tied to them, and our fates are mutually bound. It is part of our heritage as Native Americans and as United States citizens to honor the eagle as a symbol of nobility, and so it is our responsibility to protect not only our liberty, but the eagles and their habitats.[7]

Early in the morning of September 11, 2001, my sister Lynn Pritchard was working at an elementary school in an urban area near several major highways, including Washington, D.C.'s busy beltway, Interstate 495. In the center was a courtyard open to the sky, accessed though the classrooms only and not open to outside traffic. In some respects, the school's design was similar to the Pentagon, only with four sides instead of five, filled with tiny little warriors with gold stars on their papers instead of on uniforms. A coworker named Robyn said to Lynn, "Look at what's going on over there on TV." Lynn saw the replay of the first plane crashing into the Twin Towers in New York and pulled out her tobacco, which she always carries with her as part of her Mi'kmaq tradition. She went out to the enclosed courtyard to pray and ask the eagles, "What is going on?" In her tradition, it is the eagles' job to take our prayers to the Creator and to bring back answers. She heard distressed voices inside the school, calling out, and after putting down her tobacco, went to the TV again, only to see the second crash.

She found more tobacco and went again to the courtyard, this time to pray for guidance. After all, there were hundreds of little children in her care and in the care of other teachers at that moment. When she stepped out into the bright sun of that crayon blue sky that morning, she looked up and saw a bald eagle hovering just above her head. As Lynn watched in amazement, the eagle hung in the air over the little courtyard just above the one-story roof level. She put her tobacco down and offered it to the eagle, and then returned inside only to see yet another plane crashing on TV, this time into the Pentagon, only sixteen miles away.

She saw the school principal and told her about the bald eagle that was visiting the school, even as the Twin Towers were crashing to the ground in a billowing cloud of white smoke. The surprised principal said, "What does it mean?" Lynn answered, "We're okay, but this is very important, and we have to pay attention. We are protected here." The eagle's spread wings were like angel's wings at that moment, and just as baby eaglets would be protected by a mother eagle's wings, the children of that elementary school would be protected as well. As far as I know, none of their parents, including among them professional fire fighters, were injured. Both of the adults took heart seeing the patriotic bird that had taken them all under its wing, smoothing their ruffled feathers.

Pure in Spirit

Eagles are considered pure in many respects. It is safe to assume that all Native Americans who do the talking feather ceremony—and this includes all Algonkin-ode—prefer to do the ceremony with the eagle feather if available. It is generally accepted by traditionals that the eagle feather acts as a two-way transmitter between God and human beings. This is common knowledge among Native Americans.*

These are core shamanistic beliefs and practices that have existed unchanged for thousands of years. Siberian shamans thousands of years ago drew pictures on walls and rocks depicting an eagle on the branch of a high tree. According to author Beryl Rowland, the shamans of Siberia to this day wear bird costumes as they lie in trance and believe that they are descended from birds.[8]

Joseph Campbell believes this indicates that eagles were seen as messengers from the higher dimensions. The recognition of eagles as links to the Creator seems to go back thousands of years in North America as well. Many precontact creation stories show eagles in special roles: Keneu the war eagle, the eagles that carry sky woman down to Earth (though, in some versions it's geese), and the man eagle of the Hopi story of Kwatoko. The Mi'kmaq story of how Glooskap brings Wind Eagle's power into balance is, on one level, really an allegory for how Native people learned to master the use of the eagle's spiritual power.[9] In my book *No Word for Time: The Way of the Algonquin People*, I wrote down a story of the boy who wanted to fly with the eagles. He actually succeeded, but was distracted by humans below and fell from the sky, plumeting into the water, showing ancient acknowledgment that we humans cannot go into those realms that eagles can spiritually. We are not pure enough.[10]

There is a belief among Algonkin-ode of a white eagle, which is the chief of all the eagles in the spirit world. It is only seen in visions, but it is the mouthpiece of the Creator in a sense. Its whiteness predates contact with white people, and like that of the white buffalo, the white pine of the Peacemaker, and the white otter of the Ojibway, represents its purity of spirit. It is close to the great white light of the Creator, at the source of all being. All eagles of this world are emanations of White Eagle, are messengers for White Eagle, are at the service of White Eagle,

---

*The Cherokee perform a talking *stick* ceremony, so there the bird question is moot.

who is the mouthpiece of the Creator, according to Algonkin-ode belief.

One of the most sacred objects used in the sweat lodge is the eagle bone whistle or eagle bone flute. It has been used in most sweat lodges I have attended, run by elders from a variety of nations. It gives a high-pitched tone, which alerts the eagles to the prayers that are about to take place and also opens the ears of the hearers to the spirit world. It is sometimes blown outside the lodge to the four directions and sometimes inside the sweat lodge.

Heady Lifestyle of the Bald Eagle

Up in Canada, it is expected that eagles will come and circle over a sacred outdoor gathering to bless the gathering with their connection to the Great Spirit, or Creator. It also seems that they are attracted to the sound of loud drums, which is part of the secret purpose of the great drum at powwows—to help the eagles find the gathering. (This is also mentioned in *No Word for Time*.)

Eagles seldom get involved in politics, that is, unless the drumming (and the cause) is good. A few years ago, some Cheyenne were using drumming as a means of protesting a civic parade in Tallahassee, Florida, that was to feature Andrew Jackson: in fact a local couple dressed up as Jackson and his wife were to lead the parade through the streets of Tallahassee. Well, anyone who knows anything about Native Americans knows how strongly the Natives of this land feel about Jackson, even now, 180 years after he ordered the civilized tribes to walk the Trail of Tears, an earlier grimmer parade that cost the lives of over eight thousand men, women, and children. The townsfolk probably had mixed feelings about the presence of this protest group, who were drumming loudly on a huge field drum while singing a traditional Cheyenne song. Grandmother Wyakin, a Cheyenne woman, and her sister Raven, whose hair had a blue sheen the color of a raven's wing, were at the protest march, and they witnessed a pair of eagles come and circle low and slow over the heads of the protesters in a dignified manner during the song—an honor dance—and the eagles maintained their flight pattern for a long time before heading home. Wyakin felt the eagles' visit was a message from the sky world supporting the Cheyenne's position against honoring Andrew Jackson.

No bird flies as high as the eagle or sees as far, and there are twelve levels of the sky (as I mentioned in my book *Native American Stories of the Sacred*) measured by the breadth of one's hand, associated with twelve levels of the spirit world. Only the eagle goes to the highest of these levels.

According to bird-watcher Simon Mercer, bald eagles like ridges for nesting and hanging out. However they like the river valleys for food, as they like to eat a lot of fish. They can also eat a baby musk-rat, rabbit, squirrel, and so forth. All raptors eat meadow voles, moles, mice, and other small creatures. Some eagles today hang around near railroad tracks, as they appreciate a freshly killed deer. Eagles are also known to frequent lakes and ponds. When a deer falls through the ice, it can be a source of fresh eagle food for a long time. An eagle can catch a starling as it is flying in the air, thanks to its great speed. The eagle is adept at keeping control over its wings in the strongest blasts of the north wind. This gives eagles an edge over other smaller birds during a storm.

Hawks fly high during migration, but eagles (and those in the vulture family such as condors) fly high most of the time. The high place above the clouds is their home, that place over the rainbow.

Some Native traditions hold to the belief that when we pray to the Creator, or to the Sacred Powers or divine beings, they may actually materialize before us as birds in response to our prayers. While eagles are not the only type of bird form used, it is the one that most commonly comes to mind in this regard. Therefore, the appearance of any eagle is treated with respect as it might be a visit from the Master of the Universe, the Creator, or one of the Sacred Powers.

Peter J. Powell, in his book *The Cheyennes, Ma'heo'o's People: A Critical Bibliography*, explains one reason why eagles and other birds are so important in the Cheyenne way: "Sacred Persons and designs were painted on the covers of shields by the holy men possessing power to make them, and a few lodge covers were painted with holy drawings of the Sacred Persons or Sacred Powers, *who assume the forms of animals, birds,* natural forces."[11] Powell explains who some of the Sacred Persons might be, including the four Guardians of the Universe, Thunder Beings, or perhaps Ma'heo'o himself.

Cheyenne arrow priest Eugene Blackbear Sr., emphatically confirmed that living birds were sacred to the Cheyenne and that eagle feathers played a role in the highly sacred restoring arrow ceremonies. Blackbear further emphasized that the stories of Sweet Medicine and teachings (for example, about birds) must be transmitted face-to-face, and from the heart, and not in writing or over a phone. (Powell strongly echoes this in his book, *The Cheyennes, Maheyo's People*.)

The avataric figure of the Cheyenne, Sweet Medicine (named after a Native plant to which the Cheyenne attribute great magical powers, known in Europe as Solomon's Seal) spent much of his life around the Black Hills and Devil's Tower, Wyoming, where eagles lived in great numbers. According to George Dorsey, Sweet Medicine used eagle feathers in making the four arrows of restoration. Eagles play a central role in the Cheyenne way. It was reasonable for the early Cheyenne to assume that these birds would continue to fly and nest upon this land forever—as long as the grass shall grow, as long as the rivers shall flow. They put their futures in the hands, or talons, of these birds. Eagles have been in the Wyoming area since the Oligocene Period, 33.9 million to 23 million years ago, based on fossils found. It is reasonable that eagles would be incorporated into his teachings. Blackbear also said that there are hawks in that area as well. He has been going to the Black Hills (to Bear Butte sixteen times) to fast and pray for twenty-seven years.

Eagles are considered our elders and should be treated with the same respect as one would a chief or high elder of one's nation. In Mi'kmaq, the word for eagle is *geetpoo* and is the same word that is used for human elders as well.

Eagles Answer Prayers

A Cheyenne woman, Morningstar, was sitting in her car with her two daughters after school one day, discussing the BP oil spill in the Gulf of Mexico. The children had seen terrible pictures in class that day of pelicans, herons, and egrets painted black with toxic oil, still gushing out from the bottom of the ocean floor and were worried. They asked their mom what they could do to help. Morningstar told them that a prayer is often the most effective thing you can do. She explained that there are many dangers that birds face, not only cell towers, but wind towers and oil spills. and that many corporations involved are slow to respond but that prayer can speed up the process. They all started praying for the oil spill to stop and for the blackened birds to get help. Although they were in a suburban school yard, almost immediately a giant bald eagle came straight down and landed in front of their car and looked at them. His eyes seemed to say, "I hear you! I will take your prayers to the spirit world!" He nodded and took off into the sky, presumably to look into the problem.

Although the oil situation has been slow to be resolved, the little children's hearts were opened by the prompt attention the mighty eagle offered them in response to their prayers, and they caught a glimpse of how powerful prayers, to M'he'o in this case, could be.[12] According to numerous Native American traditions, this is the way a sincere prayer is usually answered. There is a Mi'kmaq song about it:

> *yo ho yo ho yo hunday, yo ho yo ho yo hunday*
> *yo ho yo ho yo hunday, yo ho yo ho yo hunday*
> *ay mizigees kotok ah medewindo*
> *peektowa singdayz geetpoohwah, peektowa singdayz*
> *geetpoowa*
> *bedjegunawadweeyay geetpoowa, bedjegunawadweyay*
> *geetpoowa*

It tells the story of how the eagle will take our prayers into the sky, fly around the Earth, and return the next day with a message.

Eagles Are Symbols of Freedom

A neighbor we will call "Max,"* who is of Saami, Frisian, Viking, and Mexican Indian blood lines (to mention a few!), was under house arrest and had to appear in court to face becoming a long-term dinner guest of the state of New York. The day of the hearing, while being driven to the courthouse in Poughkeepsie for judgment, Max prayed for a sign of hope regarding his tight situation. The symbol of freedom, the bald eagle, appeared in his path, standing in the middle of the busy highway, feasting on a raccoon that had just been hit by a car. They barely missed hitting the eagle. Killing an eagle can cost you $5,000 from a lenient judge, but it was also something you don't want to do when looking for signs from the Creator. Max later said, "The way I remember it, we were driving to court, and I was worried if I was to be sentenced to a one-to-three-year prison term that day or would I be freed from house arrest . . . and the bald eagle lifting off from the double yellow line on Route 9 in front of me was a sign that today I would go free . . . and I was released from any further confinement." Max is a free man to this day.[13]

Letting Go of Fear

Robin Tekwelus Youngblood (White Wolf Clan Mother), coauthor of *Path of the White Wolf* and member of Grandmothers Circle the Earth Foundation, told me that eagles have been very helpful to her throughout her life. Once, when she was caught up in a difficult real estate transaction that was not going smoothly, she found herself at risk of losing quite a lot of money and perhaps being homeless and began to feel apprehensive. She was standing outside a nice house, looking at yet another for sale sign, and inwardly praying to the Creator to help guide her actions and decisions. Should she buy the house just to have somewhere to go? Or wait for what she really wanted?

At that moment, a white rabbit jumped out in front of her feet and a bald eagle swooped down and caught it in its large talons. The bald

---

*Some names in this book have been changed in the interest of privacy.

eagle did not eat the rabbit or take it away to its nest. He just stood there on the grass at her feet staring with its penetrating eyes, as she most certainly was staring back at him. He stood there for twenty or so minutes, letting Robin absorb the meaning of the message. Finally, the eagle opened its talons and let the unharmed rabbit run (and I mean *run!*) away to safety. The eagle then flew away, leaving Robin to figure out the message.

Puzzled, I asked her what it all meant. She said that the rabbit had always represented the emotion of fear to her, as in the expression "scared rabbit." The eagle, on the other hand, was a symbol of freedom and power, not afraid of anything. He was seizing an opportunity but was not attached to it. "I can take it or leave it," the eagle was obviously saying. "There will be other opportunities." On another level, the eagle was showing her that fear was something that can grip you sometimes, but it is not you. It is something that runs away when you let it go.

Robin decided not to buy the house in front of her because she would have only done so out of fear or panic, the "scared rabbit" knee-jerk reaction. She decided that she could take it or leave it, and so she left it. There would be other opportunities. A little while later, she found a home that suited her very nicely.[14]

Eagles Give Thanks

Bird-lover Elfie Avery had faith in the power of nature. She lived near the Potomac River in the Mount Vernon, Virginia, area and passed away there on January 13, 1999, at the age of seventy-nine. Her family had a histori-cally significant affiliation with the Chickasaw Nation spanning seven generations. Traditions about environmental stewardship helped shape her life as a biology teacher. She spent the 1970s and 1980s participating in the effort to clean up the Potomac River—monitoring water quality, taking samples on a regular basis, and turning them over to others. Over time, her efforts were well rewarded; in the 1990s, people were able to swim safely in waters that once had been fouled with human waste from suburban expansion with inadequate sewage treatment. But there was another unexpected reward. In November 1991, a pair of American bald eagles moved into her neighborhood (Little Hunting Creek) attracted by the now environmentally safe fishing that had become available once again thanks to Elfie and her students and friends. The community also built a nesting platform just offshore that was soon taken over by osprey.

In April 1992, Elfie wrote an article about the birds in *The Beacon*, a local newsletter, championing the cause of eagle welfare, playfully titled, "Eagles Move In: Mount Vernon Home Chosen by Prominent Americans."

Late in November, activity was noticed in the neighborhood as two newcomers looked for a home in our part of Fairfax County. They chose this area for its proximity to the Potomac River and for the good homesite available for building. But these two are not typical Washingtonians—they are American Bald Eagles.

The Eagles started building in late November and could be seen dining (and also breakfasting, lunching and snacking) on the bountiful fish in the area. Mrs. Eagle is an imposing creature quite a bit larger than her husband. Between them, their nest was completed and they settled down to domestic life for good. . . . They recommend Potomac cuisine.

Seven years later, Elfie's earthly life came to a peaceful ending, and she was cremated. Her family and friends gathered to plant a tree in her honor at the edge of the Potomac, the same spot where she had spent so much of her time bird watching and monitoring the waters. Family members poured her ashes into the earth, and the tree was positioned overtop, to draw life from her bones for years to come. As one of her daughters sang a song about nature's beauty, Mr. and Mrs. Eagle dramatically appeared and circled overhead to join in the song and ceremony to honor Elfie and to give thanks for all she had done for them.

Following her funeral, *The Beacon* reprinted, in 1999, the eagle article in full, including the following explanation:

Elfie Avery penned this article seven years ago to share her enthusiasm when two American Bald Eagles took up residence in our area. This week, in silent tribute, a pair of eagles was seen circling gracefully overhead as family and friends planted a tree in Elfie's honor at the Clubhouse. It was quite a moving sight, as if the two majestic birds had come to pay their respects. Few will ever forget that perfect moment.

It was George Washington who decided on the bald eagle as the official symbol of the United States because of its strength and freedom and its associations with liberty learned from the Mohawk (his future enemies!) years earlier. He must have watched them circle his home at Mount Vernon and enjoyed their effortless flight high in the sky. If it is symbolically significant that American bald eagles were driven out of Mount Vernon by industrial pollution during the twentieth century, it is also significant that someone connected to the Chickasaw tradition helped bring them back. We are all indebted to people like Elfie Avery, whether we know their names or not. Without them, America would be impoverished, stripped of the power of nature.

Talking Feather/Eagle Phone

The eagle feather is believed by traditionals to be a two-way communication device with the Creator. You hold the eagle feather in your right hand and speak, and the Creator is listening to you through the feather. The Mi'kmaq say that the eagle is pure and cannot be misused, so watch your tongue when using the eagle feather as a talking stick! Traditional talking feather ceremonies, also called the Medicine Wheel, use a bonafide eagle feather for this reason.

Due to the new "Eagle Feather Law," which supercedes the Migratory Bird Treaty Act of 1918 (based on the Convention of 1916), enrolled members of a federally recognized nation can own and use eagle feathers in ceremony. However, this means that mixed-blood Natives who do not carry a band card cannot own an eagle feather in the United States unless they are members of the US Army's 101st Screaming Eagle Division. Although the 1918 act has helped remove the bald eagle from the endangered species list, it means that most mixed-bloods must pass the eagle feather in ceremony in the presence of a federally recognized Native American elder, or face fines up to $25,000. The Bald Eagle Protection Act of 1940 was revised in 1959, 1962, 1972, 1978 (including the Morton Policy, which protects Native Americans), and 1994. The bald eagle was removed from the endangered list in 2007. On October 12, 2012, the Obama administration's Department of Justice, Office of Public Affairs, issued a policy statement signed by Attorney General Eric Holder, making it easier for Native Americans to use the eagle feather. This policy paper stated:

"From time immemorial, many Native Americans have viewed eagle feathers and other bird parts as sacred elements of their religious and cultural traditions," said Ignacia S. Moreno, Assistant Attorney General of the Justice Department's Environment and Natural Resources Division. "The Department of Justice has taken a major step forward by establishing a consistent and transparent policy to guide federal enforcement of the nation's wildlife laws in a manner that respects the cultural and religious practices of federally recognized Indian tribes and their members."

"The Justice Department's policy balances the needs of the federally recognized tribes and their members to be able to obtain, possess and use eagle feathers for their religious and cultural practices with the need to protect and preserve these magnificent birds," said Donald E. "Del" Laverdure, Principal Deputy Assistant Secretary for Indian Affairs. "Its reasoned approach reflects a greater understanding and respect for cultural beliefs and spiritual practices of Indian people while also providing much-needed clarity for those responsible for enforcing federal migratory bird protection laws."

When the ban was placed on killing the bald eagle in 1940, their numbers were down to almost nothing. By 1963, there were 417 nesting pairs; by 1999, there were over 6,000 pairs of bald eagles in the lower forty-eight. Although the new 2012 policy clarifies the rights for federally recognized nations to own eagle feathers, the 1940 law imposes considerable hardship for Métis or mixed-blood Indians in the United States.

The eagle phone is an ancient tradition used by traditional members of most Native American nations, but similar techniques and practices can be found in other lands as well. The sender places tobacco in the hole of a tree and offers it to the eagles and sends his or her voice or thoughts into the mind of the eagle, who accepts the gift. The eagle finds the receiver, wherever he or she may be, and shows itself to the receiver. When the receiver sees the eagle, he or she immediately knows the message, perhaps by telepathy. It seems to work for traditional people. Traveling outside the body, also called exteriorization or out-of-body experience, is fairly well documented and has its roots in global shamanistic practices, but in addition, there seems to be a hidden vein of tradition among the world's indigenous people of entering into the consciousness of another and seeing through the other's eyes or temporarily working through the other. This most certainly extends to birds; in fact, birds seem to be preferred. As all beings must be asked permission before being "employed" in any way by a medicine person, it stands to reason that the eagles must be offered tobacco before asking them to help deliver a message, like a postage stamp on an actual letter. As we shall see later, there may be several situations that can arise where human and bird consciousness overlap and become, for a moment, one. This is an area for further exploration.

Thirteen Grateful Eagles

On June 5, 2010, *Clearwater* led the annual River Day flotilla, along with the *Mystic Whaler* and several other vessels of various sizes, including canoeists and kayakers. Pete Seeger and Native American friend

Apache singer/songwriter Roland Mousaa offered a musical blessing, with passengers, crew, and onlookers singing together to send off the sloop *Clearwater* from Waryas Park in Poughkeepsie to the Hudson River Maritime Museum in Kingston, in celebration of the Hudson River. When the flotilla arrived at the Rondout Creek in Kingston, there was much ceremony, with reenactors dressed in colonial garb and politicians giving the requisite speeches, including Congressman Maurice Hinchey. Meanwhile, a man named Loriman Rhodell sat on a bench looking out at the masts of the towering sloop and schooner, now docked in the creek, and what he saw was astonishing. While the celebration proceeded, thirteen eagles flew overhead, circling high above the Rondout. Seeing this many eagles in a semiurban environment is almost unheard of. They flew overhead long enough for Lori to count them and to double-check his tally. He pointed out the eagles to Manna Jo Greene of *Clearwater*, who wondered, Why were they there? And why thirteen? Then Manna realized a powerful connection—thirteen bald eagles had been killed by high-speed trains on their way up the east side of the Hudson over a period of ten years, roughly between 1994 and 2004, until strenuous efforts by the Clearwater organization to find a solution finally paid off, thus saving countless eagles' lives and assuring their successful reestablishment along the shores of the Hudson. Bald eagles had been unable to breed along the Hudson for many years, due to DDT-caused thinning of their eggshells resulting in premature death of the young. After the pesticide was banned in 1972, the eagle population began to increase slowly, and by 2004, there were about sixty birds in breeding pairs documented along the Hudson, but the loss of thirteen of these majestic birds due to train collisions jeopardized their recovery. In 2005, Clearwater raised the issue with the New York State's Department of Environmental Conservation (NYSDEC) and the railroads, sending a Notice of Intent (NOI) to sue as an illegal taking under the Endangered Species Act. The NOI brought the railroad companies, U.S. Fish and Wildlife Service, and NYSDEC, all of whom had ignored earlier entreaties, to a series of meetings, which resulted in an agreement by the railroad companies to implement a carcass-removal program to prevent the temptation a freshly killed raccoon or deer or other animal presents to eagles, whose eyesight is keen but whose hearing is not— thus ignoring the sound of train whistles warning of oncoming danger. They also agreed to develop a Habitat Conservation Plan with ongoing monitoring. By remembering this project, Manna Jo was able to offer Lori an explanation as to the appearance of the eagles they had seen. Thirteen eagles had died over the course of a decade due to the trains— these eagles had come to thank the members of Clearwater and their legal advisors for their efforts.[15]

The Famous Eagle-Mating Ritual

One of the most talked-about examples of bird behavior is also the one least seen by humans, the tumbling eagle mating ritual. In this ritual, the two lovers meet high in the sky, lock talons like two acrobats, and then form a spinning ball and make love while falling 100 miles an hour straight toward the ground. Eagles also mate in other ways, with the male bird standing on the back of the female—sort of a missionary position by eagle standards—but nothing sparks the human imagination like the tumbling mating ritual, which is both exhilarating and life threatening for the risky lovers, for a single mistake by either bird could cause death to both. Native Americans look to the eagle as a symbol of courage, and this ritual is just one reason the eagle has earned this association.

Munsee (Lenape) landscape artist Judy Abbot is a descendant of the Pacatakan (often called Pepacton) Band of Munsee, near Roxbury, New York. Their land lies in the valley of the East Branch of the Delaware, called Pacatakan (probably meaning "flat woodlands") and also called Pepakunk ("where sweet flag grows"). Today, the reservoir is called Pepacton. Judy recently went on a painting trip to Pacatakan and sat on the banks of the East Branch of the Delaware River, carefully observing the landscape and painting the scenery directly onto the boards that she sells in museums to make a living. In fact, her oils and watercolors are highly respected by art collectors across the continent.

Judy placed her painting board on the ground and stood up awhile, just to enjoy the scenery. She stood very quietly because she knew it is best to be perfectly still if one is to really observe nature. Many creatures flee at the sound of a loud noise. Judy had been painting in that spot for hours without making a sound. She heard a loud unearthly sound like metal scraping against metal. A large bald eagle came toward her from her left side, but about eighty feet up and climbing, well clear of the tops of the tallest trees. Her heart skipped a beat. Then from behind her came that same sound again, and another bald eagle appeared, also climbing.

Reaching a precipitous height, the male flew underneath the female and reached up for her. The two giant birds locked talons one hundred feet or more into the sky above the Munsee observer below. They pulled close together, forming a ball, cupping and tucking in their wings around each other, and tumbling head over heels and around and around, falling faster and faster, towards Judy. They were also rotating and turned one complete revolution as they fell, locked together side by side, until they were so close to the ground that they disappeared behind the bushes right in front of her. The two released each other's talons and flew in opposite directions without injury to either. Their timing had to be of split-second accuracy to pull off the display. The entire descent took less than four seconds.

The visual impact was so intense that Judy fell to the ground and began to weep. This was the very spot her ancestors had set up their *wikiups* in the 1600s, and she was painting the surroundings, little changed from when her great-great-great grandmother lived here, as a way of honoring the spirits of her ancestors, to whom she prayed often. Now this! She thought it could be a message that her ancestors wanted her to be more courageous and brave in fighting the reckless development going on at Ulster Manor in nearby Kingston, New York, and at other places, where native artifacts were being removed and without proper study. She certainly felt well humbled, blessed by the mating pair to be an eyewitness to a sighting that is more meaningful and rare to a bird lover than any UFO encounter; it was a bird sighting of the third kind. Of all the humans on Earth, they chose her.

This choosing was probably not unpremeditated, however. Just days earlier, Judy had been walking along a trail near that spot, and although she had not seen an eagle, she suddenly had the knowing in her mind that she was going to find an eagle feather that day. The eagles were telling her so, and she trusted their inner message with as much certainty as if it were posted on a billboard. She turned a corner, and there it was, dropped in her pathway by one of the two sky beings. She felt it was a great blessing, relaying a message of courage and hope.[16]

Eagles occasionally lock one talon each in combat or just for fun and do what ornithologists call whirling. They swing each other around as they fall, helicoptering to the ground before letting go, like a wild square dance swing. To my knowledge, none have ever actually hit the ground.

Welcome Home

My sister had moved back to our ancestral homeland in Canada and bought property near a cave by the Miramichi River where at least some of our ancestors had sought shelter, near the head of the tide. A large stone pestle was found in the river there recently, at the upstream point of an island, similar to the one that had been handed down through our generations, inherited by my brother Marc. I used to play with that pestle as a kid. Now Lynn has one, too.

Just inland from that shoreline cave is a clearing where Lynn put up a shed, but at that time, she had not yet built a house, so she had to stay with friends to make contact with western civilization. Otherwise, she had to live off the land as our great aunt Helen once did, the hard way.* There were days when Lynn felt blissfully free of all the hassles of

---

*This is no exaggeration. When Helen was first pregnant, a neighbor said it was improper to live outdoors when you're expecting, especially in Maine, where the winters are hard. So she got a hammer and built herself a house! This story is told in my *Aunt Helen's Little Herb Book*.

technology, and other days when she wondered if she'd made a mistake. Building a cabin was going to take some time. There were delays, and winter was coming.

She prayed to the ancestors every day for guidance. She kept in touch with Grandfather Turtle (whom I'd written about in *No Word for Time*) who lived down the highway. One day, he came to visit, and as they sat outside the shed talking, he drew her attention to the sky directly above their heads, and when Lynn looked up, there were exactly four eagles in a perfect circle, very high in the sky. He said, "That's a very good sign," as if to indicate she had made the right decision to follow her ancestors and move to this remote area of woods in Canada. Over previous years, he told her that the spirit of an ancestor, or another guardian spirit, can sometimes go into a bird that has given permission to do so. "Birds are that pure," he said. "They are willing to offer themselves in service to others." He told her to look for bird signs. Most Natives believe in bird signs.

On another day, she was standing by her shed when she looked up and saw two bald eagles spiraling higher and higher. Up they went, climbing into the sky. They must have ascended well beyond two hundred feet, riding a big thermal column up into the heavens, toward the Creator. They would float then flap their wings then float again. The two locked talons, and then began to tumble and twirl, plummeting faster and faster with the force of gravity, toward the spot where Lynn was planning to build her dream house some day. Just before they hit the ground, the unlocked their talons and spun off in opposite directions, completely unharmed.

What she was allowed to witness that day gave her hope that the land would be good to her. She was protected by the loving spirit of her forebears and by the birds watching over her. Over the next few years, Lynn built her dream house and now shares it with a man she loves, on a land that is powerful with ancestral memories and living birds of all shapes and sizes. The eagles were saying, "Welcome home!"

Like Judy, the Munsee woman in the above story, Lynn is out in nature all the time and has only seen the eagle-mating ritual once in her life, grateful for the experience. As for me, if I had a choice between seeing a perfect game pitched and seeing two eagles do the mating ritual, I'd choose the latter. It's the blessing of a lifetime.

Eagle Marriage Feast Ritual

Blessing Bird, of Cherokee, Tuskarora, and Lenape descent, who worked at Scales and Tails rescue center in Maryland, observed eagle behavior her whole life. She stood on a cliff at Hawk Mountain, Pennsylvania, and came eyeball to eyeball with an eagle. She saw them circling over her head, calling to her, and once an osprey whizzed past her carrying a fish at the appropriately named Eagle's Nest Powwow in Perryville, Maryland. She observed eagles do some stunning things, but nothing impressed her as much as the marriage feast ritual of the eagle, which she had heard about but then witnessed firsthand over the Susquehanna River near Havre de Grace, Maryland.

The male and female eagles flew together, then the male dived down into the river and came up with a fish big enough to feed a wedding party. He returned to the female and offered it to her from his claws. In midair, he flew upside down and boosted it up into her talons. She accepted the fish and carried it to her nest in a nearby tree to eat it. This was good news! It meant she had accepted his "hand" in marriage, a lifetime commitment for an eagle couple, who are usually monogamous for life. If she had dropped the slippery, wiggling creature, it would not have been an accident. It would mean she found the male unsuitable and would continue looking for another life mate. The male joined her in the tree to enjoy the feast. Soon they would be building a nest together, with the larger, sturdily built female and the smaller, more delicately graceful male shouldering the construction work equally. Because of their difference in size (females are much larger than males), the male and female are able to exploit two different niches in the environment, harvesting a wider variety of food sources than most other birds. Overall, larger birds are more likely to capture smaller birds in flight, while smaller birds are more adept at getting into small crevices where tasty insects might be hiding. The female's size helps her warm the eggs and fight off predators. Given the life span of an eagle, they are probably both still married with children.

It is interesting that many marriage, feasting, and entry songs in the Mi'kmaq tradition invoke the eagle, *geetpoo,* including either the eagle call or its name. The Mi'kmaq also use food gifts in the courtship ritual, as do the Creek and countless other Native peoples. Eagles are looked to as role models in both love and war, and the reasons are obvious; their relationships usually stand the test of time, and they usually win in battle.

William Strachey, an Englishmen who lived among the Powhatan in the early 1600s, wrote, "They express their loves to such women as they would make choice to live withall, by presenting them with . . . fowl, fish, or wild beasts, . . . which they bring unto the young women . . . the wooer promiseth that the daughter shall not want of such provisions."[17] We can be certain that the Powhatan woman had the right of refusal and that if she rejected the food, the suitor was rejected as well. Among the Chickasaw, James Adair, a trader who lived with them for forty years, observed in his *The History of the American Indians* (1775), "When an Indian makes his first address to the young woman he intends to marry, she is obliged by ancient custom to sit by him until he is done eating and drinking, whether she likes him or dislikes him; but afterward, she is at her own choice whether to stay or retire." He says, according to Swanton, that "the groom might divide two ears of corn before witnesses, and give the girl one, retaining the other himself, or give her a deer's foot for which she returns some cakes of bread. Another writer notes that the groom gave venison and received corn or potatoes. Immediately before the consummation of the marriage the youth and the girl's father took a meal together with no one else present. A deer was also killed and laid at the woman's door, and when she had dressed and cooked this and given the youth some to eat, they were regarded as husband and wife."[18] According to Swanton, "Bartram mentions the exchange of reeds such as they used in the corn hills as symbols of marriage, and we also hear of an ear of corn being divided by the two and of venison being given to the woman by her intended husband and an ear of corn to him by his intended wife." Swanton quotes Benjamin Hawkins, American statesman and principal Indian agent to the Creek in the late 1700s, who wrote of the Creek "that when a man has built a house, made his crop, and gathered it in, then made his hunt, and brought home the meat, and put all this in the possession of his wife, the ceremony ends, and they are married: or as they express it, the woman is bound."[19]

The Great Elder in the Sky

I was helping a client with a number of projects at once. One involved doing research on his family tree, studying the genealogy to try to confirm if there was Native American ancestry. One had to do with researching endangered birds. Another had to do indirectly with Sequoia trees. I was on site, alone on a snowy morning in an otherwise vacant bed and breakfast.

Early in the morning, I awoke and could not sleep. I was looking over my notes concerning his family tree. There was a first name in the client's early family record, Telitha, that had bothered me. It sounded like a Creek name. I thought it was perhaps linked to the ancient mound builders, the Yucchi. At 9 a.m., I called my friend Yenyahola, an author and historian who is also Creek, and asked him what the name meant. He said that it was clearly a Native American name, that Taliwa was a name of someone descended from the village of the Tali, the scribes of the Creek Confederacy, and that the *itha* ending was distinctive of the southern Shawnee band called the Takabachi, a small subset of the Shawnee sept (clan) that Dark Rain Thom calls the Talegiwa, who are related to the Hathawakila. They were a small tribe in Georgia and South Carolina that were eventually taken in and absorbed into the Creek, but there is also a settlement in Oklahoma today.

Yenyahola said that Natives living in Alabama at this time would have not claimed to be Indian because the Goose Creek men of Middleton, in northern Alabama, were rounding up all Indians and selling them as slaves or indentured servants. So Natives were giving their children code names such as Telitha, undetected by whites, while signaling to fellow Creeks that their family was proud of their heritage. I asked if there was a connection between the Taliwa and Sequoia. He said that the Taliwa became the Tuskogees and that Sequoia was a Tuskogee; he added that he could show me four different books that said so. I realized that Telitha's father was a contemporary of George Guess, later known as Sequoia, and that they might be related. That was totally unexpected.

Just then I heard the client outside yelling for me on the second floor to open the window and look out. I looked out, and all I could see was the sun in my eyes. I hung up the phone, came down barefoot, and looked up and saw a giant bald eagle circling in the sky. He said that the bird had just been circling the tree outside my window for a while. I said, "It is probably Sequoia! He's your ancestor!" My client suspected himself to be Cherokee and was a great admirer of Sequoia, so this made quite an impression. This person may not be a direct descendant, but a common ancestor does seem likely at this point. The timing could not have been more perfect. What better way to tie in endangered birds, trees, Sequoia, and the ancestors in one fell swoop!

Mountain Eagles

Stephen Larsen was once traveling around Jackson Hole, Wyoming, with his son Merlin, both doing vision quests, but Steve was down in the valley, while Merlin was on top of a steep mountain. They were several miles apart. When they met again, Merlin said, "The most remarkable thing happened yesterday, the last day of my fast. An eagle came right up to me and looked at me. It was like he was looking inside me!" His father, Stephen, looked very surprised and said, "The same thing happened to me yesterday. An eagle came close to me and looked at me in the face! It was like he could read my mind!"

Eagles and other raptors certainly like mountain ridges. In the Hudson Valley, the eagles use the Shawangunks as a passageway. Stephen says they can follow that route all the way to Georgia. Herons also fly from New York to Florida, and it is said that as they go south they turn from blue to white.

HAWKS

Hawk the Protector

The hawk, gatekeeper of the East, is associated in Native tradition with clear vision, both its own and that of others. It helps inspire clear thinking and seeing with its truth and honesty. They are reliable "warriors of truth" and can be depended on to give the message clearly as possible. Native people rely on the hawk to protect them through dozens of methods, mostly as messengers of warning. A crying hawk might be seen as a warning, while one dive-bombing the individual (as they do to a raccoon) may be seen as a challenge. The journey into the realm of the supernatural is considered a dangerous one, and it would be considered foolish to go into such realms without a protector, and that usually means a hawk.

My sister Lynn has often seen the shadow of a hawk pass in front of her as a warning or sign of danger, even between her and a stranger just before an unpleasant encounter. In other instances, a bird will sit on a low branch and stare at her and won't fly away. This is often synchronous with the death of a friend. Sometimes a hawk will fly over her head to get her attention, they "check on you," she says. The red-tailed hawk has a sharp whistle "like an eagle," which helps you "clear your mind." Some eastern peoples see the large red tail as closest to the eagle, in altitude capacity, in size, and in behavior (see color insert, plate 5).

White Hawk Spirit

The red-tailed hawk takes many forms and is sometimes almost white, with white tail feathers. In fact, according to *The Sibley Guide to Bird Life and Behavior,* "[t]he Red-tailed Hawk (*Buteo jamaicensis*) shows . . . the highest incidence of partial albinism among *accipitrids* [diurnal raptors]."[20] This description does not sound very flattering! Nonetheless, the white hawk is a very special bird; it reflects the appearance of the Spirit Hawk, which flies in the spirit world as the oversoul of all hawks. When the Mi'kmaq see a white hawk, they say, *"Bpah-cha-lai-ee!"* (Amazing!), regardless of what is written in *The Sibley Guide.*

When you see the white hawk, it means something very sacred is taking place; perhaps a message from the Creator, or a sign that a miracle is going to happen. These miracles are not events that, as the white man might describe it, violate the laws of nature; they *are* the laws of nature, in their purest form. The medicine men say, "That's the way it works!" (When you are living right!) Miracles, in Native American culture, are seen as expressions of universal truth, rather than exceptions to it. The Mi'kmaq expression, *"Nee-gehn del-li-moog del-li-ah-oh-weh del-ah-sik neh-geh"* (I am telling you the truth is happening now), is how you might say, "I have seen a miracle!"

Hawks are seen as messengers for spirit world beings, including ancestors, the deceased, protective deities, and benevolent guides and helpers. Some medicine people have an association with hawks and recognize hawks as their helpers. It is common that Native Americans will interpret the action of a hawk as a message from a deceased friend or relative. It is more an individual thing as to how these signs are read. Hawks' most significant role is as messengers for protective deities, particularly the Spirit Hawk, which is the chief of all the hawks. Some see that protector hawk spirit as a blue light behind the right shoulder. Some Mi'kmaq call it Grandmother Hawk. Naturally a real living hawk would earn respect and attention, and their feathers deserve respect as well.

Raptors are seen as protectors, possibly because they are not often attacked by other birds. They are known for their ability to flip upside down in midair, snatch a smaller bird out of the sky (from underneath in most cases), and eat it. The association between hawks and warfare is not wholly undeserved, and songbirds are not off their menu either. Understandably, smaller birds often organize to mob the hawk in the defense of a nest, and one bird lover recently saw a hawk at the top of a small tree, indignantly enduring the catcalls of a large number of small birds below him, daring him to attack. Nonetheless, hawks are seen as being extremely helpful to humans, or at least to Native American humans. According to Mi'kmaq sources, eagles and hawks cannot be misused by sorcerers; they only act as messengers of good. But some raptors, such as owls, can. Hawks, like their fellow accipitrids the eagles, mate for life—and, according to "Ecologic" radio host, Ken Gale, renew their vows yearly. If you see someone in a dream, and he or she turns into an eagle or hawk, it is good, according to Native American Bird Medicine.

New York's Finest Bird

Falcons and hawks not only warn humans, they can also bring bad news. A mixed-blood Taino woman, whom we'll call "Marlene," living in a highly urban part of the South Bronx came home on the night of July Fourth with her father, talking about the fireworks they had just seen. There, sitting on the top of the gate waiting for them, was a large falcon. The top of the gate was just below eye level, so the bird's great eyes were staring into hers. He seemed to have something to say and screamed at her; he then turned to her father and just looked at him sadly and flew away. The young girl immediately considered it a sign and mistakenly thought it was a warning about her father's health, or even imminent death. He said he was fine.

The next day, they received news that her brother and cousin were jumped in a nearby alley and beaten by a local gang, which sent them to the hospital. The attack occurred an hour or so before Marlene and her father saw the falcon. They prayed for the two family members, and the boys' recoveries were surprisingly swift. Perhaps the feathered visitor was not just warning them but reminding them to pray.

It was not until I asked her, as part of an informal interview on July 8, if she had seen any bird signs (and we had just been talking about hawks) that she made the connection and realized that the timing of the falcon's arrival must have been fairly synchronous with the injuries her relatives sustained. Tearfully, she realized that the hawk was not "saying" her father was at risk of death but was only telling them what had just happened. It is probable that the hawk had actually seen the attack and knew where the relatives lived, thanks to its tireless habits of observation and infallible memory.

Like a true New York police officer, New York's finest bird was there waiting at the door with the bad news, offering any assistance it could. The appearance of a falcon in the South Bronx is in itself somewhat miraculous, so it is only slightly more amazing that the bird seemed to have appeared at that moment in order to bring an important message to Marlene and her family.

Hawks and Their Dining Habits

Each type of hawk has a distinct style of flying, and a different flair for arriving at the dinner table. The northern harrier can almost float in the air if it wishes but can also travel at high speeds. In a similar way the red-tailed hawk can drop straight down to the ground while holding the wings still in a horizontal position. Their aim is quite good. One morning in May, I saw a red tail drop from the sky, like a spaceship making a pinpoint landing, and collapse on a narrow strip of grass in the middle of Route 95 in Maryland, presumably having spotted an unsuspecting vole or mouse. It seemed to be saying to me, "Catch the opportunity." Mice are swift but cannot turn their heads easily upward, and so a vertical drop gives them less warning. Early in the day, the hawk's long shadow coming from the east would have passed over the mouse and caused him or her to flee. But a vertical drop leaves no shadow beneath it (until almost noon). Hawks collapse over their prey to guard it from other birds who might entertain a larcenous thought or two. Like the eagle, hawks need movement in order to see a small rodent or other tidbit, but the swirling winds created by high-speed cars are not a problem for the hawk. Two sources have told me that both hawks and eagles like traffic islands; lots of mice with nowhere to go.

Hawks, in fact, do not seem to mind traffic. I saw a Cooper's hawk flirtatiously displaying its characteristic striped tail feathers to all the drivers on I-87 in New York from a nearby tree (or perhaps it was making this display only to me). It seemed to be saying, "Notice me. I am a Cooper's hawk!" The question is, what is the significance of the Cooper's hawk? Like all hawks, the Cooper's hawk tells us to sharpen our awareness of omens, signs, and signals in nature as a general practice. But its tail is uniquely like a test pattern; perhaps it was saying, "This is only a test. If this were a real omen, you would be told where to go and what to do!"

The kestrel is mistakenly called a sparrow hawk. It is approximately the size of a robin. They are known for their agility and gracefulness.

The peregrine falcon is the fastest of all and can outrace any bird and, in many cases, have it for its meal. During the late 1940s with the introduction of pesticides such as DDT, the peregrine almost became extinct overnight, because the falcon would ingest whatever toxins were in the smaller birds' bodies, after eating bugs with pesticides inside. Peregrines had to be mated in captivity and eventually were brought back into the wild but are still rare to this day.

Harris's hawks work as a team, in ways that would make the Flying Karamazov Brothers green with envy. A Harris's hawk will attack a jackrabbit larger and heavier than itself, and then fly it off to the nest with the well-coordinated help of a close relative, often a brother, who carries half the weight and who, in most cases, gets 50 percent at the end of the day.

The Northern Harrier: A Messenger from Horus

All in all, in the United States, there are twenty-eight types of raptors in the Accipitridae family, which includes hawks, eagles, and harriers, and ten types in the Falconidae family, of which falcons are members. (Ospreys are separate, in the Pandionidae family.) All these are in the order Falconiformes, or diurnal birds of prey. The Accipitridae family has been further subdivided into as many as fourteen subfamilies. Members of the subfamily Buteoninae include broad-winged hawks, red-tailed hawks, and eagles. The harriers, named after the English hunting dog, are in the subfamily Circinae.

While the northern harrier is the only one living in the United

States, other types of harriers are found around the world. The harrier has an owl-like facial disc, which directs distant sounds to its ears, which miss nothing and remember everything (see color insert, plates 12 and 25). The tall and distinguished harrier builds its nest on the ground, usually hiding it under a bush. They have wide wings and a large wing surface compared to their body, which makes it possible for them to hover almost motionless in the sky over prey or listen for messages like a surveillance satellite. They sometimes cohabitate with short-eared owls. The northern harrier is also called the marsh hawk because it frequents the water and, in fact, has been known to sink certain waterfowl in battle. Also called the blue hawk because of its dark-blue back, the name *Circus cyaneus* describes its yellow eyes and tendency to repeatedly fly in circles. Its clutch has from three to five eggs at a time.

Ahngwet (pronounced AHN-gwet), a Mi'kmaq woman, sang "Yo Ho Yo Hunday," the eagle song for her father in the downtown Washington, D.C., hospital just before he passed to the spirit world. Comments were made, asking if he would send messages from the spirit world, letting the family know he was very well, or at least okay, and that he could hear their prayers. Ahngwet was sure he would send a big, prominent sign from the spirit world.

On the morning of that last visit to the hospital to identify the body, the family—the mother and three offspring—was riding home along East West Highway and was caught in a traffic jam in a heavily urbanized area of Maryland. A huge harrier hawk circled in front of the car and landed on a big, prominent sign, and then landed on top of a telephone pole, where it continued to sit, as if listening to Ahngwet and her siblings talking excitedly about the bird, until the car had made it through the traffic jam. Ahngwet, a passenger, pointed the bird out and said repeatedly, "It's Father, coming to send a message from the spirit world. I'm sure of it!"

The same or similar harrier showed up again twice more during the next few days, in different places, as the family began preparations for the funeral. It was a choice of messenger so succinct, it was almost humorous. Her father was a tall, distinguished man with a beakish

George Washington–like roman nose. He had been a radio man in the navy, and then in the intelligence field manned Station X, a listening post in the Aleutian Islands, before going on to other assignments, so the harrier's exceptionally acute hearing (in comparison to other hawks and falcons) was appropriate. The harrier has soft feathers and large wings, rendering his flights completely silent like the owls. A remarkably quiet man known as a good listener, he had also helped develop surveillance satellites, which hovered silently over Russia, like the harrier, whose overseas territory covers most of Russia. The northern harrier is not a "people person" and spends much of its time hiding from observers, as I found out firsthand during a recent visit to the northern harrier area of The Raptor Trust in Millington, New Jersey. The harriers spent most of my visit hiding behind a small privacy barrier.

Ahngwet's father had often worn a dark-blue suit to work, wearing black wing-tip shoes, giving him a similar coloration to the harrier, who has a dark-blue back and black wing tips. While in the navy, he was among the first to use an early form of sonar to sink a Nazi submarine during World War II at close range, so the marsh hawk's ability to drown a duck in battle is a significant parallel.

Her father had also been an Egyptologist and had written extensively about Horus, the falcon-headed god who is featured in the Egyptian Book of the Dead (the original was entirely pictorial, carved at first into temple walls as hieroglyphs and only later inscribed on papyrus) and who helps Ma'at in her judgment of the dead. Among American falcons, the harrier's profile most closely matches that of Horus, second only perhaps to the peregrine falcon.

In fact, in ancient Egypt, the Egyptian marsh hawk was ritually mummified and then given as an offering to Horus on behalf of one who was dying. One town in Egypt at the time of Christ mummified over ten thousand such Egyptian marsh hawks each year, which were then distributed as offerings to the god, to ensure safe passage into the afterlife. Its closest surviving relative today is the northern harrier.[21]

Were these visits from her father "saying" that his life was lived as an offering to the Egyptian god of mysteries? Or perhaps that he was now working for Horus as a messenger? Or was this a message that he had made it through Ma'at's test and that his heart had been placed on her fearful scales and was found to be lighter than a feather and therefore pure enough to eat the sacred manna of Osiris?

Ahngwet's father had raised his family in a small, low-lying, unassuming house hidden by tall trees and bushes in suburban Maryland, in an area that had been a marshy swamp until the end of World War II, bringing to mind once again the marsh hawk. Ahngwet's father was a rare breed, a point to which everyone who knew him agreed upon, and the parallels between him and the marsh hawk had been there all along, but no one ever made the connection.

Two weeks later, after the funeral, Ahngwet's brother was in the courtyard of a New York college in a different urban area and was telling a fellow professor of the continuing visits of the Maryland harrier, with messages from the falcon-headed father who had passed to the spirit world. The other professor had just said, "Gee, I don't know . . . that's pretty *out there*," when a full-size harrier, perhaps the same one, came barreling through the crowded campus at a good speed, about six feet off the ground, and blasted by the skeptical professor, nearly touching his shoulder, as the bird made a dramatic swoop toward the two figures. The harrier then landed on a big, prominent *sign* above the student union and looked at the disbelieving scholar, who blanched in shock. He recognized the harrier from the story and knew, as a loyal bird enthusiast, that this bird was not only on an endangered list but also not in the heart of its migratory path, as this was not a marsh or prairie. The young professor ran wide-eyed in the other direction, as fast as he could, glancing repeatedly at the harrier, who was staring back at him. It was a memorable moment.

Red Tails Understand Mohawk

Kevin Deer, a Mohawk ceremonial leader from Kahnawake Mohawk Territory, knows from experience how red-tailed hawks can dramatize connections with the departed spirits of good friends. There was a ceremonial gathering of elders and traditional-minded people at Victoria Harbor, about one hour's drive north of Toronto, Ontario. They were gathering to do a spring seed ceremony involving some Iroquois, Cree, and Ojibway people. However, the recent loss of two of their beloved elders, who had passed on, was occupying their minds, and the executive director of the healing lodge asked if there was something that could be done to deal with the grief that they were feeling.

Kevin decided to conduct the condolence ceremony to honor the grief they all felt. This ceremony took place beside a garden surrounded by beautiful trees, with the main house and some offices situated nearby. In the morning, Kevin's father began the traditional thanksgiving address, spoken in Mohawk then English, and then translated by the Ojibway clan leader. The Mohawk *kastowah,* or headdress, that Kevin was wearing had three eagle feathers.* Since no wampum strings were available, Kevin decided to improvise and use each one of the feathers from the kastowah, passing them across the fire to the Ojibway elders on the other side. The first feather, he said, dealt with the eyes and with tears that were being shed. The second feather, he said, dealt with the ears and nose. Then the third feather, he said, dealt with the lump in the throat. Those three feathers and the words associated with them were intended to help lift the minds of the grieving party. The feathers then crossed the fire, and the speaker on the grieving side of the fire then repeated the words associated with the small condolence ceremony to help pick up their minds. And then they broke for lunch.

Kevin stated that the first part of the ritual, which they had just completed, had dealt with the physical aspects of grieving and cleared their minds. Now, they would deal with the spiritual aspects of the planting, addressing, and honoring Great Spirit and the spiritual elements of the upper world. Then, when addressing the upper world elements—the four winds, thunder beings, and other sky world elements—Kevin acknowledged and thanked each of these elements in nature. At that moment,

---

*All Mohawk kastowah have three feathers. See illustration on page 217.

two red-tailed hawks appeared and circled over their fire. Kevin looked up, offered tobacco, and thanked them for showing up. As soon as the ceremony was over, someone started to ask questions: Is there a connection between the fact that we were reaching out to the spirits of the two elders who'd just recently passed on, and the fact that two red-tailed hawks circled low over our fire? What is the connection? Why did that happen? Kevin answered that some events seem to be complimented by the power of spirit, and that when we see these things, we can be assured of the reality of the Great Spirit's presence. These moments are sacred revelations. They do not happen all the time. We have no control over them. They just are. Kevin understood that they, as witnesses to such an event, would want to tell the story to their friends as soon as they got home, but reminded them that no one could share the feelings of sacredness they felt the minute the red tails made their entrance. That feeling of awe was to be theirs alone, and he urged them not to be too disappointed if friends and neighbors failed to understand.

Kevin Deer experienced a similar visit from three red-tailed hawks at Grand River, Ontario, on the Six Nations territory back in 1988, during a June strawberry ceremony, which they had decided to conduct outdoors in a forest. Although the strawberry festival is usually held in a longhouse, this was a special occasion. Twenty-five people were in attendance. It was midmorning, and Kevin was conducting the Mohawk ritual widely known as "The Giving of Thanks Address," subtitled "Greetings to the Natural World," and commonly described in Mohawk as "Words Before All Else," because nothing is done in ceremony without giving thanks first. "There is a section that reads, 'We give thanks to the birds that still we hear. The good songs they carry, and the big one, the leader. The eagle is his name. We give thanks that he watches over the cycles of life. So then it will be in our minds.'"*

---

*This is a quite literal translation, based on my interview with Rainbow Weaver on December 14, 2012 in Highland, New York. I also recommend the booklet rendered beautifully in English by the late Jake Swamp, in which the ending is ". . . and now we will be of one mind."

As he said the words acknowledging the bird life, three red-tailed hawks seemingly jumped from out of the forest about twenty feet above the participants' heads and cried out, screeching like eagles. The timeless words of thanks continued to be spoken, but some upwardly cast eyes filled with tears as the hawks completed their graceful circles of flight just above the fire, then left. It was a moment that defied explanation.

Birds connect the land world and sky world; wings denote that one can go from one world to the next, to travel from the air to the land and back. Angels, as sky beings, are portrayed with wings, as they travel between the physical world and the spiritual. Native American people understand that although they are in physical form, birds are emissaries at times from the upper worlds in a deeply spiritual sense and therefore have a lot in common with angels.[22]

It often seems that birds are just waiting for the right moment to communicate with us, waiting for us to ask them (in the right way and in the right language) to join in our circles and ceremonies. They have been waiting for thousands of years, but thanks to new environmental hazards such as electromagnetic waves and pulses, toxins, increasing water and noise pollution, and tall buildings, we may not have much more time to keep them waiting.

Moon Hawk

Tony Moon Hawk of the Unkechaug is a man who really loves birds. "Birds carry life; they protect the planet!" he said. "Especially eagles and hawks. Waterbirds are very sacred. Certain birds make the wind blow or stop wars. Eagles bring us good signs. All the birds are important to the Unkechaug."

I asked him how he got his name. He said he was originally named Silver Bison, but the name didn't work for him. For one thing, bison hadn't been a part of life on Long Island for thousands of years. One day while praying, Spirit told him it was time to change his name. Tony was going through a difficult time in his life; his marriage wasn't working out, and he had a lot of problems with money and at his job as a housing cop. He wondered about this for a while, then finally, one night at about 10 p.m., at a beautiful spot, he sat down and prayed to the Creator to tell him his name. Just then, he saw the silhouette of a hawk gliding across the face of the pale blue moon, the second full moon of that month, and he knew what his name was supposed to be. He had always felt a kinship with the hawk nation. His name from then on was Moon Hawk. The hawk, he says, is a backup bird to the eagle, and yet they are different. The hawk is a fighter, yet is very helpful and brings good signs.

Exactly one year after he got his name, he met his future wife, Marcey. People stopped bothering him at work. He divorced, moved out of New York City to New Jersey, and began to spend more time in nature, out in the wilderness. Marcey encouraged him to go to powwows, and gradually he became a renowned maker and vendor of Native craftwork. Everything in his life changed for the better. His understanding of the Unkechaug way grew stronger. If he saw a hawk fly in front of him on the way to a powwow, he would always do well and be successful. If no hawk appeared, it was going to be iffy. This pattern remained very clear to him for six years, and the closer to the

Tony Moon Hawk and his wife, Marcey, by the Hudson River

wilderness the venue was, the more dramatically true it was, especially in Pennsylvania.

Tony had always said that he "would never have any more kids." That, too, was about to change. Marcey soon became pregnant, and they were both happy, but there were problems. She was delivering prematurely, and the baby's heartbeat was barely registering. Tony took Marcey to a hospital in Pompton Plains, a highly urbanized area where a band of Wappingers had migrated late in colonial history. The doctors were calling for a C-section but were afraid of losing either the baby or Marcey. Marcey told him to call her mother to help pray for her. Tony took his cell phone and went outside, in front of the lobby, to make the call. A doctor, not related to Marcey's team, walked up to him and said, "See that bird?" Tony was very distraught and looked at him like the doctor was the one under too much stress. "What bird?"

The doctor pointed to a giant bird that was sitting on the corner of the roof about two stories above Tony's head. It was a hawk. The doctor made sure Tony could see it, and then said, "I've never seen a hawk here in all my years. That is amazing!"

Tony looked at the giant bird, and the hawk turned his head and looked straight at Tony, who got the clear message, "Don't worry!" The two indigenous "hawks" looked at each other for five minutes. It was the biggest red-tailed hawk he'd ever seen. In fact, at first he thought it was a turkey. The janitor came up and looked where Tony was looking. "Red-tailed hawk! That is the biggest I ever saw!"

Tony ran back upstairs, and the doctors were jubilant. Everything was fine. The baby, Cheyenne, had arrived. She was certainly a preemie, at only seven and a half months and weighing in at only five pounds—much smaller, in fact, than the hawk. But Cheyenne has grown to normal size and is a healthy and rambunctious child today.

That night, it was the second full moon of the month, a blue moon. Once you start looking for signs, they appear in flocks, like so many birds.[23]

Hawks Love Drums

Hawks, like eagles, are attracted to powwows in part because of the drums. Etaoqua, a Mohican, was with Mohawk Jake Swamp as he performed a Tree of Peace planting ceremony at New York City's Orchard Beach. Orchard Beach is a modest public park surrounded on three sides by tall buildings. There were few birds in sight as they began the ceremony. Jake Swamp pulled out a small hand drum and sang a song to open the ceremony. As he did, three hawks came and began to circle the tree and continued to circle at low altitudes until the ceremony was done. Then, as Jake closed the ceremony, the three emissaries from the sky world disappeared into the cityscape.

Etaoqua and her husband, Sagamore Mike, were visited only once by a hawk at their Rahway home, sitting on a telephone pole in front of the house, but it stayed long enough for Sagamore Mike to go inside, get a camera, come back out, talk with the bird, and then take a photo. As soon as he snapped the picture, the bird left. That hawk had a good reason for visiting; Sagamore Mike passed on into the spirit world shortly thereafter, taking his ancient Mohican language with him.[24]

Red Tail Protection from Above

As I was driving to my first interview at a new university, I was having doubts as to my good sense. It was a hundred miles from my home, and gas was at its most expensive. I looked for signs to tell me if I was on the right road, literally and figuratively. Suddenly, I see old Red Tail the hawk riding in the "eagle's nest" position, directly above and just in front of my car's windshield. He is looking from side to side as if protecting me, guiding me, and making sure I don't change my mind. Shortly thereafter, I met Elaine Henwood, who told me a similar hawk story about one of her clients, and she told them that, as Rolling Thunder would say, Red Tail was "clearing the way" for me as he flew, an apt description. Red Tail flew with me for about a mile and then disappeared into the sky. I knew I would get the job, and that it would be important some day in the distant future. Although I had to move closer to work, I taught in several capacities at this school, which offered me a variety of intellectual stimulation. That connection led to a course in Native American Literature, and the authorship of several books and PowerPoint presentations (including one on Bird Medicine) much of which is still in progress.

Food for Thought

One of the secrets Aunt Helen knew somehow was that when feeding raptors such as hawks, you couldn't just feed them meat from a can or hamburger. If you did, you needed to mix crushed bone or bonemeal into it, or the raptor would eventually get sick. They need to make the pellets in order to clean out their system and also need the calcium from the bone. As quoted in her biography by Eleanor Noyes Johnson, the feeding of young wild creatures was one of Helen's favorite subjects. Young hawks, she would say, "need more than meat. They need bone. Hamburger has too much fat in it, but liver rolled in brown bone meal will help grow strong legs and wings. Above all, hawks mustn't be kept on a hard surface or the legs go out of joint, and they will grow crooked like legs of rickety children."[25] Helen saw the birds in her care as her own children, and she took good care of them. I recall wondering as a child why many of the birds had no cages: the distinction between tame and wild would become very blurry sometimes at Helen's White Animal Farm.

Dream Hawks

Robin Larsen has run a Jungian dream group with her husband, Steve, for many years and says that many people have dreams about birds, hawks in particular, who give them guidance. She commented that geese have been considered sacred birds for thousands of years and pointed out that geese migrate across the Atlantic Ocean, from Finland in Europe to North America. In Mi'kmaq, we say, *"Geezoolgh, ge-gun moo-ee la-maik pboogh dju-wa doo-ee naht-koh-way!"* This saying is in the old high language, but it means roughly, "Creator, give me the teaching dreams!"

The Prisoner and the Peregrine

"Nathan" and his wife lived in New York City, on the top floor of a forty-story East 72nd street apartment between York Avenue and the East River. Being a birder, Nathan was familiar with a breeding pair of peregrine falcons that lived on the top of New York Hospital at Cornell University Medical Center, a couple of blocks away. These birds were described in *Red Tails in Love,* a book that mentions Pale Male, a hawk that lives at a swanky building at 927 Fifth Avenue. Fifth Avenue is part of an old Native American trail known as the Tulpehocken Trail, which stretched from Montreal to Louisville, and which was then designated as Route 22. I believe many "gatekeeper" birds still follow the old trails.* It also mentions the secret "bird book," which records in longhand the sightings of rare and wild birds by New Yorkers and is kept in a secret location at a news stand, a secret which is known, nonetheless, to thousands of New York City bird enthusiasts.

Nathan would often marvel at their aerial acrobatics, especially when going after pigeons. He had also spent some time on a Shoshone Reservation in Idaho and with the Samburu of Kenya and had learned a few things about animal signs. Both he and his wife had looked to those falcons for signs and for inspiration before.

Nathan got in some trouble and was sentenced to four months in federal prison at Fort Dix, New Jersey. July 9, 2002, was the day chosen for Nathan to be released, but his wife was not notified. He was let out late in the morning, not knowing how he would be able to communicate with his wife, but she was in his thoughts.

Late that afternoon, Nathan's wife was ironing in the living room when she noticed a bird making a beeline for the apartment. It actually scared her, and she went to close the large glass French doors thinking

---

*We will explore this idea further in the section "Crow Councils: The Return of the Corvid Tribe" (page 73).

the bird would fly in. The bird landed on the corner of the terrace railing and just sat there looking at her, and to her surprise, she realized it was a baby peregrine falcon. It stood looking at her for a while before flying off. She knew it was a message letting her know that Nathan wished to make a beeline for home if he only could and would be arriving soon. The bird seemed to say, "Nathan is okay!" Although Nathan couldn't call, because of the falcon's visit his wife felt at peace. Her husband made it home in one piece a few days later after some last-minute peregrinations.

CROWS

Corvidae, Gatekeepers of the South

Now we turn to the South of the Medicine Wheel of master birds and honor the ravens and crows, which nations of the Matouac of Long Island place in that direction (see color insert, plate 3). Ravens and crows belong to the Corvidae family, which includes jays and magpies. The corvids are great communicators, but like winged Hermes in Greek mythology, they are also associated with keeping secrets. There are forty-one species of crows worldwide, and the common or northern raven, *Corvus corax,* is one of them. What people in America call crows are really American crows, *Corvus brachyrhynchos.* Many Native Americans I talked to are not always specific and don't always distinguish between a raven, which is a large crow with a notch in his tail that can "speak," and an American crow. Nevertheless, it seems that the ordinary common crow, four times smaller than the raven, is one of the most respected birds in Native American culture. Crows are smart birds with a lot of admirable qualities. Among the Omaha, black birds are very important. One of the major Omaha historical figures is Chief Blackbird, and there are many tribal members with the family name Blackbird today.

Crow Councils: The Return of the Corvid Tribe

According to the late Narragansett elder, Big Toe, eastern Native Americans watched crows very carefully for teachings about holding council. At certain times, and for reasons unbeknownst to us, crows will gather in the hundreds or even thousands at a certain spot, covering field after field to the horizon. They will remain there for hours or even days, without fighting or strife, and then all depart at the same time.

In old times, Native American leaders, and this is apparently true in particular with Iroquoian clan mothers, would see a council of crows as a sign that it is time for them to call a council as well. These crow councils would not always be in such great numbers, but might be perhaps five or six or seven crows with their heads together, but stationed near the elder's window or doorway where they were conspicuous, and therefore unusual.

David Fescier, a Wappingers descendant and a student of Big Toe, has always been connected to crows and has been sensitive to their messages. He says, "We learn to gather in council from Crow, just as we learn about the family from Wolf. Big Toe saw a grand council of crows only once. It was in the back country on the way to Foxwoods, in eastern Connecticut. There were thousands of crows covering several adjacent fields. I knew of their significance from my elder, Big Toe's teachings and took notice."[26]

A few years ago, a council of crows picked downtown Middletown, New York, as the site of one of their biggest gatherings, and over ten thousand were in attendance. The *Times Herald-Record* ran a story on it because of the impact on the city. The approximate location for this gala event was near the Paramount Theatre just north of Orange County Community College. Similar crow festivals have been occurring every year during the winter months near this location. Although little is known about Middletown's Native history, this spot is near the geographic center of town where North Street would have become South Street and East Main would have become West Main. It is also near Monhagen Street, Waywayanda Avenue, Mount Hope Road, and Mulberry Street, all thought to be old streets of Middletown. These streets are linked to 17 M and 211, which approximate two longer trade routes from Native times. Route 6, the Sagamore Trail, which runs from Cape Cod to California, is also nearby as is the Wallkill River. Just to the north is Thrall Park. All of this suggests that the crows were gathering at the site of a Native American village at the crossroads of many trails. The odd thing was, there were no more crossroads and no more Native American villages! (See color insert, plate 28.)

Nathan Brown, a columnist for the Middletown *Times Herald-Record*, began an article, published February 29, 2012, with the ominous words, "Around sunset, a black, cawing cloud descends upon downtown." Brown noted that the crows had been roosting in the Benton Avenue area and around the former Horton Hospital earlier that winter (and Mulberry Street) but had moved to James and West streets and would likely disappear by March. Dropping his Poe-like prose, he turned to "black" humor and wrote, "Cisco Velez, owner of the Havana House of Cigars at James and West Main streets, said he first started to notice large numbers of crows hanging out across Main Street and in the James Street parking lot three or four weeks ago. Velez said he hasn't had too much of an issue with them, and hasn't heard many complaints from his customers about them. 'I guess they're helping out the (car washes),' he joked."[27]

In the end, it's all about business, and the ancient ritual of the crows comes into conflict with plans for an economic recovery. Brown wrote, "Over the past decade or so, the city has relied heavily on Bird Gard amplifiers—which play the sound of a crow in distress—for crow control. These don't seem to be working as well this year. 'We just can't stay on top of it,' [Mayor Joseph] DeStefano said. 'We don't have enough machines for the number of crows this year.'"

According to my reckoning, James and Main streets and Mulberry Avenue all lie within five hundred feet of an ancient crossroads where a village once stood. The crows still remember.

Crows regularly gather in White Plains, New York, in December and January, near the junction of two important Native American trails, Route 100 (Potituck Trail) and Route 22 (Tulpehoken Trail), a few hundred feet from the Quorropus Road (Quarropus is Wappingers for "where dew lies white on the plains"), next to the Bronx River (Aquehong) near Battle Hill, the site of a colonial skirmish with Natives. Many thousands of crows will gather there at sunrise and sunset, particularly around the solstice, according to several sources. This is near the site of today's County Center Building. The website www.crows.net reports that one unusually large gathering occurred on February 20, 2009, with thousands and thousands of crows—with the greatest population of these partiers concentrated between the north- and southbound lanes of the Bronx River Parkway. As evidence of the struggle between human and bird at these times, the Staples store has cut off all the branches of all the trees on their property, presumably to discourage roosting. I arrived just before solstice at Battle Hill with some friends to see if we could spot some crows, but it was already too late in the day, and none were to be found. We asked two local teenage girls walking by if they had seen any crow councils, or big flocks of crows, an odd question to ask total strangers. Their answer was telling: "Yeah, all the time. Aren't they amazing?" I learned the hard way that crow councils are generally held early in the morning, perhaps to "sing up the sun" as Natives do, following the corvine way of wisdom.

I have also seen crow councils in Poughkeepsie, on both sides of Route 9, just before sundown, in January and February. They gather at the edge of the Central Hudson Gas & Electric property (on Phoenix Street, ironically), just below the junction of Route 9 (the old Mohican Trail) and Routes 44/55 (the old Plymouth Rock Trail) and near the stream called Valkill (Winnakee in Algonquin), which is also near Winnakee Falls.* The Central Hudson building was excavated in the days before cultural assessment codes, and so far no evidence has reached me of a village site having existed there, but it is just north of the safe, sheltered spring the Wappingers called Apookeepsing, which gave the town its name. It is also near Poughkeepsie rural cemetery,

---

*Benson Lossing writes in his classic book *The Hudson*, "between two rocky bluffs was a sheltered bay (now filled with wharves) into the upper part of which leaped, in rapids and cascades, the Winnakee, called Fall Kill by the Dutch." (Lossing, *The Hudson*, 187). Winnakee means "beautiful land" in the old Mohican, and was adopted by the Wappingers as a name for this river and falls. Cranes and herons still gather at the bottom to snare fish coming down the chute.

across from Vassar Brothers Hospital. The website www.crows.net lists the site, describing it as near the Metro North Train terminal and placing the count in the thousands for a council that occurred right on the winter solstice of 2011.*

Winter solstice is a time in Algonkin-ode culture when families honor their ancestors. It is the "night of the year," when the veil between this world and the next is very thin and people receive messages from the deceased. They may create altars in their homes using the belongings of the departed and honor them in some way and may look for dreams about and visits from the ancestors. It is likely that a visit from a bird at this time, specifically a crow but any kind of bird, would be seen as a visit from a grandfather or grandmother.

It is interesting that the Midewiwin and other medicine societies generally meet for four days of gatherings. It is also interesting that long ago Algonkin-ode people gathered on the solstices and equinoxes in large numbers to honor Earth and the Creator and to do ritual. I know this from family tradition, oral tradition, colonial history, and current practice. Even those without clocks or calendars can identify these four days of the year without any trouble and know to meet annually at these times. If the crows are an indication, this habit apparently lingers long after death of the participants. I have taken digital photos of a number of sites I felt might have been sacred to the Esopus Munsee (in one case, before dawn on the equinox) and find numerous clearly defined orbs in my pictures, which some might speculate are the souls of the departed, *o-tchi-tchan-hau-mitch-(oo)* or shadow soul in Mi'kmaq and other Algonquian languages.

It seems to me that, given the number of stories I have collected of deceased Native and non-Native people as well appearing as birds

*Platt's *History of Poughkeepsie,* published in 1799, shows that many of the earliest colonial homes were built along the east side of this stretch of road. This suggests that the drinking water available here was somehow preferable to that of the Winnakee (now Valkill) and this we can surmise would have been true for the Wappingers people as well. In my experience, the Wappingers today still seem to have a special fondness for the crow.

to their family members, the apparent desire by Natives both living and dead to meet on solstices and equinoxes; given the tradition of having meetings at important crossroads near streams (so that both canoers and walkers could find them without a map and without street addresses); given people like Rolling Thunder who "travel" outside their body and "ride" birds while they live; and given crows are almost universally seen as occasional messengers from the dead, especially at winter solstice, the surprising but intuitively satisfying conclusion is that these giant crow councils are, in some cases, continuations of human gatherings from long ago, by the same souls who went on before. No one has told me that this is a Native American belief, but the other "beliefs" are from highly reliable and corroborated sources, and they add up to a somewhat startling conclusion. The pieces of the puzzle fit together, and we have to accept the picture that appears when we are finished—that these crow councils are "class reunions" of Native American tribes and nations who have since passed from history. For a slightly more "scientific" approach to the study of crow councils, log on to www.crows.net/roostlst.html.

There is an old saying, "Animals are equal." We are told we should not play God with animals or birds but respect their sovereignty. Many Native American traditionals believe that we have not only been animals and birds in past lives, but that we might reincarnate as such in the future, so we had better treat them as we would want to be treated in the future. Given the acceptance of what is called shapeshifting among certain groups and circles, that future might be just around the corner. In the fictional work *The Eagle's Gift,* by Carlos Castaneda, the character Benigno gives expression to this deeply held Native belief when he says, "You must have been a tiger and you are definitely going to turn into one again. That's what happened to the Nagual, he had been a crow already and while in this life he turned into one again."[28]

Dr. Dennis Hastings, cultural authority on Omaha traditions

for the Omaha Nation of Nebraska and Iowa, is a member of the Small Bird Clan, the official name of which is Tha'tada (pronounced LA-ta-da) and a member of the Waça'bezhinga (pronounced WA-sa-bay-zhin-ga) Little Black Bear subclan of the Tha'tada. (The Omaha call them clans, but the academic world calls them gens, since inheritance goes by the way of the father.) He says that the crow is a death bird to the Omaha, similar to the owl.[29] Death birds, in general, do not cause death, as some of the more superstitious might suppose, but merely report of a death that is about to occur or one that has just occurred. In fact, these death birds can communicate to the living messages from the other side or the underworld and tell us of those who have passed on.

Quoth the Raven

Edgar Allan Poe, a great storyteller whom I have long suspected to be of mixed-blood Lenape or Wampanoag ancestry, wrote the poem "The Raven," depicting this bird as the messenger of mournful tidings. He was invoking this aspect of the Corvidae family, as understood by some Native Americans. One of the most dramatic stories I have heard illustrating this aspect of Native American crow lore comes from the civil rights community. At the time of the incident, which was April 4, 1968, Manna Jo Greene was living in the East Village in New York City just a few blocks from the Poe House at 85 West Third Street, where the poet wrote "The Raven." In 1963, at the age of eighteen, Manna had helped bring the Reverend Dr. Martin Luther King Jr. to Bridgeport, Connecticut, to help organize the local chapter of the Congress of Racial Equality (CORE). As secretary of Bridgeport CORE, Manna was present for Dr. King's triumphant "I Have a Dream" speech at the August 1963 march on Washington, D.C., and then went back to Washington to lobby with Dr. King, James Farmer, and the many other great civil rights leaders of the day to lobby for the passage of the Civil Rights Bill in 1964.

By 1968, Manna was married to a TV reporter/journalist and was eight months pregnant. Walking in the park that evening she noticed joyfully that the buds were just starting to bloom with new life. Over to her left, she saw an unusual sight: a large black bird fell from the sky, as if shot, landing with a thump in the center of a nearby intersection. It fluttered for a moment and then was still. As she walked over to the bird to see if it was dead, and perhaps to help save its life, there was a massive contraction in her womb. She went into labor with such sudden intensity that she had to turn around and find a telephone to contact her husband. She struggled up the stairs to their fourth-floor apartment. Now sure she was in labor, she called her husband to tell him to come quickly and take her to the hospital. His answer surprised her. Choked with emotion, he said, "I can't come right now. Can you hold on?," explaining that Martin Luther King Jr., her hero and source of inspiration, had just been shot in Memphis and that he had been assigned by CBS-TV to interview U.S. senator and civil rights sympathizer Jacob Javits. Some involved expected there might be rioting in the streets before long and that a sensitive interview with Javits expressing compassion for the black community might help save lives and property in the days to come. Minutes later, Robert F. Kennedy gave a timely speech in a black community in Indianapolis, considered one of the finest speeches in U.S. history, comparing King to his own brother, and it had a healing effect on the city. Although many cities were torn apart by rioting that week, New York City and Indianapolis were not among them. As it turns out, the fall of the raven occurred at the same moment that King fell to the floor of the balcony of the Lorraine Hotel in Memphis, Tennessee, at 6:01 p.m. Though blinded by tears for Dr. King, her "elder," as she calls him, Manna Jo delivered her baby the following day, in the company of her husband. Although a few weeks early, and slightly underweight, it was nonetheless a healthy baby girl, named Khadejha, which means "sister of love" in Arabic. If the raven was carrying a message to Manna Jo, it was a clear one: she would nevermore see her beloved Dr. King again.

The Brilliance of Black Birds

According to Dr. Margery Coffey, assistant director of the Omaha Tribal Historical Research Project,* the crow and raven are among the most hated birds in mainstream society in part because they are so intelligent. She has seen a black bird, possibly a crow, "cuss out" a cat to the point where its furry ears were pinned back, and then found another black bird joining in the cussing. The cat hid under Margery's chair, but the "roasting" did not stop until the cat had retreated inside. Another time Margery saw a cat bother a black bird, which then repeatedly dive-bombed the angered feline down to a height just an inch away from the cat's uppermost leaping extension.[30] The rivalry between cats and birds is the stuff of legend. A Canadian elder told me of birds (crows, perhaps?) she observed that thought nothing of dive-bombing a pesky neighborhood cat, ripping out a tuft of the cat's fur, and feathering their nest with it. Repeatedly. Nothing like cat fur to make the nest more comfy for the little ones!

Corvine intelligence is now well documented, with the New Caledonian crow leading the class with straight As. In the August 9, 2002, issue of *Science* magazine, New Caledonian crows were credited with primatelike intelligence and reported that one such crow, called Betty, had learned to make tools. Betty was captured as a juvenile in March 2000 and in 2002 was soon observed displaying remarkable problem-solving abilities, gaining admission into an exclusive club that at one time only included humans (as far as scientists were concerned)— the tool-makers club. On several occasions, Betty bent a piece of wire with her beak to make a hooklike tool, which gave her the ability to reach food at the bottom of a tube. The crow figured out the solution to the puzzle in a minute's time, placing crows on the short list of animals that shape and use tools.[31]

---

*This project is an independent 501(c)(3) multicultural agency working with the Omaha Tribe of Nebraska and Iowa as the designated Omaha Cultural Authority in perpetuity by formal resolution.

A crow was recently filmed as he repeatedly sledded down the icy metal roof of a city building on a large jar cap, apparently attempting to extend the length of the ski slope each time. The crow showed great agility balancing the cap on the peak of the steep roof, then jumping in as it was sliding downward. Eventually, the bird placed the cap in his beak and flew away (see www.wimp.com/crowtubing).

Crows can also hoist a piece of meat, hanging below them on a string, by coordinating their beak and feet together.[32] Scientists at Yale are now studying crow brains; there is a theory that they may be our closest relative in terms of brain structure. They think ahead more effectively than primates. We like to think of ourselves as a species that thinks ahead better than other beasts; but given our lack of success at heading off climate change and the crows' success at prescience, perhaps that conceit needs to change.

It is said that crows can carry a grudge. I heard a story of one man who had a pet crow he and his younger brother kept in a parrot's cage when they were growing up. His brother started to tease the crow, and the crow in turn started to bite the brother, but not other family members. Although the brother stopped mistreating the crow, the crow continued to peck at the younger brother for the rest of his bird years. And we thought dwelling on the past was a human trait!

Sharing the Banquet

Crows and ravens are not hunters, interestingly enough. They live off the prey of other hunters, including bears, humans, and wolves. In the old shamanic stories, crows direct hunters to their prey—not only human hunters but wolves and bears. They lead them to living game animals, and then wait patiently for the deed to be done. Unlike raptors, crows don't have hooked or serrated beaks to rip and tear apart flesh; they can only pull, and usually as a team. That is why crows like roadkill only after the eagles, vultures, and several more cars have gone over it. After the hunters have taken what they want, ravens swoop down and enjoy the leftovers. It is said that ravens warn of bears' presence to help keep unarmed humans safe from harm, but they also may be hoping for a meal down the road, in case the human wants to take down the bear. Not all crow warning behavior is selfish; most of it seems to be truly neighborly. Debbie Bahune raises chickens and feeds them in a large pen that is opened to the sky. She has noticed that crows surround the pen sometimes and guard the chicks against incoming hawks, warning them with their loud caws. By the time the hawk comes near, the chicks have run inside, thanks to the early bird-warning system.[33]

Although ravens are viewed as solitary birds, a study by academic field biologist Bernd Heinrich of ravens wintering in Maine, showed that these birds share with each other quite generously, even when food is scarce. He writes, "I had often noticed a pair of ravens. I now saw the birds . . . doing something solitary animals are not supposed to do: They were sharing valuable food—those who had, it seemed, were giving to those who needed. It was the most left-wing behavior I had ever heard of in a natural system."[34]

Heinrich goes on to recount his observations of ravens who found the carcass of a moose fallen into the ice and proceeded to make loud calls; other ravens heard the calls to dinner and came from miles around to share. Fifteen ravens at once were soon eating the moose meat. I feel sure the principal characters in Heinrich's book *Ravens in Winter* were working as a team to use their unserrated beaks to cut up the moose meat, which would have been difficult to do individually.

Crow Warnings, Crow Scolds

Crows are masters at communication. They are universally recognized as bringers of warnings, and their caws are understood by all animals as warnings of danger. Their movements can also be warnings.

Tony Moon Hawk's mother was a Pamunkey woman from Virginia and watched birds for signs. She said, "If you see a crow and it comes down and looks at you and walks slowly in front of you, it's a warning. It may mean that someone you know is going to die." Not everyone agrees. There is no one standard way of interpreting bird movements as signs; it's personal. One person, Cathy, has seen a white crow in the

Ottawa area. Opinions may differ as to the significance of such a bird or what kind of message it was here to give, but any white animal draws attention to itself as sacred. Over time, different Native people develop their own relationship with a certain species of bird, and whatever system of sign reading they develop, it tends to work for life.

Sometimes, when we are running a little late for a meeting, it may be spirit telling us that everyone else is also starting late and that it's okay to get other things done first and arrive on "Indian time." However, there are meetings that start right on time, gatherings for which it is very bad to be late, possibly causing embarrassment and rejection. This is a source of distress, especially for some who travel in both Native and non-Native circles. Heather Wiggs, an aboriginal Canadian who is the director of the Asinabika Women's Drum Circle of Ottawa, has a unique relationship with crows. She travels in both worlds, and her concern for being late inspired her to seek additional help from spirit regarding these issues. The crows, the warning birds of the skies, came to her rescue. When they fly across her path far in the distance, it is a very gentle warning that she might be just a little late. When they fly somewhat closer, it means she is late. When a crow flies right in front of her car or across her windshield, it is a warning that she better step on it. They are telling her she'll be ruffling some feathers if she doesn't fly as the crow flies and arrive on time. On one occasion, Heather was looking for such signs in a downtown urban environment, and there were no crows in sight. At that moment, a pigeon swept across her windshield to tell her she'd better hurry up—a substitute crow as it turned out. She took the hint.[35]

Robin Larsen insists that crows speak English. When her short-legged cat got stuck in a tree trying to chase a baby owl, a murder of crows mobbed the feline, yelling, "Come and see, cat in a tree!" At least according to the best of her recollection. The cat, needless to say, was humiliated. Grandmother White Wolf, a Mi'kmaq descendant, recently watched as a raccoon climbed a tree to about eye level to get a really close look at her. As the two stared at one another, White Wolf wasn't sure if it was a good spirit or a bad one that was staring back. At that moment, a crow came up and started screaming at the raccoon in a loud and commanding voice. The crow continued to insult the raccoon, scolding and yelling at it without stopping until the raccoon scampered away.[36]

My great aunt Helen bred animals and kept mice in cages, but the birds flew free and traveled when and where they pleased. I remember the crow that used to live in the shed with the mice, and I'll never forget how hot it would get during the summer in that shed, easily 120 degrees. Respectable townspeople and scientists from the universities would come in to look at the thirty-five species of mice, including rare purebred whites. Too polite to mention the unavoidable stink of the cages, they would comment on the heat. Helen was always polite and ladylike around the neighbors and never swore or complained. She would smile and say, "Well, heat doesn't bother me!" Whenever she would say something like this, that crow would chime in lustily like an old sailor with "Hell it's hot! Hell it's hot! Hell it's hot!," with great aunt Helen's Maritime accent intact. It didn't take a rocket scientist to figure out where he heard those words. It was a betrayal of the highest order, and she could do nothing to stop him.

The question is, Was Aunt Helen's crow really a raven? It is said that in order to speak, crows have to have surgery, whereas the English raven does not. A birder I know, who attended Helen's funeral in 1994, said that her father told her that when he was young, his father—an old-time duck farmer who found that chickens laid more eggs when fed dog kibble—cut the pointed end off a crow's tongue and cut the finlike membrane that stood below the crow's upturned tongue, thereby liberating the crow's considerable propensity for human speech. To my boyhood memory, Helen's black bird looked more like a crow, and he could certainly talk, so perhaps it was Helen herself whose surgeon skills gave life to this acerbic tongue from hell.

Aunt Helen had a crow during World War II named Tim that could speak and said hello to each customer as he or she entered her store on the pier in Old Orchard Beach, Maine. Tim could also catch nickels and dimes on the fly, and the sailors would come and toss coins into his cage or as he was strutting about; he would prudently hide these silvery objects in the cracks between the boards, saving them for a rainy day. He apparently had a way of cocking his head, winking at the customers, and moving his beak that let the customers know he wanted more such sport.[37] The crow I met at Helen's farm in the 1960s must have been the grandson. The Mi'kmaq word for crow is *kaw-ha-gootch*. It is loosely translated as "Old Grandfather that says caw." In fact, Tim said more than caw and was the grandfather of the bird I knew as a child.

Ta Ta Grandfather Black Crow and I

We met in Dream—a different Place
a Hawk and a Crow, seeing Eye to Eye and Face to
    Face
sharing a branch on the Great Tree—Side by Side
Star-Hawk and Light-Crow with nothing to hide
Knew each other well with our own keen Sight
Crow-Friend and Hawk-Friend—Brothers in the Light
go on, my Friend, flying, laughing, to new heights
to new ways to See, in a place always Bright.

DAVE HOLDEN, MI'KMAQ
WOODSTOCK, NEW YORK, JULY 2010

OWLS

Owl: The Night Eagle

We now turn to the West and honor the owl (see color insert, plate 2). Eagles and hawks are not the only birds who bring medicine; the owl is also a favorite bird of shamanic healers around the world, North Americans included. Almost any bird can be a divine messenger at times, according to tradition, but the four master birds are supreme. While the integrity of the eagle and hawk messages are beyond question, the same cannot be said for the other two, the crow and owl. One must be careful, even with the other raptors, as they can be misused. In the Winnebago story, "Cono, the World's Greatest Gambler," Owl was used by the evil Cono as his representative in a game, gambling for the future of the planet. Fortunately for us, he was defeated in a game of "Stare" by Wakjankaga, Raven Boy.[38] But a number of nations have taboos against using owl feathers because of their associations as messengers of death.

When my mother was a young girl, her father took her out in the forest with a bow and arrow to teach her to hunt birds for food. He probably didn't think she would actually hit anything, so did not go deeply into taboo animals and birds and why some were hunted and others not. Suddenly, a white arctic owl flew over her head, and before giving it a thought, she instinctively fired her arrow at the bird and killed it. The bird dropped to the ground before her. My mother screamed. She looked horrified at the bird and cried and swore she'd never hunt again and kept her word ever after. I believe that this owl was an ancestor, trying to discourage her from taking up hunting birds, for whatever reason. In any case, nothing bad happened to her afterward. In fact, I suspect her father was secretly proud of her budding abilities as an archer.

Many believe that when you hear the owl call your name, you are the next to face the passage to eternity that awaits us all. This encounter with the underworld might take many forms. All birds are our allies. Each specific tribe or nation has a favored bird that looks out for it, and this special relationship can develop in a number of ways and even change over time. Of course, the clan of a specific bird would have a taboo against killing that bird, and owl clans exist that forbid their members to kill owls. Owls are commonly thought of as messengers from the land of the dead but are often misunderstood. Owls are associated with both black and white magic.[39] Tony Moonhawk has stated that to the people of his Unkechaug nation, the owl is not about death but a bird of wisdom and a sign of good fortune. Unkechaug do not eat owl, but there used to be quail on Long Island and they would eat them, and they still eat pheasant when they can.

Owls are sometimes called the night eagles, as they generally fly at night and have excellent night vision;[40] however, owls can be seen at all hours of the day sitting on the limbs of trees and watching all the proceedings with a sort of sleepy, half-interested bemusement, like gatekeepers to the doors between the rational and irrational worlds. They are deeply connected to the shadow side of our psyches and can help us unlock the messages of our dreams, helping us look with larger eyes into places we dared not venture into in the past. They help us listen with sharper ears to the fleeting messages from the spirit world, directives that sometimes prove very helpful. They are at ease in the realm of the subconscious, where the deeper truths lie, hidden behind our fears and personal demons.

Many who are afraid of owls are phobic about other things—afraid of their own dark side and what might be lurking in the deep dark forest of their own mind. It is within this forest that we face the fact that each of us must die some day in order to fully enter the spirit world and be reborn anew. The irrational realms of dreams and of death are not so far apart, and when we see one we see the other, both reflected in the pale moon-yellow eyes of a night owl.

According to Mircea Eliade, some shamanistic societies see the owl as a possible apparition of the Creator, in answer to prayer, similar to the eagle. According to some beliefs, the owl can also transmit power to the healer as the eagle can. He writes, "Thus for example, among the Cahuilla of Southern California (Cahuilla Desert), shamans are considered to obtain their power from Mukat, the Creator, but this power is transmitted through guardian spirits (the *owl*, fox, coyote, bear, etc.), which act as the god's messengers to shamans"[41] (italics mine).*

Both shamanic healers and warriors often dedicate themselves to the task of "gathering power" before undergoing a difficult task in order to bring a boon to the village. There is evidence to support the idea, shared by some shamans (and refuted by others), that the night is a good time to connect with this power. Eliade writes: According to some Paviotso shamans power comes to them from the "spirit of the night." This spirit "is everywhere. It has no name. There is no word for it." The eagle and the owl are only the messengers that bring instruction from the spirit of the night. "Water babies" or some other animal can also be its messengers. "At the time that the spirit of the night gives power for doctoring, it tells the shaman to ask for help from the water-babies, eagle, owl, deer, antelope, bear or some other bird or animal." Then, in a footnote (140) Eliade adds: "The spirit of the night is probably a late mythological formula for the Supreme Being, which has become partly a deus otiosus and helps men through 'messengers.'"[42]

Owls are thought of as the ultimate nocturnal animal, hence associations with the dream world, but in fact the barred owl and certain

---

*The footnote on that page is very interesting as well. Eliade writes, "Among the Mohave and the Yuma power comes from the mythical beings who transmitted it to shamans at the beginning of the world. Transmission takes place in dreams and includes an initiatory scenario. In his dreams the Yuma shaman witnesses the beginnings of the world and lives in mythical times. (132: A.L. Kroeber, *Handbook* . . . C.D. Forde, *Ethnography* of the Yuma Indians, pp. 201 ff. Initiation into the shamanic secret society, the Mide'wiwin, also involves a return to the mythical times of the beginnings of the world, when the Great Spirit revealed the mysteries to the first 'great doctors.' We shall see that these initiatory rituals include the same communication between earth and heaven as was established at the creation of the world."

other species come out at about 3:30 p.m. and hunt and socialize until about 10:30 p.m., and then go to bed with the rest of us.[43] Others, however, such as the long-horned owl, are strictly nocturnal. Though one may overlook their presence in the night sky, the *who who whooo* of a hoot owl is anything but subtle. In fact their "Who?" almost sounds comical, as if they were literally talking to you.

One way Native birders trace the whereabouts and habits of owls is by hunting for their pellets. These pellets are pithy summaries of everything the owl has eaten in the past day or two, made up of bones, scales, fur, and feathers, all rolled up into a little ball and vomited from the owl's beak. Owl pellets are much different than hawk pellets, which contain less bone content thanks to a more powerful digestive system. The number of pellets can indicate how many owls are in the area, and the contents tell the story of who and what the bird has been able to invite over for dinner, its guest list and barf bag all in one. In several European studies, the radiation from cell towers has been shown to reduce the size of litters of mice living within 300 meters of the transmitters in just two or three generations. Although these studies may suggest that raptors such as owls and eagles have little trouble flying clear of the cell tower's area of disturbance, these towers decrease the populations of insects, mice, and small birds through a variety of means, thereby affecting the diet of the raptors* and their vomit, of course.

Owls have binocular vision; not only do they turn their head 270 degrees, they can turn so fast to the other extreme that a human watching them might think their head swiveled completely around. Perhaps this is one reason why owls have been unfairly marked as demonic. They have a long flexible neck hidden by feathers, which allows them to twist and turn while flying without losing their focus or sight of their prey. In fact, I have heard from numerous bird handlers that owls are a little slow, due to their small brain size. They are highly specialized, and much of their cranial area is devoted to acute vision and remark-

---

*See part 6, summarizing the Balmori studies from Spain and other European studies.

able hearing. Special facial feathers direct the sound to their ears, which move separately. Diurnal raptors' eyesight can be eight times as powerful as humans' in some cases, and hearing is of similar clarity. On the other hand, they can hardly smell at all.

But wisdom is not a matter of braininess and quick thinking, it has more to do with being calm and thinking big thoughts, which the Mi'kmaq call *un-kee-das-see-wa-q'n*, another word for wisdom. Owls, with their big eyes, look like they are thinking those big rounded philosophical thoughts, thinking several steps ahead before acting. Legend has it that Merlin kept an owl under his peaked hat. If he did, he probably didn't ask it for advice, but you never know.

Owls and My Aunt

My great aunt Helen Perley was famous for her ability to communicate with birds, both wild and tame. Many years ago, she trained owls and worked with them in school shows and assemblies to teach children about how intelligent birds were. She knew of their associations with the underworld and was quite comfortable with that. As she got older, more and more of her best friends went to dwell on the other side. She ran the White Animal Farm on Seavey Landing Road in Scarborough, Maine, for many decades, and owls would sometimes come and roost on the roofs of her animal sheds and watch her work. She used to tell the story of how her owl introduced her to the chief of the Old Town Penobscot Indians, who spoke owl language. One year there was a sportsmen's show in the Exposition Building in Portland, and the young Helen was invited to bring her "Mickey Mouse Show" of trained mice, as well as some of her birds and animals. It was there that Helen met a kindred soul. Eleanor Noyes Johnson writes about this incident in her biography of Helen:

> By happy coincidence, her display area was right next to that of the Old Town Indians. Mrs. Perley and the chief were soon the best of friends. The chief learned that Mrs. Perley knew more about and was more appreciative of the arts and skills of Indians than most

members of his tribe. Mrs. Perley found that the chief was, in his own way, as close to the animals as she was. He talked to the owl in his language while Mrs. Perley talked to the mice and the other animals in a language they could understand.[44]

She credited the owl with helping her make that friendship. The man was presumably Chief Poolaw, who was *sachem* at Old Town during the 1930s, but I never asked her specifically.

The Voice of the Owl

Aunt Helen Perley's neighbor and good friend Cheryl Aranovitch had retinitis pigmentosa and was gradually going blind, but enjoyed the birds around Aunt Helen's farm and the sounds that they made. She and her husband, David, would spend every Christmas eve with Helen. David would help around her White Animal Farm, insulating the doors and windows of the animal houses so the little dears would not freeze to death. There was an owl that lived in a tree between their houses, and as Helen slept on her porch every night, year-round, she listened to its distinctive *hooo* as she was going to sleep. Cheryl could hear it, too, and that soothing musical sound was a regular topic of conversation between them. Someone said the owl was white in color. Owl watchers might comment that if it sat hooting in a tree, it was probably an albino. Arctic ("snow") owls don't tend to perch in trees; they prefer sitting, as they would in the arctic above the tree line. And barn owls don't hoot, they screech. Did Helen know? Could she tell what kind of owl it was? The sound of that bird connected Cheryl's world with Helen's in a unique and joyful way.

David and Cheryl found an opportunity to open a hotel on the beach, about five miles from Helen's ancestral property, and sold the house on Seavey Landing Road. Cheryl could not drive any more, so her busy husband would drive her to meet with Helen and her birds, enjoying the visit himself. Helen ate healthful herbs her whole life and was very vigorous through her eighties, but then was given the wrong medication, so she says, from a doctor and was in and out of the hospital the last six months of her life. Cheryl, no longer a frequent visitor to the White Animal Farm, would call Helen on the phone every week to see how she was doing. Were there any owls out Cheryl's way? Not one. Twelve years passed without hearing that sweet *hooo!*

One October evening, just after 9 p.m., as David was out walking the dogs and Cheryl was working in her upstairs kitchen, she heard a loud and distinctive *hooo* repeating outside the upstairs kitchen window. It was the first time their beachside hotel had been visited by an owl in a dozen seasons. She said the owl "told her" that Helen had just died. There was no doubt in her mind, but she called Helen anyway and got no answer. She called some mutual friends, but no one had heard anything. Shortly thereafter, the phone call came from Helen's relatives: Helen had passed into the spirit world at 3:30 p.m. that same day.

When I stood in that kitchen back in 1994, looked out that window, and heard this story, I was waving my hands, filled with questions. David and Cheryl agreed that because of the dramatic timing and the fact that there were no owls living nearby it did seem extremely coincidental and believe to this day that there is more to the story. Cheryl said that she felt that Helen "was riding around in the form of an owl to say hello and good-bye, the only way she had of letting me know it was her, and that she had passed on." The hoot owl in the tree had become their symbol, a sign that Cheryl would not miss. Since then I have learned more about owls being messengers from the other side. Helen had told me a lot about birds and bird lore, but never mentioned that she rode around in them.

In 1994, a Cree woman named Lisa Petagumskum, of Chisasibi, paddled down Lake Champlain and then the Hudson River in a canoe called the *Odeyak*, with a crew that sailed as a part of a demonstration against Hydro-Québec's proposed flooding of Cree lands to build hydroelectric dams and to bring awareness to the fact that the flooding had released high levels of methylmercury, which had bioaccumulated in fish and wildlife—important sources of food for the Cree and Inuit.

While staying at Manna Jo Greene's center in Cottekill, New York, Lisa had shared a meal with *Odeyak* crew and supporters, many associated with the Clearwater organization, and then asked if she could take a walk in the nearby woods. There were hundreds of acres of preserve land beyond the property; of course, she could take a stroll. So Lisa went deep into "bear country" that night by moonlight. A while later, she returned and, with a touch of urgency, asked to use the phone to place a call to James Bay. She explained, "An owl spoke to me and told me my grandmother just died." She was handed the phone and, upon completing the call to Canada, found that her grandmother had, indeed, just passed onto the next life. The owl's message was confirmed. This is exactly how traditional people describe their experiences with owls, as messengers for those who are passing on into the spirit world.[45]

Owl as Oracle

One German woman involved with Native American culture, Barbel, tells the story of how an owl smashed into the windshield of their car late one stormy night the moment of her father-in-law's death in another state. The bird hit it from an angle, sliding across the rain-slicked glass, from left to right, leaving a trail of blood across the window. It was hard to tell the species of owl as the bird vanished quickly and fell to the roadside, but she remembers the underbelly was white as a ghost, a sight she will never forget. The owl does occasionally earn its keep as a messenger for those who are making the leap into the world beyond, to send messages to loved ones not to worry. Owls are often bringers of tragic news, as this story suggests, and this role is not confined to Native American culture, where it sometimes is taken to excess by the more fearful.

Another woman told the story that an owl visited her right before and right after her father died. To me, this shows the owl in two different roles. The first role was as a messenger of death itself, not necessarily a warning. The owl was certainly not a cause of tragedy, but simply a sign of an imminent passing. This has always been the owl's most famous role and one reason why many Native American nations have a tendency to avoid owls and their feathers. It can foretell a death in the family, and some people don't want to know. Also, the owl is not considered "pure" like the other raptors; it can be misused.

The second appearance of the owl, right after the man had passed away, demonstrated its alternate role, as a messenger between the dead and the living. The father's spirit was in the bird, in harmony with the bird's own spirit, and, moving it through the great power of the Creator, came to that woman to tell her that he had died, that he was okay, and that there is an afterlife after all. It may have also been his way of saying good-bye, although there is no word for good-bye in most Native languages.

The Mystery of the Owl Platter

I once witnessed a situation in which owl energy was used to harm someone, but it was done in a very sneaky, silent way. Indeed, which of our elders would allow open misuse of this noble bird of the night? A Native grandmother was having an ongoing quarrel with her boyfriend over the responsibilities of the house. He said that to make it up to her he would mount a row of beautiful Indian collector plates along the wall, just under the ceiling, which he did. The last four plates depicted white wolves, and hidden within the design of each was a letter: W, O, L, F. These were meant to be displayed with the letters in order, left to right, to bring helpful, positive wolf energy into the house.

The day I arrived in the house, the woman was very sick and needed healing. Not only was her vision failing, she was going to have major surgery the next week on her knee and shoulder. She was in a lot of pain. I asked her to sit down and close her eyes. I sang a song and told her to let go of human thoughts and become of one mind with the white wolf. She did so. We did a healing ceremony together, and asked the Creator for help. Looking up, I noticed the plates. I said, "There are your white wolves! Become of one mind with them. They are strong in spirit and can heal themselves!"

Then I noticed that the plates were in the wrong order, F, O, W, L, and that the F was covered up by a large doll in Native American dress, standing on a high shelf. The remaining plates spelled out owl. I climbed up on a chair and, while smudging with sweetgrass, switched around the order of the plates until it said wolf, as its creator intended. I felt quite sure her boyfriend had placed a great deal of intention, harmful intention, in the deliberate misordering of the plates. Some Natives call owl feathers "deceiver feathers."[46] This owl man had deceived the sick woman in several ways, for one thing, he knew her vision was too poor to notice the mixed-up plates and the word *owl* on her own wall. I said, "Owls can be tricky birds!" She answered, "That man was pretty tricky, too!"

I said, "Would you say the man who put those plates up there was praying against you at that time? Would that theory work for you?" The woman said, "It sure would! He left me right after that. For another woman!" He flew by night, leaving an arrow in her heart, and was never seen again.

I told the woman the story of the young brave who went to the house of a medicine man with an arrow sticking in his heart. He said, "If you're a medicine man, you can tell me who shot this arrow and why the Creator let this happen!" The medicine man only answered, "I think you're asking the wrong questions!" The young man said, "See, you can't answer the question. No one can. It makes me so angry." The medicine man looked the youngster in the eye and said, "Take the arrow out of your heart!" The young man jumped back with surprise. "What? Take it out? Why?" The medicine man commanded, "Just take it out!" The boy pulled out the arrow and offered it to the medicine man, who broke it over his knee and threw it into the fire. Right away, the youth felt quite a bit better. The medicine man said, "Now about the two questions . . ." The youngster answered, "What two questions?" He no longer needed to know why the Creator had allowed him to be injured. He was merely grateful to be alive.

Within a single day, the woman reported remarkable progress in her recovery from illnesses that had gotten worse since the collector's items were hung in the wrong order. And then she added, "Oh by the way, I took the arrow out of my heart!" Although no healing is without its reverberations and illnesses tend to reoccur in lesser forms, that grandmother has been much better since the plates were moved.

With the owl, we have now completed the Medicine Wheel of the master birds, as used ceremonially by New York's Matouac people. The owl is the guardian of the western gate. Most would consider Native Hawaiians the gatekeepers of the West among Native North Americans. They hold the owl in the highest regard. The white owl that flies at night is called pueo, and it is the messenger of the kahunas, the powerful shamanic leaders in Hawaiian culture.* Still further west, aboriginal Australians revere the owl as their master bird and, by the way, don't believe he can be used to do bad things.

We have now discussed the four sacred birds of the four directions, eagle, hawk, crow, and owl. But there are countless other species of birds in North America, each of which have a message for us and a story to tell. There are no boring birds once you get to know them. They are all interesting. In this next section, we will look at other species of birds that were able to convey messages of concern from beyond the veil.

---

*Conversation with Woody Vasquel, Elders' Spiritual Gathering at William Commanda's place, Maniwaki, Quebec, Canada, August 7, 2010. He also noted that in Hawaiian the "little people" are called *menehune*.

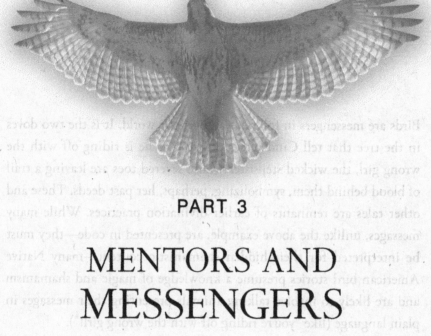

PART 3

MENTORS AND MESSENGERS

MESSENGERS
AND CARRIERS OF SPIRIT

Birds are messengers in folktales all over the world. It is the two doves in the tree that tell Cinderella's prince that he is riding off with the wrong girl, the wicked stepsister whose severed toes are leaving a trail of blood behind them, symbolizing, perhaps, her past deeds. These and other tales are remnants of earlier divination practices. While many messages, unlike the above example, are presented in code—they must be interpreted for their hidden shamanistic content—many Native American bird stories presume a knowledge of magic and shamanism and are likely to involve talking animals presenting their messages in plain language (like "you're riding off with the wrong girl!").

In "real life," birds seldom speak in audible sentences.* But according to the traditional lore of Bird Medicine, they speak volumes through their songs and motions. These messages are mainly meaningful in relation to the environment and the observer's situation at that time. It could be said that no two bird "signs" will ever be exactly the same. The variations seem infinite and ingenius.

How can a mere bird give us messages that might change our direction in life? They can cause their shadows to cross our path or our faces as a warning, or fly in figure eights over our heads as if to say good-bye, or appear in numbers that have special meaning to us. Their migration patterns give us milestones that welcome us to new seasons, as big and clear as a state border crossing sign to the trained eye. Birds may appear to us in dreams, or first in dreams and then in real life, providing additional information. They can bring messages from those we have lost,

---

*However, see my story "Blue Jay Answers a Prayer" on page 131.

just as we are thinking of them, and even apparently give us clear signs as to who they are speaking for. Birds get our attention by possessing the timing of a comedian and the dramatic flair of a storyteller. They save their appearance for the exact moment that will make the meaning unmistakable and even funny.

Each species has its own associations—thanks perhaps to its observable strengths, weaknesses, and colors—and according to Bird Medicine lore, these swift and unfailing bird volunteers use these associations as part of their message, mirroring from above our best or worst behavior or modeling how we should strive to be. They are teachers who model for us our saner courses of action. In fact, they often arrive as harbingers of a human message that is about to arrive. The species is almost always an important part of the message, as in the case of robins, which are often associated with messages about family and relationship. If different species appear together, it is thought to constitute a more complex message, probably about alliances. The four gatekeepers are bold birds, and will not be shy if they need to send a message from beyond; flying beside your car, staring into your eyes, crashing into your window or fender, or saluting you with their wingtip. They might even dance for you in a way that has special meaning to you; anything to get your undivided attention. According to the teachings of the elders, it means there is something you need to know. Some species, such as the hummingbird, have very specific associations for different tribes and nations, and knowledge of these will help the observer decipher the message. These particular birds appear to the elders in visions, perhaps carrying symbolic objects or tools of shamanic power, to show approval about a decision—often in answer to a prayer.

The color of a bird has meaning according to the Medicine Wheel teachings of each tradition, but these meanings change from village to village, or even person to person. Red usually embodies the Creator's life-giving power and the sacred gift of fire. White often embodies air and the wild wind, and also wisdom. Yellow can represent love and joy. Black may embody the power of the earth, of rest and going deep within. Green embodies the power of Mother Earth and blue embodies the detached and expansive power of Father Sky. The variations are endless, but the color of a bird's feathers are an integral part of the message.

Birds teach us how to pray at dawn, how to attract a mate through dance and song, how to raise a family, how to deal with adversity, and even how to look for bird signs. They teach us to give a great deal of space and freedom to our fellow humans, and they show us how to love and share without trying to own someone else. And yes, at times it really does seem like they are talking to us directly, speaking our language in a way that stops us right in our tracks. All we need to do is listen.

The late Russell Means, Native American rights activist and actor, once said that nothing is by accident. This even extends to the passing of a bird or its shadow across your path. These are considered signs in Native culture, especially if they are unusual. I lived in a house for eight months that was next to a forest where a very loud hawk lived. Just before I moved out, I explored the forest and visited the hawk's abode, and he made his usual racket. A few days later was my official moving day. As I was standing out in the driveway, he came out over my head and did figure eights over me for a while, singing his farewell song. For the first time, he wasn't one hundred feet in the sky, but was low above my head. It was my last day living there. The next day, I had to come back for a few more items. He brought two friends with him—hawks I'd never seen before—and they flew high overhead making noises. It was a memorable *bon voyage*!

In response to my query, "What is the significance of birds in Native American life?" Ken Cohen wrote:

The observation of birds and natural bird migration patterns are absolutely essential for the survival of Native American healing, spirituality, and culture. Hunting, planting, and ceremony are often coordinated with the appearance of particular birds. Birds also remind storytellers that it is time to teach children about the lessons learned from the eagle, the hawk, the heron, the dove, and so on. A bird such as the eagle does not simply represent flying close to Creator or seeing from a higher perspective. Rather the eagle teaches and is this value and power. This is very different from the perspective of Euro-American culture in which birds and animals may symbolize human values. There are numerous examples of bird symbolism in the Bible. If Native Americans only valued birds for their symbolic value, then they might be satisfied to read or think about them or view them in an aviary. But they are not, because birds must be observed in their natural state in order to learn directly from them.[1]

The belief that birds carry the spirit of a deceased relative is widespread and takes many forms. This may relate to the crow council phenomenon, wherein crows tend to gather at places where the Native peoples gathered years ago and at the appropriate times for ceremony. My question was, "How can this happen?"

I gain insight into Algonkin-ode culture whenever I connect with the Nyoongar and other aboriginal people of Australia. The similarities are striking, and the Nyoongar excel at expressing their views of Dreamtime; how they explain these ancient teachings make so much sense. Bente Hansen, author of several books, including *Messages from Beyond,* worked for seven years with Australia's Aboriginal and Torres Strait Islander Commission and worked with the Nyoongar and other native aboriginals in western Australia. She adopted the practice of going into meditation, entering into Dreamtime, and traveling inside an eagle, to look through its eyes and see what it sees. She was very successful with this, and yet soon found herself inexplicably traveling inside an American bald eagle, a bird she had never seen, flying over the landscape of the United States, a country she had never visited in her physical body. This unexpected phenomenon kept happening over and over, allowing her to visit different places, especially in the midwestern states. One day, she got an opportunity to move to the United States, and she took flight, on a jumbo jet. She lived in the United States for many years and eventually did visit the Midwest. Not surprisingly, a lot of it seemed familiar to her human eyes. I took her story as an answer to the question, "Why do the crows gather where the ancestors did?" Is it because the Lenape of the Atlantic coast were working through birds during their life and are still channeling through them now they are dead?[2]

According to Elaine Henwood, trusted friend of the late elder Rolling Thunder, RT would go into an altered state of consciousness where he would become one with a bird in the sky and see through those eyes as they were his own. He had Bird Medicine, a set of spiritual gifts and abilities all having to do with birds. This technique was a sacred tool he used and a gift he was born with. He was trained practically from birth to use these healing gifts for the good of all, although it's something that gets easier with practice. RT was especially attuned to eagles and their habits and used eagle feathers in healing. When Elaine first met Rolling Thunder, he was healing a young man with an open ankle wound using an eagle feather. This was at the Association for Research and Enlightenment center in Virginia Beach. Rolling Thunder and others in his circle eventually reached a point where the need for borrowing a bird dropped away and became unnecessary. They could "go direct," their spirits flying on their own with a high degree of accuracy and recall. As mentioned earlier, some might say that our spirits or souls are what fly from place to place in these situations, similar to a bird. This, too, is part of Native American tradition and may be counted as an advanced form of Bird Medicine. Rolling Thunder, whose father marched along the Trail of Tears, was born Cherokee in the hills of Oklahoma, but married a Western Shoshone woman and later became a spokesperson for that nation. In fact, he spoke for all Native American nations when he said, "Birds are our brothers and sisters and need to be respected!"[3]

Given the still-prominent use of the eagle phone (described on page 45), it seems probable that the ancestors who lived on the East Coast a thousand years ago practiced this technique of out-of-body travel while they lived, so that when they died, they could continue to watch over Turtle Island (or North America) in the bodies of birds. Now instead of gathering in the bodies of eagles, which have become few, they gather in the bodies of crows, which are many.

Birds as Oracles of the Dead

A Mi'kmaq relative, Grandmother White Wolf, said that when her mother's body was being laid to rest at the cemetery, a small bird came and perched on the back of the headstone. The minister said his eulogy, and the bird turned its head, listening to what was being said. As the body was lowered into the earth, the bird continued to sit there, looking down into the hole, watching. As the ceremony was about to end, the bird chirped a few times, as if to say something definitive about the proceedings, and lifted off and flew away. White Wolf (Wabay Bachtezun) always felt that her mother's spirit entered into the bird at that time to say good-bye to everyone, but also to remind them that death is not the end and that the soul lives on.

A Club-Footed Messenger

One of the most remarkable stories I ever heard about a nonraptor becoming a messenger for the dead at the moment of passing involved a pigeon. There was an old man named Ed in Poughkeepsie, and no one seemed to know if he was Indian or not, but he loved birds. He especially loved pigeons and was not averse to eating pigeon eggs for breakfast. (Some Native Americans believe it is bad luck to eat a robin egg, but pigeon eggs are fair game.) In New York, it is illegal to own a pigeon unless you are part of a pigeon club, and this man was one of the regulars, a lifetime card-carrying member of the Poughkeepsie Pigeon Club.

This man had a clubbed left foot from birth; he didn't hide the fact and was not ashamed of this unusual feature, which set him apart from other males of his species. He gave up his collection of pigeons when he reached eighty-five years, feeling he was too old to do a good job of feeding and caring for them, but he was known to feed wild pigeons in his own yard.

The day Ed died, at the ripe old age of ninety-two, his brother walked out into his own yard to find a pure white pigeon staring at him. He had never seen a pigeon in his yard before and has never seen one since, but this large white pigeon spent the entire day standing in the backyard, staring at the brother of the man who had just died. The brother went out into the yard to get a better look at the bird, and yet it did not fly away. It was then that the bird showed the brother his left foot. It was a clubbed foot, just like Ed's. Even the skeptical brother had to admit, this was no ordinary bird. He told the story many times and reported, "It was Ed. He was saying to me, 'Everything's okay!'"[4]

A Robin's Timely Message

Kevin Deer, a ceremonial elder of the Kahnawake Mohawk Territory near Montreal, received an important message from a fledgling baby robin a few years ago. One day, his dad came by to visit and Kevin decided to greet him at the rear entrance door, and adjacent to the rear door was the clothesline. Suddenly a fledgling robin landed on the clothesline, a foot away from his head. That's when they looked at each other, the robin and Kevin. Kevin said to his father, "That's odd! We're going to get a message shortly. I don't know how it's going to come."

The robin departed. Within five minutes, Kevin's friend, Tom Porter, was on the line with a message. The baby daughter of a family in their close circle of friends had just died. The funeral would be very soon. Tom had an obligation to conduct the ceremony, but unfortunately he had another obligation that took precedence. He called to ask Kevin if he could do the honors. Kevin said yes, and almost immediately left the Montreal area, headed for Albany. He attended a funeral parlor in Albany and then a church service. Then he traveled to a small town called Red Rock and to a beautiful country cemetery laid out on the bottom of a sloped hill at the edge of a forest. After the Catholic priest finished the service, he then introduced Kevin, who shared some perspectives about Native American rituals regarding death. In the Mohawk worldview, death is predestined. When it is our turn to leave, we leave and that's it. No ifs, ands, or buts. There is no would have, could have, should have. This eliminates any kind of guilt that individuals may have regarding the loss of the departed. Some people may go through a lot of second-guessing—if only I had done this or that for the person, if only they had had more time, and so on—mounting up personal guilt about all the things that could have been different. In the end, all that doesn't matter, and in fact, there is nothing to worry about. When we die, we go back into spirit, into the realm of the Great Spirit.

Kevin stated, "Our elder brother sun in his journey every day, teaches us about life. If we follow it from sunrise to sunset, it is a reflection of our life. At sunrise, it looks like the sun comes out of the earth. He reaches a midway point and begins to set, and then goes back seemingly into the earth. But tomorrow, the sun rises again. Similarly, with us as human beings, we come out of the earth, we reach a midway point and begin to grow old and start to set, but our face will rise again, only in spirit this time, just as the sun rises again tomorrow." He then added, "Our people look to the natural world—to creation—to understand the Creator. We find our answers in the natural world."

As he gazed out compassionately at the audience, he extended his left hand toward the edge of the forest. As if on cue, a tiny fawn leaped out from behind the trees and danced on the green grass in the very spot that Kevin was pointing to. The fawn was having a great time and had no worries as she cavorted and played amid the reminders of death. He said, "*Nia:wen!*" (Thank you!). The fawn stopped, locked eyes with Kevin for a moment, and then left to find her mother. The priest, who had been standing next to him, exclaimed, "How did you do that?" But there was no explanation that could do justice to the moment. It was an experience, a shared feeling of the closeness we have to the spirit world, which those gathered together will not forget.

Moments later, Kevin met with the grieving mother, who expressed her gratitude for everyone's support. She said that it was a bittersweet moment for her. Although she had lost a daughter, she was also now reassured that her baby was all right, dancing in the sunshine of the Great Spirit.[5]

Bird Language

Alexie Kondratiev was a birder, but also a scholar and linguist who worked with indigenous populations, including the Ojibway, and as I recall, the Innu of northern Quebec. He could speak thirteen languages with complete fluency and was considered functionally fluent in sixty languages. One of the languages he spoke was that of birds, and he had an encyclopedic knowledge not only of birds but of their songs and their symbolic meanings. He passed away in the wee hours of Saturday, May 28, 2010. He had been writing about the Celtic goddess Bridgett while riding on the Long Island Railroad when he experienced heart failure and tried to make it to his house in Queens before time ran out. He only made it as far as Crocheron Street and 167th. He lay down on a patch of grass and breathed his last, looking toward the full moon, his latest writings on Bridgett, his patron saint, in the book bag still clutched in his hand.

It has been said, by Ken Gale and others, that when he died it was as if a library of rare books had burned down. His sister Valeria, and five other people, including two of his students, went on a pilgrimage to the place where he died to offer their prayers a few days later. Though just a patch of grass, to them it was a shrine to Bridgett herself. As they arrived, they watched a crow and a mockingbird fly down side by side and land on a rosebush, visiting them and then flying away. The crow was a bird closely associated in Ireland with Bridgett, and Alexie had often called the mockingbird the multilinguist of birds, one he had always closely identified with. The arrival of the two together was a message to the six pilgrims that Alexie was flying beside Bridgett in the spirit world, that they were together at last. But the rosebush—ah, that was a puzzle. Someone pointed out that the mockingbird's wings flash white when it lands, the color of Bridgett as a young maid, that the rose petals are red, the color of Bridgett as a mother, and the crow's wings are black, the color of Bridgett as an old crone. These three colors came together when the two birds landed on the thorns of the rose, also a symbol of heartbreak and parting. White, red, and black are the colors of the triple goddess, of whom Bridgett is a prime example. In Ireland, a crow or raven eating fresh kill on snow is considered one of Bridgett's signs, as the three colors meet. The students felt that Alexie was reaching out to them, showing that he could still teach them from beyond the veil and that the language of birds was still in his remarkable repertoire.[6]

Bird Dog

One person told me that a certain hawk flew parallel to their automobile, staring at them through the passenger window for quite a while as they drove. Needless to say, it got the driver's attention. A day later, the same hawk dive-bombed the same driver while she was operating a school bus, then followed the vehicle down to the school yard. I knew that a Native elder would ask if someone important had died in the days preceding the event, so I inquired, and the person answered that a favorite family dog had just died a few days earlier. She did not know about such beliefs or have them herself, but the loss of the dog had grieved her at that time. She was easily convinced that the persistent hawk was somehow connected to the dearly departed family dog, whose loss was so much on her mind.[7]

Hummingbird: Courier of the Fallen Warriors

The tiny hummingbird is the only bird who can fly in one place or fly backward. This extraordinary rainbow-feathered bird can fly to the left or right as well. It is not only beautiful in itself, but works hard to bring beauty to the flowers, by sucking their nectar and pollinating them. The Maya say that the hummingbird is a good-luck bird for traders and traveling merchants, who move quickly from place to place exchanging small treasures. It is also a bird of diplomacy as it can back up and move from side to side, to get a perspective on what is being offered. The Maya also have a teaching that when warriors die they visit their loved ones as a hummingbird. This tiny hovering bird has often been seen right after someone dies, and the departed is not always a Mayan warrior.

One woman claims that at the very moment of her young son's death, a hummingbird hovered in front of her face and stared at her. She immediately felt it was a greeting from her son. I have heard similar stories, often from people who have no connection with Native Americans that they know about.

A Mi'kmaq grandmother named Heather Sole (also called Eaglewoman) told me that while delivering her father's graveside eulogy, a hummingbird hovered behind her shoulder, standing watch. The bird appeared as soon as she started speaking of her father, Reg McEachern. It fluttered behind her head as she prayed to the Creator and left as soon as she was done. The wife of Charlie Labrador, a teacher of Mi'kmaq lore who was present at the eulogy, knew the bird was significant and asked Grandmother Heather, "Did you see it?" Because the bird stayed just behind her ear, she never saw it. Charlie told her the hummingbird is the rainbow bird because of its bright colors and that she could connect with Reg and her mother, Doris, through the rainbow bridge, which links this world to the spirit world. I told Grandmother Heather that the Maya and many other nations say that the hummingbird appears to honor a fallen warrior. I asked her if her father had been in the military. Her reply gave me goose bumps. "He was a lifetime military officer. He was in the navy during World War II and afterward, and spent the last twenty-five years of his military service in the army," she answered with surprise.

I asked my sister if she had known Charlie Labrador, and she told me he was in charge of the petroglyphs and burial ground in Kejmajink, Nova Scotia, after he retired (from the army) and invited her to see them. He knew we were Muis family on our mother's side. He pointed to an island and said, "That's called Muis Island because when the white people took over, that's where they put all the Indians!" A sad story, but what better proof that you are Indian than to have a Native American Internment Camp named after you? Charlie passed away in 2003. Todd Labrador, whom I watched build birch-bark canoes using only traditional materials with William Commanda at Maniwaki, is Charlie's son.* Small world.

Why is the fragile hummingbird associated with a warrior? Legend has it that if a bear tries to steal the eggs or young from a humming-bird's nest, the hummingbird mother will attack the bear and peck his eyes out.[8] The bear's big paws and teeth are no match for the speedy hummingbird, whose flight is quicker than the eye. A small bird cannot kill a large mammal, but the folklore about birds pecking the eyes out of villainous thieves is based on some truth and has reached even the Brothers Grimm, who had doves peck out the eyes of the two mean stepsisters at Cinderella's wedding to the prince.

Someone told me that hummingbirds gather near the sacred burial grounds at Kejmajink where many great Mi'kmaq warriors, called *madn'ach,* which means "defenders," had been buried many centuries ago and that the hummingbirds all arrive on May 15 and leave each year on Labor Day. They are disciplined, to say the least. I have yet to make the journey and see for myself.

---

*See the DVD *Good Enough for Two* by Valerie Pouyanne.

BIRDS AS TEACHERS

Birds Can Change Your Flight Plans

Author and healer Kenneth Cohen told me that one day long ago, while undergoing a difficult fast as part of a vision quest, he saw an eagle fly over his head. It was a time when he had chosen a path of continual self-abnegation and suffering in order to purify himself. This fast was part of that. The eagle seemed to say to him, "Don't seek suffering for its own sake. The suffering that comes along in the course of living is enough." That message, subtle as it was, changed the course of his life. Ken has since become a more gregarious and outgoing person and spreads his knowledge of indigenous healing practices as he travels coast to coast, on eagle's wings, as it were, living a remarkably full life.[9]

In Ken's book *Honoring the Medicine,* he quotes late Seneca Grandmother Twylah Nitsch as saying, "In the Wolf Clan Teaching Lodge, the gift of seeing is symbolized by the hawk, a bird known for its speed and sharp vision. Grandma Twylah says that the hawk teaches us to appreciate the importance of imagery, dreams, stories, and myths. The hawk, like the eagle, reminds us to view life from a higher and wider perspective and realize that, as in a dream, all events in our lives are connected in mysterious and meaningful ways. We can use our intuition to discover life's plots and subplots."[10]

Anishinabi elder Eddy Stevenson and I were in Canandaigua, New York, years ago, undergoing a vision quest, not together, because it was a solitary experience, but separately, under the protection of a pair of capable elders from Canada. Eddy had been fasting for several days, as I had, under cold and overcast conditions. Looking up in the sky, he observed the dense cloud cover, then watched as a hole appeared in the clouds and a brilliant beam of sun shone through, reaching Earth below with its miraculous golden light. At that moment, he had a vision in his mind of a great hawk circling in that spot, carrying a medicine shield with symbols written on it, which he knew to be a teaching shield. He knew what the message was: it was time to pass along his teachings. He had been in contact with Native ways his entire life and had been a helper to a number of traditional elders over the many years that had turned his hair to white. Teachers had blessed him with wisdom from the ancestors, but Eddy had always been rather shy about taking on that position himself. Here was a mandate from the heavens; the winged ones were insisting that he become a traditional teacher.

His life changed in that instant. He knew that the role carried with it great responsibility, that one had to know what one was talking about before speaking. He began to travel around the United States and Canada, looking for elders who would train him and correct any misunderstandings he might have accumulated along the way. A few years ago, he began teaching in earnest and now teaches Native Americans (and others) in correctional facilities in the Northeast.[11]

A Change of Heart

One of the most famous stories of a bird visiting a human being and bringing with it a life-changing experience was told by William Commanda, an Algonquin (Mamawinini) elder who received the Order of Canada on November 5, 2009, in the company of Prince Charles of Britain. Commanda was the carrier of three wampum belts: the Seven Fires prophecy belt, the Jay Treaty belt, and the Friendship belt.

He became a master birch-bark canoe maker, worked in lumber camps, and got married. He drank, swore, and smoked. Then, in 1961, he had to stop the booze. "I had cancers in the abdomen. It was malignant."

Doctors told him they could operate, but they would not be able to heal him entirely, and he would need to use a colostomy bag. "Oh no, I said, I don't go for that. So I came home, I called my wife, she came and got me."

He started drinking herb tea made by his wife while receiving injections from a faith healer.

Early one morning, he heard a bird singing outside. Opening the curtains, he saw the bird and fell to his knees by the couch, reeling in pain. He said of that moment, "I knew that bird was not just a bird. He was more than that. I asked that bird to save me."

He said to the Creator, "If I have something I could do for you in life, I want you to save me. If not, I want you to take me away now. I don't want to live another hour."

He stopped drinking and got over his anger. He forgave everyone who had made life so difficult for his people. He was better in six months.

His wife was amazed. "You're not the same person anymore, what did you do to yourself?"

He answered, "My life does not belong to me, it's not mine. It's borrowed time. It belongs to my Creator."

Two years later, he held the first Circle of All Nations, a gathering on his land to restore aboriginal culture and spirituality. This annual meeting has come to include anyone for whom ecology is part of living in harmony with the planet.

In 1970, members of his community presented Grandfather Commanda with three sacred wampum belts that had been held by his great-great-grandfather, Pakinawatik. It was clear the people thought he was the leader who should have the belts.

He began taking them to meetings with government officials, explaining the message of the Seven Fires prophecy belt (relationships with creation), the three-figure 1700s belt about sharing, and the Jay Treaty border crossing belt about borderlessness, which emphasizes that, for the nomadic First Nations, "territory is as the river flows, as the bird flies and as the wind blows."

The Oka Crisis of 1990, in which the Mohawk nation protested a proposed golf course, was a wake-up call for the Canadian government. Suddenly, they wanted to appear to respect aboriginals. Over the years,

Commanda was invited to more and more ceremonies honoring human rights; he met with the Dalai Lama and Nelson Mandela.

I traveled with Commanda for fourteen years and stood in for him on several occasions when he was not feeling 100 percent. William Commanda passed away on August 3, 2011, at the age of ninety-seven.[12]

I asked William Commanda on more than one occasion what species of bird brought the message from the Creator that day in 1961. Although Commanda was an expert on wildlife, the answer did not seem to be a simple one. Whatever it was, it was something quite unusual, all the more astounding that it was not your average *Peterson Field Guide* songbird. In fact, he insisted it was, speaking in the French language, a *rossignol*. This is generally translated as a nightingale, some Natives say the bird was a gold throat, or what birders call a common yellow throat, who usually says *witchity witchity* (or ratio ratio ratio ratio). However, the nightingale is not a North American bird but Eurasian exclusively, and if this was the case, it must have been imprisoned in a cage and shipped to the New World before escaping to run free with its indigenous brothers and sisters. It may have been some kind of thrush, but one of a most rare and unusual nature, physically as well as spiritually. It was apparently a messenger as unforgettable as the message.

Speaking of gold throat, a popular bird among Canadian Natives, Anishinabi bird caller Madeleine Saiga was once visited for over an hour by what, in her language, is called a *silabeekway*, which means "it sits on the cedar branch." It climbed all over her and drank water from her cup. She said the European name is gold throat. She wondered if it was telling her she needed a cedar bath.

Bird of Four Colors

A Guatemalan Mayan man living in eastern Canada got a change of flight plans from a bird as well. He was home alone one evening, and he heard someone knocking on his window upstairs, so he climbed the stairs and went to the window to see who was calling. There he saw a bird with feathers of black, white, red, and yellow, the colors of the four cardinal directions (no pun intended) and the colors associated with Native North American culture. He didn't know what kind of bird it was, but he knew that he was supposed to spend more time with real aboriginal people, especially those who still respected those colors.

It also seems that the dominant color of the bird was one he associated with the West, so he went straightaway to Alaska and worked there for many years, before returning East. It was a very successful and profitable adventure. The male eastern towhee is a red-eyed bird that brandishes these four colors of the Medicine Wheel. Their call is "Drink your tea tea tea tea tea!" However, they are rather rare in New Brunswick, Canada, and in Mi'kmaq territory in general (where people apparently drink enough tea as it is) and prefer to spend their winters in Mayan country on the Mexican border, around Hidalgo County, Texas, and throughout the Deep South. Was this the bird the Mayan man saw while living among the Mi'kmaq? When the Native American is ready, the feathered messenger appears, regardless of climate. In any case, that bird flew a very long way to deliver that message in a language that a Mayan man could understand.

BIRDS AS MUSICIANS

Birds have always been associated with an incredible variety of sounds. In Grant Foreman's book *Sequoyah,* he quotes Samuel Lorenzo Knapp, lawyer and statesman, in an article published in the *Cherokee Phoenix* (1828):

> From the cries of wild beasts, from the talents of the mocking-bird, from the voices of his children and his companions, he [Sequoyah] knew that feelings and passions were conveyed by different sounds, from one intelligent being to another. The thought struck him to ascertain all the sounds in the Cherokee language. His own ear was not remarkably discriminating and he called to his aid the more acute ears of his wife and children. He found great assistance from them. When he thought that he had distinguished all the different sounds in their language, he attempted to use his pictorial signs, images of birds and beasts, to convey those sounds to others or to mark them in his own mind.[13]

It is not surprising that a keen observer of life like Sequoyah would see a link between human speech and birdsong and use that insight to create the first alphabet or syllabary for the Cherokee language. Gisela Kaplan, the brilliant Australian scientist, once wrote:

> Birds have inspired human imagination. . . . Birds feature in many human dances—many cultures have prided themselves on being able to mimic birdsong and bird displays. Human fascination with birds may also arise from having something in common with birds—humans and birds share a strong investment in communication by vocalization. In fact, the complexity of songs and communication

systems developed by birds and by humans has no equal among vertebrates, except for whales and dolphins.[14]

So by listening to birds more closely in order to understand the Cherokee (Tsalagi) language, Sequoyah was merely taking down ideas from our closest relatives in the domain of speech, the birds.

Dawn Song of the Birds

There are countless stories about birds and their music making. To the Mi'kmaq, the sun is "the closest thing we can see to our Creator," and they teach that birds sing their prayers to the Creator each morning as the sun rises in the east. In fact, they may be praying to help the sun rise up so that creation may continue.

If songbirds are all eliminated in the silent spring that some scientists are already observing in certain hot spots near transmission towers, who will sing the sun up? And how do we know the sun will rise again without the birds to cheer it on? According to Native tradition, we don't really know as much as we think we do about nature.

Dennis Hastings and Margery Coffey wrote in their joint dissertation "Grandfather Remembers: Broken Treaties/Stolen Land; The Omaha Land Theft" about the lost sounds of morning on the prairie in the days when indigenous birds sang the praises of the Great Spirit as it came up in the east. In a section titled "Dawn Song of the Birds," the authors reveal a shocking truth behind the seemingly happy sunrise chorus we enjoy today in America as we look eastward over woods and fields—that even this is not as it should be.

While listening to an elder one afternoon, in a moment of quiet small talk of the prairie and how it was in the old days, he shared a view of the past.

"My great-grandfather told me," he related shyly, "that when he was a small boy, his great-grandfather told him that he had truly heard the dawn song of the birds."

"The birds always sing at dawn," someone commented, "even today."

"But then, before the white man came, it was only the aboriginal birds that were here. These birds were so accustomed to singing with each other that each had its own spot and part to sing in a grand melodic chorale that praised Wakonda.* The alien birds that we have with us now don't know either the words or music to the prairie song of dawn."

"Like the pheasants, sparrows, and starlings?" another offered.

"Precisely. My great-grandfather said his great-grandfather told of the incredible harmony that one could hear at that time. This was sung at dawn when traditionally the prayers were always said and the pipes smoked. It was a song that died in his lifetime and we will never hear it again."[15]

I have been told that the birds have a certain preordained order of entry as they begin their morning motet. Each section of the chorus has its own invisible cue to tell it when to enter. Over the centuries, since the coming of European birds, the song has changed. Immigrants from England insisted on bringing over "the birds of Shakespeare," and many other nonindigenous birds have arrived from all corners of the globe over the years. In their dissertation, Hastings and Coffey suggest that these birds do not have a natural part in this chorus of song and that the original sunrise symphony enjoyed by the ancestors has been lost.[16] However, I have since learned that though the English sparrow marginalized the eastern bluebird, which is sacred to the Navaho and other Native American nations, the bluebird is starting to make a comeback as of 2012.

---

*In an e-mail on December 13, 2012, Margery Coffey explained this term, which has a nasal n sound: "Wakonda is often defined as 'The Creator' by Euro-American cultures who are God-focused. The Omaha see Wakonda as the collection of all spirits. It is not limited to humans but encompasses all life forms of plant and animal including the spirits of water, rocks, soil—the part of the planet that Euro-Americans do not see as alive but the Omaha do. Wakonda is not limited to this planet, it includes the spirits of the Universe. As such it contains all wisdom."

Musicians of the Forest

Most advanced ornithologists (including the late Alexei Kondratiev of Columbia University and Anthony Bledsoe of the University of Pittsburgh) rely mostly on sound to identify birds in the forest, as most songbirds are small and fleet of foot and remain high up in the canopy of trees to avoid capture. Many songbirds themselves rely on sound rather than line-of-sight recognition in determining who their neighbors are. Birds have an additional advantage in "caller ID" situations, as other neighboring songbirds can recognize the tone of voice of a particular male songbird even when he is crooning a new tune they have never heard before."[17]

The winter wren has a ten-second song, described as tinkling, a twittery series of squeaks. He sticks his tail straight up when he sings. The Blackburnian warbler is more rare and is hard to see, but makes a *chitchit* sound or *tsitsi*. The mourning warbler is yet more rare. The hermit thrush has an enchanting ethereal echo to his call, which sounds like R2-D2 in an echo chamber (okay, perhaps a Baltimore oriole in a cave), but which rises as an ascending melody of one measure of pure happiness. A wood thrush has a similar call, but it more resembles a high-speed modem in an echo chamber.

The young indigo bunting (*Passerina cyanea*), which is not yet entirely indigo blue, has an incredibly long song. I once found myself sitting next to one on a mountaintop near Breakneck Ridge in New York's Hudson Valley, not a place you expect to see such a bird. It was sitting on a rock repeating a string of thirty notes, over and over again, calling out into the void before us as if expecting an answer from the Creator. It was a musical moment. According to ornithologists, the song undergoes editorial improvement as the summer wears on, until it is honed down to much fewer notes. The bunting tours South America during the winter and comes back to New York the following spring, ready for the big time; the song is brief but honed to perfection.

The red-eyed vereo (*Vereo olivaceus*) has a number of very musical songs, which more than one European court composer has probably appropriated for his work. Imagine a half note C natural preceded by an upper E natural grace note. Then imagine a half note E natural preceded by a lower C grace note. Then imagine an F natural above that, preceded by D and E as a gliss to F. Then imagine eighth notes D and E, followed by eighths E down to D, leaving us with unresolved longing, as popular in the art songs of the romantic era of Vienna. That's a song I heard from a red-eyed vereo. There is also a blue-headed vereo who is not a solitary bird at all and has no time for all that unresolved longing.

A cheerful bird by nature, the black-capped chickadee (*Poecile atricapillus*) symbolizes hope, among other things, and is featured in the Mi'kmaq creation story about the two brothers who gamble for the world using the *woltis* game, also known as the peach pit game. The peach pits turn into chickadees and fly away, preventing the good brother from losing. The peach pits are black above and white below, like the head of the chickadee. That story is told elsewhere and in my book *Native American Stories of the Sacred*. The chickadee has a very distinctive whistle that can actually be played on the flute or other woodwind instruments. One I heard in Pennsylvania whistled an A natural quarter note followed by a lower F sharp eighth note slurred to a G natural above. Was it really an F sharp or was it a quarter tone below G? Another chickadee, recorded by Kroodsma, whistles a C quarter note followed by two A eighth notes, then, after a repeat, sings a quarter note A followed by two eighth note Gs, similar to the figure above.[18] Either way, one can hear the universally appreciated words of welcome coming from the mouth of this bird of peace, "Hi, Sweetie!" According to Native American folk legend, when the chickadee sings the second "Hi, Sweetie" at a lower pitch, it means it is going to rain. This bird also says its name, *chicka-dee-dee-dee!*

The Mi'kmaq of New Brunswick hear a lot of warblers in the summer, but rarely see them, as they stay high up in thick tree canopies and eat bugs. Their warbling woodwind section rises to a crescendo in early June and dissipates to almost nothing by July 1. The Mi'kmaq also hear the hermit thrush's magical song in summer, but rarely see this very private creature in person. Kinglets are around in summer and sing all day long. The Berwick's thrush is rare elsewhere, but its song is commonly heard in New Brunswick during the early summer months. These male birds sing when seeking a mate or protecting their territory.[19] Later in the summer, they have found their better half and are "out with the kids" or "going shopping" and doing errands.

Another call heard among the thickly leafing branches of the dense forest is the screech of the broad-winged hawk. It is the only hawk that can fly through leafy foliage because its wings, pale when seen from below, are very short, making up their wing surface in breadth. The Cooper's hawk cannot follow the broad-winged hawk into the trees. Its wings are too long.

The brown creeper has a curved bill and has a very high-pitched song of only three seconds. There are many stories and songs in the forest above our heads.

Blue Jay's Gift of Song

My niece, Beverly, was in her front yard talking to her young son. Out on the lawn, a mother and father blue jay (*Cyanocitta cristata*) were teaching their baby blue jay to fly. Three cats entered the yard, drawn to the scene and the helpless young bird. One was Beverly's own cat, a pet, and the other two were feral cats who lived in the garage. Beverly stood guard over the three blue jays, continually chasing away the three persistent cats, while keeping an eye on her own child.

Her son got hungry, and so she had to go inside for a while to make lunch. She won the trust of the blue jay's parents and was able to take the baby bird in her hands and place it high in a tree where the cats would not get to it easily. Awhile later, when she came outside again, she saw that the bird had fluttered down to the ground (part of its flight-training program, no doubt) and also that the three tough cats had reentered the yard, intent on capturing the bird. Again, she stood guard and chased the persistent cats away.

Finally, as evening was falling, she took her son up to bed. While tucking him in, she heard a sound at the window. She went to the sash and found the blue jay parent sitting in the window looking at her. He began to sing a remarkably beautiful song, a type of song rarely associated with blue jays, who usually attempt no more than a short curving *cheep,* either a short curving *jay,* a double *jay,* or an occasional *queedle.* This lovely and musical song went on for quite a long time. It was a way of showing thanks for Beverly's hard work and valiant efforts for saving the life of their child. It was a song of thanksgiving.[20]

My mother says that blue jays are protectors for other birds. If a cat is on the prowl, a jay will yell out a squall that sounds, at least to her, like the word *cat.* Three other people have told me this, so I believe it. Some West Coast Native Americans call the blue jay an evil sorcerer, but in fact, they are among the most intelligent of birds and, like us, are prone to the temptations that come with free will. Blue jays and parrots test well against squirrel monkeys and dogs on animal IQ tests, and probably some people, whereas cats are no match for them.

In *The Mishomis Book,* Edward Benton-Banai has the following story:

> Waynaboozhoo began walking carefully through the land. It is true that he felt a special reverence for the Earth, but also he wanted his arrival in the land of his people to be a surprise.
>
> Just then, Dee-deens' (the blue jay) came to rest in a tree just ahead of Waynaboozhoo. Dee-deens' started yelling as loud as he could. Waynaboozhoo pleaded with the blue jay to be quiet and even tried chasing him away, but Dee-deen's only flew a little bit ahead yelling louder all the time. Waynaboozhoo sighed helplessly. If this kept up everybody throughout all the land would know he was coming!
>
> Today, the Ojibway regard the blue jay as a gossip and tattletail. It is true that he offers an alarm when a stranger approaches, but it seems that Dee-deens' gets a little carried away sometimes.[21]

My Wild Bird

The Mi'kmaq Indian word for wild bird is *zizeep*. It may be used occasionally to refer to a person who has a desire for freedom. *Zizibem*, which literally means "my wild bird," refers to a sweetheart or beloved companion—a tender morsel of ironic wit for a society that prides itself on personal freedom. I asked the expert birder Dr. Anthony Bledsoe of the University of Pittsburgh what bird makes the sound *zizeep*, which would have been known to the ancient Mi'kmaq people of the Maritimes. He did not hesitate to answer. He said that the black-throated green warbler (*Dandroica virens*) says *zizeep* and is quite common in New Brunswick during the summer. (See color insert, plate 11.) It is in this province where *zizeep* and the respectfully possessive *zizeebem* are common expressions among the Mi'kmaq.

Given the flirtatious connotations in Mi'kmaq of *zizeebem*, my wild bird, I was amused to read the following description of the male black-throated green warbler in Donald Kroodsma's *The Backyard Birdsong Guide:*

It's easy to read the mind of a singing male Black-throated Green Warbler. Early in the season before migrating north from the Caribbean or Central America, he begins singing the song that he uses to attract a female. It's a wheezy, slightly hoarse song, containing four or so notes on one pitch, then a single lower note, and ending on the highest and somewhat more raspy note: *zee-zee-zee-zee-zoo-zree*. It's fairly fast-paced, each note about a quarter-second long but the last note slightly longer; the entire song lasts about a second and a half. The unpaired male arrives on the breeding ground and continues this song all day long.

A week or so after he arrives on his territory, he begins to use his second song in an intense dawn chorus. It's slower, lazier, and overall, more wheezy, like *zreee-zreee-zoo-zoo-zree*. The first two *zreee* notes are nearly a half-second long, followed by two of the lower, more tonal *zoo* notes, ending with a higher, rising *zree*.

Before sunrise, he sings rapidly; inserting hoarse, double chip notes between the songs. These songs are typically used near his territorial boundary, too, especially during aggressive interactions with other males. It's the song best described by the often-used mnemonic "*trees-trees-murmuring-trees*."[22]

On some small islands off the coast of Maine, there's space for only one territory. On such islands, a male rarely encounters another male and so rarely uses his aggressive *zreee-zreee-zoo-zoo-zree*. Given this ornithological scenario, I can understand why Mi'kmaq men living on those islands in Maine, or farther up the coast, call to their prospective sweethearts with the word *zizeep*, or the more presumptuous *zizeebem!* Perhaps there was an old teaching tale about a *meegamooatch* who went a'courtin' and was turned into a bird, or to be more exact, a black-throated green warbler.

Migratory Songbirds and Their Struggle to Be Heard

Migratory songbirds have no voice if they do not have a territory. It is well known that male songbirds don't sing if they are not sounding out and claiming a territory. Such have-nots are called floaters, and with their habitats in both the North (during summer) and the South (during the winter) being uprooted in so many insidious ways, it seems that more and more birds are falling silent, either through the lack of a "soundstage," or as the inevitable by-product of death. Migratory songbirds are some of the most popular types of two-leggeds pursued by birders of every stripe and feather, but they are also a subject of growing concern, as their numbers seem to diminish year by year. The great ornithologist Terborgh estimated that the number of migratory songbirds left in the United States in 1990 was a mere one-quarter of that enjoyed by Native Americans before the invasion of the white man.[23] We can only imagine what dawn was like in those days, with the great chorus of birds that greeted the red fire of the sun in the east, at least four times greater than the one we hear today. Dennis Hastings, in

"Grandfather Remembers," hints at how great this mighty choir must been and states that the elders tell us it was a different set of voices as well, without interlopers from afar.

Two study sites near my childhood home, the Cabin John Island site in Maryland and the Rock Creek Park site in Washington, D.C., have been the locations of highly regarded migratory bird studies since the early 1950s. In both sites, songbirds known to travel to the tropics and back declined by a full 45 percent by 1990. During that time, non-migrating birds stayed steady.

In 1965, Chandler S. Robbins of the U.S. Fish and Wildlife Service began a continent-wide bird tally known as the Breeding Bird Survey. In this study, counters make fifty stops at half-mile intervals listening for singing males. Robbins announced in 1998 that "between the years 1978 and 1987, twenty species of migratory songbirds experienced drastic declines. The populations of Wilson's warblers were declining at a rate of 6.5 percent per year, yellow-billed cuckoos, 5.0 percent; wood thrushes, 4.0 percent; northern orioles, 2.9 percent; American Redstarts and Scarlet Tanagers, 1.2 percent; and Ovenbirds, 1.0 percent."[24] These are shocking statistics.

The cause of the decline during that time seemed to be deforestation in most Central American countries. In fact, Haiti is a major winter haven for the songbirds that frequent the northeastern United States all summer, and it is a country plagued by the worst of environmental devastations, earthquakes included. But most other countries in the area are headed in that direction.

Fifty-seven species of migratory birds have been in jeopardy since 1990 or before, according to *The Birder's Handbook* based on the work of John Terborgh and David Wilcove. They include Mississippi kite, swallow-tailed kite, broad-winged hawk, Chuck-will's-widow, whip-poorwill, yellow-billed cuckoo, yellow-bellied sapsucker, great crested flycatcher, yellow-bellied flycatcher; Acadian flycatcher; eastern wood pewee; wood thrush; Swainson's thrush; gray-cheeked thrush; veery; blue-gray gnatcatcher; black-capped vireo; solitary vireo; yellow-throated vireo; red-eyed vireo; Philadelphia vireo; black-and-white warbler; prothonotary warbler; Swainson's warbler; worm-eating warbler; golden-winged warbler; blue-winged warbler; black-throated gray warbler; golden-cheeked warbler; Bachman's warbler; Tennessee warbler; northern parula; magnolia warbler; Cape May warbler; Townsend's warbler; black-throated green warbler; cerulean warbler; yellow-throated warbler; Grace's warbler; Blackburnian warbler; chestnut-sided warbler; bay-breasted warbler; blackpoll warbler; ovenbird; northern waterthrush; Louisiana waterthrush; Kentucky warbler; hooded warbler; Canada warbler; American redstart; northern oriole; western tanager; scarlet tanager; hepatic tanager; and black-headed grosbeak.

Of all the bird species that build nests in the eastern United States, about 66 percent while away their winters south of the Tropic of Cancer, from the north of Mexico to northern South America. Altogether, about two hundred fifty species fly south when it gets cold as part of their survival strategy. Western songbirds are less likely to make the trip, but the Vaux's swift and Townsend's warbler do.[25]

Does the change in latitude make songbirds change their tune as well? That isn't clear, but what is remarkable is that there is a difference between the types of songs one hears in bird populations in the far North and in the far South, a difference that cannot as yet be explained. In her blog entry "Native Melodies," which appeared in 2008 on the website of *The Austrialian* newspaper, Gisela Kaplan, author of fifteen critically acclaimed books, made this stunning observation: "High latitude birds in the northern hemisphere seem to have perfected major scales while Australian birds often sing chromatic scales. Moreover, Australian birds are immensely accomplished percussionists. [Elsewhere she says many specialize in dissonance.] In Europe, excepting starlings, examples are relatively hard to find."[26] This observation makes the sweet diatonic song of the chickadee all the more captivating; its Aussie cousins to the south would be singing (and drumming) a very different tune, but arguably one still playable by modern orchestral instruments.

Just as folk music varies from continent to continent, shamanistic practice finds notable variations from place to place as well. If human music and shamanic practice are both inexorably influenced by, even derived from, birds, our elder brothers on the planet, it would stand to reason that our songs and rituals would vary from place to place as the species of birds do. The folk music of France is solidly diatonic and, in fact, quite often in the major scale, similar to at least a few birdsongs of French climes, whereas the folk music of Bali and the Balinese gamelan orchestra is strikingly percussive, dissonant, and chromatic, as are the birdsongs and bird beats of the Australian continent (and Micronesia).*

She Who Sings Like Birds

Among the Mi'kmaq of Maine and the Maritimes, there is a rich tradition of bird calling that does not involve any kind of device other than the hands and mouth of the caller. The results are remarkable to hear and certainly do not sound human. The calls and whistles so closely resemble those of countless species of songbirds, raptors, corvines, cranes, and other field birds, that the birds are drawn to the call. One may think of this practice as an attempt to "fool" the birds, as is the art of building bird decoys,† but it is an attempt to communicate with them. Natives say it's a way of relating to one's environment. Just as one would not think it deception to speak French in Paris, or Italian in Rome, so Mi'kmaq walking in the woods may burst into the florid song of an indigo bunting, or the piquant cry of a whippoorwill, just

*Bali and Australia were once united by the ancient Sunda Shelf, which is now three hundred feet under the ocean. That water rose a mere 9,000 years ago, whereas the birds have been singing those chromatic songs for 60 million years at least. Stephen Oppenheimer was able to trace the migration of the Sunda Shelf's human gene pool northward from Australia by linking it to its most unusual feature—immunity to malaria—and plotting the appearances of this remarkable quality out into the Pacific Ocean. Along this trail, we should expect to find musical and linguistic markers as well.
†The duck decoy, a staple of Americana and primitive art, is actually a Native American invention. In 1924, eleven canvasback duck decoys were found in Lovelock Cave, Nevada, estimated to be 2,160 years old. For more about duck decoys, see my article "American Art Before 1609: The Fine Art of Fooling a Duck" in the Fall 2009 *Hudson River Museum and Gallery Guide* (pages 26–39).

to show respect for the culture. Some of the best bird callers I know are members of the Mi'kmaq side of my own family, but I'm sure there is a dues-collecting society of bird callers somewhere and a Latin word for the time-honored practice. In any case, it is a seldom-documented aspect of Native American Bird Medicine.

Helen's niece and nephew, Kay and Roland, are expert warblers. They can whistle in imitation of a large number of songbirds, but also enjoy an all-purpose warble once in awhile. They both learned it from their mother, Violet, but I suspect that their father, Clinton, who must have been a fine warbler, had something to do with it, as well as his sister, my aunt Helen, as she was my first teacher in matters avian, and she was the first human I ever heard burst into whistling song while outdoors.

In the book *Mrs. Perley's People*, by well-known author Eleanor Noyes Johnson, there is a brief segment that reveals my great aunt Helen's love of birdcalls.

Gingerly Helen leaned over and put her hand into the cold water. Behind her a bobolink whistled and trilled. A bobolink in April! That was strange. For a brief second Wild Chief [the name she was known as within her "Squaw Tribe," and in fact a descendant of a Miramichi chief] was bewildered, and then she started to laugh.

"Come out from behind that tree, Gray Fox," she shouted. "If you want to fool me with bird calls, be sure you choose one that's in season."

"More fun to puzzle you," answered Gray Fox, alias Phyllis Hough.

As she joined Wild Chief by the brook, Gray Fox whistled again—this time the call of a white-throated sparrow and was answered from the thicket by a feathered white-throat.

Some mornings, Helen would have kept her friend whistling, for Phyl had a real gift, and she loved to listen to her. This morning, however, she had other fish to fry.[27]

Elsewhere, Johnson describes Helen so joyful at the sound of two whippoorwills calling to each other at evening that she wanted to "dance and sing."[28] That was back in 1920, when Scarborough Marsh, the largest salt marsh in Maine, really was "the way life oughta be." Today, it is unusual to hear whippoorwills; modern technology—and apparently the deforestation of Meso-America where they spend the winters—has been very hard on them, and Helen, if she were still alive, would be the first to complain and sign a petition.*

I have heard a number of Native American friends make the calls of eagles, hawks, crows, and seagulls—all with varying degrees of ability. But Helen excelled, apparently, in songbird whistles. Madeleine Saiga of the Anishinabi, who performs the best eagle, heron, crow, and loon calls I've heard, told me her mother is a great warbler and birdsong caller, but only does it when she is happy. It is not appropriate for solemn occasions. That seems to be true for Helen and her relatives as well.

---

*A Native woman living in New York City said she heard a whippoorwill calling in Central Park in the spring of 2012.

BIRDS SPEAK
OUR LANGUAGE

Blue Jay Answers a Prayer

Soon after Joseph Campbell's passing, I was working with his widow, Jean Erdman, to help establish the Joseph Campbell Foundation, which now exists in Hawaii, Jean's home state. I had been involved in some limited aspects of planning, but now it was time for everyone involved to donate some money in order to become a member. I was not working at the time and didn't have much money. I was quite torn up over how much to donate. I knew that donating too small an amount would seem hypocritical, after all the words of praise I had heaped on the name of the deceased. I called Jean and asked her exactly how much I should give. She said, "That's not the kind of foundation this is. You have to decide for yourself."

I answered, "I really have no idea at all. I know some are giving thousands. I don't have anything like that. Just tell me what to do!"

Jean answered like an indigenous grandmother would, "Evan, what do Mi'kmaq do when they don't know something or can't decide?"

I said, "They put out tobacco at the base of a tree and pray for the answer to be provided. Then the eagle or some other bird comes within twenty-four hours and brings the answer."

"Well, why not try that now?"

I stuttered, "But, but . . . How can tobacco tell me how much money to send in?"

"Trust the process," she answered.

I took some tobacco and went out to the yard and held it in my hand, praying for the Great Spirit to tell me exactly how much money to send to help the Joseph Campbell Foundation. Feeling awkward and silly, I was about to place the tobacco at the base of a tree, when a strange thing happened. A blue jay–like bird flitted up and perched in the low branch of the tree I had been praying in front of. It was two feet in front of me, and we were eyeball to eyeball. He looked at me with the most piercing gaze I have ever seen in a bird, and it said, very clearly, "Sixty! Sixty! Sixty!"

My mouth dropped ten feet. I held tight onto my tobacco. I responded, "You want me to send sixty dollars to the Joseph Campbell Foundation?" The bird cocked his head for just a second, then peered at me again and, with some urgency, repeated himself, nodding slightly, "Sixty! Sixty! Sixty!"

I was speechless. The bird popped into the sky and disappeared. I stumbled back inside to call Jean and tell her what had just happened. She was excited at the news, almost twittering with delight. She said, "That's just how Joe would have wanted it. A bird told you the answer. How perfect! He would have loved that story. Send in sixty and you will be a founding member of the foundation!" I did so. As it turns out, that was how much I had in my wallet. Sixty. That was back in 1992; it was probably the first twitter message ever received during the cell-phone era.

Twitter Messages

Everyone can relate to the experience of hearing a bird going into its patter and making what sounds like words in their own language. While I hear messages in English when birds twitter, the Ojibway may hear birdcalls in the Anishinabi language. For example, the robin is called *o-pe-che,* so when it says this, it is stating its name, to the Creator in prayer and to us as well. When o-pe-che chirps its long call, the Ojibway hear *n'doan-watch-e-go! n'doan-watch-e-go!* which means "A stranger is coming! A stranger is coming!" When no one comes, he hides in the rushes and curses *"Che! Che! Che!"*[29]

When I need to sprinkle a little bit of humor in my talks about birds, I talk about twitter messages. A lot of people talk about twitter messages these days, but for me, it means something a little different. I like to keep life simple; I don't use a lot of text messaging, but there is one kind of twitter message I do read, those I receive from the birds.

In general Native American belief, birds bring signs and messages in dozens of ways, and this is in answer to our prayers. Are they speaking our language at these times? Is it a miracle? These are the wrong questions to ask. What is important in the mysticism that surrounds the shaman's relationship with birds is the impact on the human. The traditional person is always saying, "If this were a dream, what would it be teaching me?"

This summer I was greeted each sunny morning by a wide variety of songbirds, each with their own distinct message. One, a Carolina wren, had the mysterious message, "Twenty . . . twenty . . . twenty . . . twenty-two?"

Another, probably an ovenbird, called for me, beseechingly, "Teacher? Teacher? Teacher?" Yet another took a look at that beautiful sunrise and said, "Swwwwweeet! Swwweeet!" Of course there was one house sparrow that didn't like my country décor and said, "Cheap! Cheap!" All were entitled to their own opinions!

Twitter messages have been recognized for a long time. According to American folk interpretations, the male Carolina wren, always thirsty for some good herb tea, says, "Teakettle!" (Carolina Wrens say a lot of funny things, but the teakettle seems to be a mating call). The white-breasted nuthatch, a truly American bird rarely seen outside the United States, says, "Yank, yank!" (See color insert, plate 7.) The tufted titmouse, perhaps looking for Peter Cottontail around Easter says, "Peter, Peter, Peter!" The willow flycatcher, a bird after my own heart, says, "Pizza!" The downy woodpecker, who seldom stands still, invites us to look quickly, saying "Peek!" The flirtatious black-capped chickadee says, "Hi, sweetie!" while the Carolina chickadee says its own name, as does the jay, the whipoorwill, the killdeer, the sora, the bobwhite, and the eastern phoebe. The eastern wood-pewee is less sure about its name, it says, *Pee-wee-uhr!* The eastern towhee says, *TYO-hee-hee-hee-hee!*

There is a bird called Chuck-will's-widow (*Caprimulgus carolinensis*) down in Georgia, because it says that phrase. But who is Chuck Will? And does his unfortunate wife know he's dead?* The Latin name of this bird is derived from an old folk belief that this class of birds drank milk from goats' udders, causing the milk to dry up. The Chuck-will's-widow apparently has a habit of clinging to vinyl siding.[30]

The barred owl lives east of the Mississippi, but also lives year-round in eastern Texas, Louisiana, and the states to the north of those (see color insert, plate 8). The cantankerous barred owl's call has been translated as "Who cooks for you? Who cooks for *yaaall?*" He then can go into what has been described as "maniacal laughter," which sounds like *wuh-uh-uh, uh-ow*. The killdeer knows Morse code, and sometimes it clearly sings the letter B: *deeee-dit-dit-dit*. Perhaps it is secretly trying to tell us to "just be" ourselves, or maybe it is a clue to the location of the murdered deer its name refers to. Speaking of Morse code, Navy radiomen/telegraph operators during World War II tapped out CQ, the call of a prominent eastern bird, a code meaning, "Is anybody listening?" When radiomen hear this lonely bird calling in the wilderness, they want to call out, "I am! I am!" The eastern bluebird says "few" and "fewer," as if lamenting the fate of his species in recent years. The white-throated sparrow says, "Hee sweet O Canada Canada Canada Canada!" One eastern meadowlark's song has been interpreted as "The spring of . . . the year!" The house finch looks out over the fields from the safety of the eaves and says, "Wheat! Wheat!"

John Burroughs associated the beautiful song of the hermit thrush with a mystical experience. The veery, whose summer habitat focuses on Maine, seems to say, "Now! Now! Ayup! Ayup!" The catbird can meow like a cat, while the northern mockingbird can reference the great-crested flycatcher, the bluebird, the cardinal, and the pewee in one song. The tiny blue-winged warbler, which summers in New York state, says, "See?" and then gives us the most delicate of "raspberries," as if trying to

---

*In fact, there is an author and historian, Chuck Wills, who writes about everyone from Lincoln to Jerry Garcia, but he is very much alive.

prove us wrong. The yellow warbler says, "Chip chip chip chip *tchetcher tchawit!*" but at dawn can sound more like an electric typewriter, typing out his morning prayers to the Creator. The black-and-white warbler sounds to me like it is saying "Itchy itchy itchy!," hissing in and out like a baby's squeeze toy. The scarlet tanager says, "Chip-*per!*" Then whistles like a sailor calling a buddy over, one presumably named Chipper.* The field sparrow says "Here, here, here, here!" Then its call comes faster and faster like the sound of a Ping-Pong ball when you try to stop it from bouncing with your paddle.

I grew up in Maryland, home of the golden-chested Baltimore oriole, its sunny state bird. In one recording, it is as if the poetic yet acquisitive oriole is singing, "What treasures you adhere to, here here here, heap!" The last part of this intricate melody is sung in an ascending sequence of upper appoggiaturas, like a soloist in the Maryland Opera Company. Orioles have dozens of songs, apparently, but this one seems almost Buddha-like in nature.

Sitting Bull of the Hunkpapa was a tough-skinned elder, but his relationship with birds was remarkably tender and loving, and he communicated with them intimately. He was especially fond of the western meadowlark and would berate those warriors foolish enough to make fun of his attachment to them. Robert Utley writes, "Two Bulls recalled an incident when Sitting Bull interrupted a feast to succor a wounded meadowlark. When chided by others, he lectured them sternly on the meadowlarks' special friendship for the Sioux and the sage counsel the little birds offered those wise enough to listen. 'Let us teach our boys to be kind to all the birds,' he concluded, 'especially to our meadowlark friends that speak to us in our language.'"[31]

Sitting Bull was a singer/songwriter within his culture and highly regarded by his people. Many of his songs were about birds and animals. One of his songs was a celebration of the bobolink, which he wrote while watching one with his nephew One Bull. According to

---

*Some of these descriptions are from personal encounters; some are based on live recordings included in Donald Kroodsma's *The Backyard Birdsong Guide.*

one source, "He would imitate the songs of the birds. He was said to understand what the meadow-larks say."[32]

One of Sitting Bull's songs recalls sleeping beneath a tree, dreaming that a bird of great beauty was watching over him from the hollow tree trunk. In his dream, the noise of a great bear crashing through the bushes nearby reaches his ears. The bird knocks on the trunk and advises Sitting Bull to lie very still as if dead. Although the young man is filled with fear, he does what the bird says to do. The dream bear walks right by him without taking notice and disappears.

In the song, the singer awakens and looks up to see a golden-winged woodpecker pecking loudly on the tree and looking straight at him. He extends his hand to the bird and sings to him, "Pretty bird you have seen me and took pity on me / amongst the tribes to live, you wish for me / Ye bird tribes from henceforth, always my relation shall be." This song seemed to be based on a true story, perhaps the moment that Sitting Bull began treating birds as his intimate friends.[33]

According to One Bull, his uncle, Sitting Bull, composed a thunderbird song in order to bring an end to a long drought. Sitting in solitude on a high hill throughout the night, he sang about thunderbirds flying across the night sky announcing: "Against the wind I am coming / Peace pipe I am seeking / Rain I am bringing as I am coming."[34]

Sitting Bull belonged to a fraternity made up of those who had dreamed of thunderbirds, the Heyoka (literally, coyote). Once a man dreamed of the thunderbird, he had to undertake a Heyoka ritual one time. Robert Higheagle writes: "Sitting Bull must have had a dream of the thunder bird because he painted his face with lightning. Only those who dreamed of Thunderbirds . . . painted their faces with lightning. . . . Sitting Bull must have performed the ceremony of the thunder bird one time."[35] Utley states:

> Wakantanka [grandfather in Lakota] conferred no greater honor than a thunder-bird dream nor no more fearsome obligation. Failure to perform the Heyoka ceremony attracted lightning strikes that

could kill. The thunder-bird dreamer had to abase himself publicly through dress and behavior, inviting ridicule by acting the fool and conducting himself in ways the opposite of normal. Heyoka might dress for cold in summer and heat in winter, walk or ride backward, cry amid humor or laugh amid sadness. A regular feature of the ceremony, against the backdrop of special dances and songs, was to thrust hands and arms in a kettle of boiling soup and retrieve choice pieces of meat. A man performed the Heyoka ceremony but once, after he had dreamed of the thunderbird, but he participated in all subsequent ceremonies of others.[36]

Bird Dreams

Mystics around the world honor the messages in their dreams, and according to Jungian therapist Stephen Larsen and others, a large number of dreams involve birds, most notably hawks. This is nowhere more important than in Native American culture, where the belief continues to this day. The Mi'kmaq say, "Dreams are powerful, but they can make a fool of you if you're not careful." And yet, as mentioned, eagles and hawks are the most reliable dream messengers.

Jean de Brébeuf, a canonized Jesuit missionary, said to have written the first Huron dictionary for Europeans,* wrote in the 1630s of the Huron that (as summarized by W. Vernon Kinietz)

the faith in dreams surpasses all belief, that the Huron looked upon them as ordinances and irrevocable decree, the execution of which it was a crime to delay. Dreams were their oracles, prophets, physicians, and absolute masters and often presided in their councils. The same writer continued his account of dreams by saying that in theory all dreams were not held in great credit. Regard was had to the

---

*Brébeuf "spoke their language" and was so popular among the Huron that his charismatic presence helped to create a rift between "traditional" and "missionized" Huron. Bruce Trigger of the Smithsonian has commented that this split, along with smallpox, left them vulnerable to attack from the Haudenosaunee.

dreamer, poor persons' dreams availing little. In order to have his dreams obeyed, the dreamer must be a person in fairly good circumstances and one whose dreams had been several times found true.[37]

Assuming Brébeuf was correct, this same criteria would not necessarily hold among the dreamers of the False Face Society of the Haudenosaunee, or the Midewiwin Lodge of the Algonkin-ode. In these lodges, dreams certainly hold a high place as a source of revealed truths, but not all dreamers are equal. Over decades, some people's dreams prove to be more reliable than others, and these men rise to higher rank than others, regardless of their wealth. No one wants to be fooled by a dream! In other words, *Caveat morpheus!* Dreamer beware!

Kinietz writes, in summarizing Paul Ragueneau's 1636 "Relation" (*Jesuit Relations: Journal of the Jesuits*) or report on his experiences at the Huron mission: "Shamans received their power through an oki or powerful genie who entered their bodies or appeared to them in their dreams or immediately on their awakening and showed them their power. Some claimed the genie appeared to them in the form of an eagle, a raven, or any one of numerous other shapes."[38] Although the Arabic word *genie* hardly fits, there is no English word for these *oki*, a Huron word, or *manitouak*, the Algonquin word.* Brébeuf said, perhaps overstating the case, that a Huron became a medicine man through power received from their familiar spirit or oki in a dream. Elsewhere, he states that in the old times, a Huron would have to fast for thirty days to receive the appropriate dream to attain this high office, but that by the 1630s, the authority of his post had become diluted, possibly by missionaries, and so it was becoming more rare for someone to fast thirty days for such a dream. Perhaps this was the beginning of the trend that ultimately led to the "weekend shaman certification" programs of our current time.

Among the Ottawa, a war chief, such as the famous Pontiac,

---

*The word *manitou* (or the plural, *manitouak*) is analogous to "a spirit." When capitalized, *Manitou* can be considered short for Kitchi Manitou and refers to the Great Spirit.

relied on dreams as well, and of his *manitou,* which were often birds. According to Antoine de la Mothe Cadillac's *Relation with the Indians,* an undated manuscript archived in Newberry Library, Chicago, and quoted in Kinietz's *Indians of the Western Great Lakes,* "A war chief abstains from eating and drinking and fasts sometimes for a week . . . ponders his dreams night and day, praying to the spirit he has chosen as his guardian or patron to give him men. This spirit, in which he trusts, is sometimes a raven, an eagle . . . it is always the one which has appeared to him in his dreams and visions."[39]

Many readers will remember the dreams I had while fasting in New Brunswick, Canada, at the Eel Ground Reservation with Grandfather Turtle in 1989, which I described in my book *No Word for Time.* During that same time, my sister Lynn was in Maryland, going through a very difficult time of her life, and she began to dream of eagles frequently over a period of months. The eagles would appear in different stages of life and spiritual abilities. Sometimes the eagles were juvenile and led her to children, sometimes they were very old, and one appeared in the brilliance of the sun's corona, as if part of the blinding white light. The dreams concluded with one vision that would have an impact on her for years to come.

She looked out upon a stark, white landscape of snow as far as the eye could see. Outside her window, she saw bare branches coming up through the snow, a small bush of twigs that appeared to be dead. While she watched, the twigs began to grow and sprout leaflets and golden flowers budded and unfolded in the winter scene. At that moment, an eagle flew across her view, low to the ground, and suddenly out of nowhere a large truck came barreling by, and the eagle flew directly in front of it and was killed while she watched. She woke up disturbed and upset, never understanding why a magnificent creature with sharp eyesight would allow such a thing. She asked a spiritual advisor, who said she should go back and ask the bird himself. She did, and the bird said, "If I didn't do that, I couldn't have gotten your attention." But why was her attention needed? It took years to unravel the puzzle.

Twelve years later, she was visiting New Brunswick and traveling in Nova Scotia, when she met a chief, very likely a relative (whom we will call James), who had a similar experience at that time. He began to tell her of a time when he could not eat or go to work, and during that time, he had vision after vision of eagles, young eagles and old eagles and eagles in the sun. James said that the dreams were so intense, he could not eat for two weeks. During this time, neighbors noticed that birds and other animals, including eagles, were constantly surrounding his property and his house. This led him to reconnect with his ancestors. The chief said his Grandfather taught him things during that time, so that he could see through his eyes.

The eagle in the dream was her ancestor trying to get her attention to guide her to move to Canada. She had always had a compunction to spend time in the woods, connecting with the plants and animals, and she had come back to Canada to learn more about spiritual and natural medicine from gifted elders, another important step in her transition, as she would have to live by her wits off the land while building her house. More eagles appeared.

About this time, she went to the famous three-thousand-year-old Red Bank burial mound, to pray. As she was praying, she noticed a bald eagle feather perched up against a nearby tree, and then saw two golden eagles circling by the burial mound. The connection between eagles and ancestors was now clear in her mind. Perhaps the dream eagle was showing her he was among those who had already died. She felt that he was showing her that through small deaths, we emerge into strong and wise creatures ourselves. To give up all that one knows, to follow one's spirit, to respond to invisible nudges from the Creator's messengers toward an unknown future, this was the life the dream eagle wanted her to live. This was her lesson. Her faith in those messages through hard times led to incredible changes later on. In addition, the mound, the museum, and the people associated with it were to play a critical role in her relocation to Canada. Twelve years later, the pieces of the puzzle were, indeed, finally fitting together.

Lynn had gone to New Brunswick to retire and study the traditions, but there was another surprise. Unexpected circumstances forced her to apply for a job. Her résumé was rejected by the people she was applying to, but the paperwork fell by accident into the hands of someone looking desperately for a person who was cool in a crisis to work with at-risk schoolchildren, including Mi'kmaq children across the region. A brief interview revealed her extensive experience in crisis management involving young people and, separately, her extensive experience with Mi'kmaq traditional life. To make a long story short, she now works as a guidance counselor with children of different cultures, including Mi'kmaq children in several reservation schools, and the need has never been greater. The knowledge about birds and Native tradition she has learned from Grandfather Turtle and others, plus the connection with the ancestors, comes in handy in her work every day.

The Mi'kmaq children are of the greatest concern to the elders and ancestors. It is they who must carry on the ancient traditions of the people, not scholars or writers or reporters. Without them, these spiritual traditions and many others will perish. Lynn's lifelong interest in raptors and in her Mi'kmaq heritage and her remarkable rapport with little children have all come together to play an important role behind the scenes in helping tomorrow's elders get through a dangerous and difficult time in their lives. As they make the transition to social acceptance, many of them choose to leave their Native American tradition behind in order to feel like they are "making it" in the burger-and-fries world of fast cars and easy money. In fact, these Bird Medicine teachings, and other traditions, open the doors to inner guidance from the Great Mystery that people of all ages and walks of life can benefit from. They can even help young Native people succeed in the white world! It was a long journey of many miles, but it all started by paying attention to a bird sign in a dream. "Follow the Spirit, and you never know where you will end up!" is a Mi'kmaq saying.[40]

BIRD WARNINGS

Magpie Burglar Alarm

I asked Magpie, the husband-wife folk duo originally from Takoma Park, Maryland, if they had any stories about magpies and their famed messages, and I was not disappointed. But I was not prepared for what I was to hear. Greg Artzner and Terry Leonino related a story, which I published in 1992 in *Resonance Magazine*.

In September of 1990, the pair went to England on a concert tour. They stopped at Avebury, and pulling their rental car into the parking lot, they spotted an Asian woman feeding a magpie, who was getting closer to the bird than Greg or Terry had ever seen a wild magpie allow. They grabbed the camera and jumped out of the car. When the Asian saw how interested the two Americans were, she gave the bread to Terry and followed a friend of hers into the village of Avebury.

Terry began feeding the magpie, and it came even closer to her. At one point it perched on a guardrail, and jumped toward Terry to retrieve the bread she had thrown. She was startled and passed the bread to Greg, taking the camera to record on film the encounter, as the bird came even closer to Greg. It hopped on top of a car, and Greg went around to the back of the car to entice it further. The bird hopped down on the back trunk and took the bread, but instead of eating it, the magpie stuffed it under the flap covering the zipper of his hip pack. The zipper was open, and the magpie jammed the bread into the pack. Greg took out the bread and handed it back to the bird, thinking maybe the intelligent creature didn't understand it was a gift.

The British bird had not made his point quite clear enough. He finally ate the bread, then hopped over to Greg and began to peck furiously at the zipper, where he had previously stuffed the piece of bread.

Since he had already given away the last piece of bread, Greg began to walk away. The bird hopped down off the car and over to Greg. The magpie picked a small pebble off the ground and carefully tucked it under the lacing flap of Greg's Converse All Stars. He proceeded to perch himself on Greg's foot and wouldn't leave, at least for an embarrassing minute or so, and then hopped off and walked away. Greg and Terry, the human magpies, said good-bye to their feathered counterpart and made their way to the entrance of the stone circle monument.

He was trying to say something about the car, but neither Terry nor Greg could figure out what. Greg checked the unzipped pocket of his hip pack, remembered it was where he usually placed the rental car keys, and discovered that the car keys were not there. He then checked all his pockets; finding them devoid of keys, he next checked the car door. There he found the keys hanging from the door lock, for anyone to take.

They took the keys and walked toward the stone circle, a place of enchantment from long ago, from a time when wizards took the form of birds and sent messages through animal and bird spirits. Soon they came across a sign that said, "Your car is at risk for theft. Be sure to lock your car and take your valuables." Underneath the warning was a picture of a magpie with a string of pearls in his beak. The implication was that magpies are thieves. Perhaps it takes one to know one, but the little magpie had saved them from losing their valuable instruments, which were piled up in the car.[41] Magpie has recorded a medieval song about the magpie and fascinating lore about other English birds called "The Magpie" on their outstanding CD *Living Planet.*

Rockin' Robin

Robins can be warning birds, too. On June 23, 2010, Monique Renaud, an officer of the Alliance Metis de Quebec, was conducting a healing session with a client in Gatineau, when they both heard a most unusual robin song, one that went on and on. Though quite tuneful, it was so unusual that they both ran to the window to see what was wrong. There they found a lone red breast sitting on a clothesline tree near the house, one that Monique had never seen a bird sit on before, as it was so close to the building. The singer was looking at them and at the house in general and was belting out a loud, high-pitched melody that seemed endless in variation, as if there was a long message in it. The man exclaimed, "It's saying there will be rain! That's a rain song!"

Monique thought, "If *that's* a rain song, there's going to be quite a deluge," and yet when she looked up to the sky for thunderheads, she noticed that the sky was completely clear and sunny. This didn't make sense. Monique said, "I'm going to remember that song. It must be some kind of warning!"

The tiny little thunderbird lifted up its wings and fled, leaving the two puzzled humans in a state of alarm. Immediately, the earth began to shake violently, and the floor heaved up and down in the house where they were standing. The walls rolled in and out, and shelves tossed objects onto the floor, as framed paintings rocked from side to side. The earth made a sound like a hundred jackhammers with the volume turned up high, and it seemed to go on forever without stopping. That drum roll officially lasted only seventeen seconds, but in fact it seemed to Monique and her friend to go on for ten minutes, as they ran for the door frame and held their breath. When the mayhem finally stopped, Monique quipped, "I'm going to pay more attention to bird signs from now on!"[42]

That earthquake was first estimated at 6.0 on the Richter scale, but later lowered to 5.0. Nonetheless, it was felt as far away as Chicago, Boston, and even New York. The bird was successful in getting them to come to the window but not to leave the building. The robin modeled the appropriate action by fleeing the scene, but sometimes interspecies communication isn't easy and things get lost in translation.

Storm Warnings

The late Oannes Pritzker, a descendant of the Wolf Clan of the Wabanaki, was director of the Yat Kitischsee Nature Center in Naples, Florida, host of the Wolf Mountain Radio Show, (still streaming online), and was formerly an employee of the National Park Service. He once told me: "Hawks and eagles and other birds are our meteorologists. They give us indicators of weather changes. A well-trained hunter, trapper, or fisher can look at their behavior and know if a storm is coming. Birds know and indicate an approaching storm well before most mammals, such as chipmunks and squirrels. This is a primary reason why Natives cultivate a relationship with birds; it can be life or death in the bush."[43] This is related to how Natives look to birds for other kinds of signs as well. Oannes added: "Eagles and hawks send our prayers to the sky world. They also teach us by example how to get along with each other. They also are part of our prophecies."

In the Bird Medicine of the Kickapoo of Mexico, an Algonquian-speaking nation closely related to the Misquakee, birds foretell changes in the weather. "The arrival of geese announces cold weather; when the cranes fly over the river, it is a sign of rain; the arrival of starlings and swallows announces the approach of warm weather; the cry of the whippoorwill foretells the death of a member of the group . . . when an owl hoots it tells them a witch is nearby."[44]

BIRDS AS ROLE MODELS

Role Models for Responsible Parenting

When asked what his favorite bird story was, White Deer of Autumn answered, "Grandmother Sarah Smith of the Mohawk tells a story about the role of birds in our lives." The following is as it was told to me by White Deer of Autumn.

> A young girl had tried to commit suicide, but failed. Her Mohawk grandmother came for her and took her to the woods. On the way, the grandmother asked the girl why she tried to throw away the great gift of life. The girl said, "I have no role models. My father left us, and my mother is an alcoholic." The grandmother brought her to a tree and showed her some cardinals building a nest. "See how they care for their young, and teach them. They teach us as well. Our role models are not just humans, we learned how to live from the birds and other creatures. Without them, we forget how to live."[45]

Male cardinals help build the nest and give it an effort equal to the female's. To the Cherokee people, cardinals are also associated with prophecy.[46] They teach us self-respect. Many other birds are good role models as well. Baby ducks have to be taught by parents how to swallow; it also seems that they don't recognize the difference at first between edible food and other inedible objects—mother and father have to teach them.[47] Birds will often fake a broken wing to lure predators away from their babies.[48] Woodpecker parents act as a team; one will go searching for ants while the other babysits. After the young have grown up and left the nest, the two both go together to search for their food.[49] When baby woodpeckers reach the age of four weeks, they start to learn limited flight and follow behind their parents on hunting trips. If the brood is large, each parent will take some of the offspring on individual training maneuvers. If the brood is small, both parents teach them together. It takes several months for the parents to teach the young to search for bugs in the interior of dead trees and stumps, and in the heart of old logs. Then in the fall, the young go out on their own. By this time the good role model parents have also taught the young the art of self-defense, showing them how to outwit hawks and other predators. One technique woodpeckers use is to scurry frantically back and forth like a squirrel, to fake out the hawk, perhaps to make the nasty raptor think they are too crazy to be worth all the trouble. It works for squirrels! Perhaps a wily cardinal learned it from the squirrel a long time ago and taught it to their young who have passed it down to our day. Like squirrels, woodpeckers gather acorns and hide them in trees. Woodpeckers may cache as many as fifty thousand acorns in a single tree.[50]

Role Models for Choosing and Creating a New Family

For many Americans, and birds, the old-fashioned nuclear family model does not apply but principles of mutual sharing and support still do. The cowbird is a North American bird that Native Americans have been familiar with for millennia and is a great role model for families of choice. The cowbird lays its eggs in the nests of other species, leaving birds of other species to raise the young cowbirds. Of course, the problem with this system is that the adopted (or some would say hoodwinked!) parents can't teach the cowbirds how to be cowbirds, or even how to sing mating calls. What happens is fascinating, and somewhat modernistic, by sociological standards. As young fledgling cowbirds leave the nest, they gather elsewhere in flocks (gangs and intentional communities) to explore the world. Like *American Idol* contestants, they learn to improve their singing by responding to feedback from nonsingers. According to Gisela Kaplan, "The female performs a display of 'wing stroking' when she is attracted by the song of a young male. This apparently reinforces the male because he is more likely to sing the same song again if the female has performed this display. Therefore, in time, the songs of the males become matched to the preferences of the females. The females train the males to sing the correct song even though they do not sing themselves. If the males are put into a flock with females of a different group of cowbirds, they learn, also in response to wing stroking by females, to sing the song of that group instead of their own."[51] I meet an increasing number of young people who feel, sadly, that they have nothing in common with their biological parents and, after leaving home, form "families of choice" selected from their larger peer group, which they treat as actual blood relatives. Like cowbirds, these young people train each other how to survive in the real world and give nonsupportive signals when someone in the group starts to act harmfully, steering them nonjudgmentally toward a more productive route.

Male crows sometimes encounter a similar problem of having to leave home and find a new family. When there is an overabundance of them in a small area, some of the males travel to unknown regions to better their chances of finding a mate. When they come to a new set of crows, the chances are that the new group is singing different songs from what the folks at home used to sing. They have to adapt and learn the new songs in order to attract a mate and do so with relative ease.

In a 2011 article published in *Zoo Biology*, a group of researchers presented their findings concerning how vocal cues affect the mating habits of some birds:

> The goal of this study was to increase reproductive behaviors in a captive colony of Northern Bald Ibis (*Geronticus eremtra*) at the Bronx Zoo. The Northern Bald Ibis is classified as critically endangered by the IUCN, with only about 100 known breeding pairs in the wild. Our analysis of zoo breeding and colony size data confirmed earlier observations that small captive colonies of this species do not breed as well as larger colonies, possibly because of

insufficient social clues. Using principles from social facilitation theory, we attempted to provide such social cues by presenting acoustic enrichment in the form of conspecific breeding vocalization playbacks.[52]

According to the article, these ibis had been reproducing until 2007 but stopped mating behavior. The first attempts at "acoustic enrichment" in 2009 increased mating behavior but did not produce eggs for reasons that were not clear at that time. However, higher quality recordings acquired from Austrian sources produced a dramatic result when used in 2010: mating behavior increased, and five pairs produced thirteen eggs. Six chicks fledged successfully.

Message from a Robin

My understanding is that robins are "relationship" birds. (See color insert, plate 24.) Their messages are about courtship, home, family, and the loving heart. I never saw a robin do anything mean to another bird or a mammal. They are not high fliers, but stick close to the ground, close to where humans tend to live, making them highly susceptible to cats, insecticides, and radiation from cell towers. Natives never hunted them for meat.

Brenda, a Lenape woman living in Rochester, tells this story: "I was in a relationship that needed to end. I was resistant because I loved the person very much and knew the suffering that would ensue as a result of my decision. It was spring. This robin kept trying to get into my house. It battered the sliding door repeatedly. I remember talking to it, trying to explain that it did not belong inside my house, that its life was elsewhere. Eventually, it ceased and I believe found an appropriate mate, for a pair of robins started building very near my deck. . . . But I still wouldn't listen and kept on with the troubled relationship. At the end of the summer, I discovered that a bird had tried to establish a home within the mesh around the arbor vitae. Most birds knew not to build there. This bird's mistake led to its death. . . . It was not to build there.

"My mistake with this person would have led to my spiritual and psychological death. I ended the relationship and dealt with the suffering. . . . In my dream world after ending the relationship, the ancestors and my psyche were furious with me and admonished me repeatedly for such a dangerous mistake. . . . I try to listen more closely to animal messengers now and utilize them during meditation time."[53]

Do You Take This Duck?
The Mandarin and the Art of Dating

Ducks and eagles seem to be role models for many Native American mating rituals. It is interesting to compare duck behavior (as observed by white scientists) with Native American mating rituals (as observed by white colonists). Male mallards are expected to instigate mating with the female, and sometimes the pressure to make the right moves causes tension in both male and female. (See color insert, plate 26.) To reduce the tension, the male will turn his head completely away from the female and preen his specialized colorful feathers on his back to make them stand out more, feathers associated with mating. This both increases his attractiveness and his confidence and also reduces tension in the female, as it gives her more time to "think" and perhaps excuse herself. The mandarin duck has a preening display that ornithologists, among them Gisela Kaplan, describe as ritualistic, involving raising his crest as well.[54] These are courtship displays that are similar to those young men learn from older men and use when the tension of approaching a female gets too high.*

---

*Preening is a cornerstone of bird self-maintenance. The bird ruffs its feathers, squeezes preening oil from the base of its tail, rubs the oil on its feathers with its bill, and then uses the bill to correctly align the substructures of the feather (something like the way a zipper works) to make sure they are interlocking. The oil keeps the feathers from drying out and also prevents mites, lice, and fungus from eating away at the feathers. There is a possibility that the radiation from cell towers dries up the preening oil in birds, based on the change in the feathers of exposed birds, but no studies have been done. Nothing in this section is meant to suggest that preening has only psychological or ritual uses. Kaplan is merely suggesting that there are additional dimensions to the everyday grooming process. (See Kaplan and Rogers, *Songs, Roars, and Rituals,* 19–20.)

I have been told that, at least in some Algonkin-ode nations, the male always initiates courtship, except in the case of an arranged marriage. This is done in an indirect and noninvasive way that allows the female to reject him on that level of intimacy without rejecting him on other levels as a member of the community. Much of the initiation and the response is therefore ritualized and nonverbal. Swanton says, of the Creek custom, "An offer of marriage seems to have emanated sometimes from the youth [he means male] sometimes from the people of the youth's clan, and sometimes from the people of the girl's clan."[55]

In some Native American societies, there are taboos against looking directly at a stranger, while in others it is expected. In yet others, there is an appropriate time for both. The wood ducks are interesting because they don't like too much eye contact with strange ducks. If two wood duck boxes or birdhouses are placed across from each other with the entry holes facing each other, neither box will ever have a chance to welcome an occupant. A wood duck would rather be homeless than risk being stared at by another wood duck while in the privacy of his own home. This is even true at great distances; a pair of wood duck boxes across a lake or pond must still not face each other. If they do, no wood duck will go near them.[56]

Once the first signal receives an encoded green light (as I mentioned in No Word for Time), the next courtship signal goes out, a little more bold and assertive. He may play the lonesome flute near where she is standing, an indirect invitation to "take it to the next level."[57] This is clearly parallel to the universally recognized mating calls performed by male birds as opposed to "vocalizations," which are more individualized, like conversation, and are enjoyed by both genders. Just as the birds teach this mating call to their young male offspring, the successful lonesome song that leads to marriage is used as a lullaby for the children, and then taught to them, which they would be free to use in their own courtship.

The male duck may, at any point in the approach, look away from the female to preen his feathers. He may circle the female duck to introduce himself to her and let her get a good look. The human male circles around the female at a respectful distance, both at the powwow and later verbally, in conversation, and then gradually comes closer until they are face-to-face. It has been compared to hunting a moose. If he senses the tension is too high, he may turn his head away, not look at her, but preen for a while, perhaps grooming or combing his cockscomb hair, or retying his braid, polishing a badge, or doing something totally irrelevant to put her at ease. I have also heard an eyewitness account of a much more aggressive approach to wood duck courtship, the male in hot pursuit of the female. According to Swanton, the Choctaw incorporated this approach into the marriage ritual as well. He writes, "Just before the marriage ritual, the girl was pursued and caught in a ceremonial race by her intended, each assisted by the respective relatives, and this gave the woman an opportunity to change her mind if she so desired. Usually, however, she allowed herself to be caught after an exhibition of formal reluctance, and was seated on the ground with her intended groom near at hand."[58]

Whether between ducks on a pond or Native American humans at a powwow, this pursuit, either seductively circular or passionately linear, may lead to a phase of courtship where either the male dances for the female, or they dance together. The male duck is known to dance for the female a short distance away. At a powwow, a male may engage in a fancy dance and may attempt to win a prize to impress the female intended, who in fact is the actual prize he is pursuing. More likely, however, both may engage in a rabbit dance, which they perform hand in hand, but with arms crossed, moving clockwise and counterclockwise in harmony with the entire circle or community.

Mating dances among male birds are legendary, some approaching in artistry the oeuvre of Michael Jackson. One plain-looking species of bird of paradise of New Guinea creates a large blue mask by inverting his feathers, and then dances side to side to impress the female. Some birds spread their wings and throw their heads back and forth, while hopping and doing steps. A number of fancy dances now popular in the powwow circuit are surprisingly similar to actual bird courtship dances. When these birds strut their stuff, it is often rather fancy. Competition dancers who want to win the big money would do well to observe bird-mating behavior.

If successful, both the duck and the human may move on to feeding rituals. In a classic avian gesture, he may feed her, placing food in her mouth. According to scientist Gisela Kaplan, when birds do this, it is called "displacement ritual," because the goal of the moment is not to feed the female, who may not be hungry, but to mate with her. The feeding is displacement as it serves to distract her from his ultimate intentions, but it is also a signal, because it helps them bond together in a sharing ritual that also shows how he will take care of her when she is on nesting duty.[59] This has become part of the wedding cake ritual at non-Native weddings, but it is certainly understood on lesser levels of commitment as a nonverbal gesture of interest in the female among Natives. It is also very "ducky." Like the eagle, human males may offer fish to the female of the species (perhaps at a surf-and-turf restaurant) or a variety of other foods. And might I mention that, for all its cover stories as a religious holiday, St. Valentine's Day is really the time of year when birds of opposite sexes pursue each other and mate. As Beryl Rowland wrote, "Birds give their wings to angels, and they sing like angels. Their harmony reflects the harmony of heaven itself. Especially on Valentine's Day do they sing 'with voys of aungel' in their harmony. Just as St. Valentine followed God's Command to procreate and multiply when he strove to increase the number of the faithful, so the birds implement God's decree by mating on the Saint's day."[60] Earlier this year, the week leading up to Valentine's Day, I saw a female eagle streak across the path of my car like a cannon ball at low range, pursued closely by a male eagle, who chased her down a long wooded path to my right. Later that day, I asked an old mixed-blood Nanticoke buddy, with a great interest in birds (and women), what that was all about, and he said, "Valentine's Day's acomin'. Eagles are in matin' mode all week. That male'll prob'ly wear down that female's r'sistance in about four days!"

Swanton quotes Strachey, who wrote that Powhatan men initiated courtship with the women "by presenting them with the fruits of their labours, as by fowle, fish, or wild beasts, which by their huntings, their bowes and arrows, by weeres, or otherwise, they obteyne, which they bring unto the young women, as also of such somer fruicts and berries which their travels abroad hath made them knowe readily where to gather, and those of the best kind in the season." John Smith further noted that the Powhatan chiefs draped a string of wampum over the joined hands of the couple to be married and perhaps even tied their hands symbolically together with it. Also according to Swanton, in the Creek confederacy, as elsewhere, ducks were eaten and their body parts used to make highly ornamental clothing. The Creeks made blankets out of mallard heads, while the Caddo would sprinkle duck down on the hair, sprinkled with red ochre.[61]

The bowerbird male actually builds a structure for the female as part of the courtship, one which will at no time serve as a nest, but she finds the gesture highly impressive, perhaps because it shows her that he would know how to build a nest at the moment one was needed, when eggs are on their way. Male ducks and other birds apparently also give gifts to attractive female ducks. Single Native American males (this is not exclusive) often engage themselves in handicrafts, which they shower upon their beloved as part of the courtship ritual. I knew one Ramapough man who showered his beloved with the most amazing beadwork as a way of keeping her interested and wrote numerous songs praising her great qualities, but there was a great age difference between them, and he died of old age before the marriage, however ill advised, could take place. A Native man may take his bride-to-be camping, creating a bower of sorts in the wilderness for her, to show off his great skill at building shelters and his survival know-how, a big turn-on for many close-to-the-earth brides-to-be.

I have observed each of these courtship phases among Native American friends and associates from time to time. Native American courtship rituals vary according to each nation's traditions. But it does seem to have a lot to do with ducks!

Woodpeckers Are Good Builders

The red-headed woodpecker, one of the birds Native Americans look to for signs, is now listed as endangered in the state of Connecticut. Algonkin-ode people of New Brunswick, the Mi'kmaq say, "The great feather is called *uk-tchee-ghun,* this feather is from the chief of the birds, and is quite honorable to have. It is from a red bird, *gyewsoonedj.* It is around trees that are fallen."[62] Its Mi'kmaq name, *dyew-a-soon-idj,* seems to be shorthand for both "a little blanket of fire" and "a little blanket of blood," either *buch-dyew-a-soon-idj* or *maughl-dyew-a-soon-idj,* respectively. It is poetically ambiguous, as both are accurate descriptions of the red mark on the bird's head.[63] Note that woodpeckers are not killed for their feathers; the feathers are found and collected. (See color insert, plates 9 and 10.)

Woodpeckers are the home-builders union of the avian nation. The holes they peck out of trees each year may be used by four or five other species of birds over the course of a few summers. They are also known for debugging complex network systems, so techno nerd birds of the human variety take note.

Woodpeckers are also the rhythm section for the forest symphony each morning. Sometimes I wake up wondering who is playing the temple blocks in the bushes outside my window, some escapee from the Hudson Valley Philharmonic, no doubt. Before I get a chance to call HVP's conductor Randall Craig Fleischer to see if he is missing a percussionist, I see the woodpeckers gleefully dancing around on the tree limbs just beyond the short stone wall below the sash. Their funny little ballet always brings a smile to my face. Mystery solved. Woodpeckers are the role models for humans involved with drumming, home building, digging deep to find "bugs," and removing problems. They are energetic little fire birds that, like the mythic bird in the Stravinsky ballet, seem to be making a comeback. At the very least, the magnificent ivory-billed woodpecker resurrected itself in 2004 after being pronounced dead a generation earlier.

I have not been inclined to read books on Bird Medicine traditions, content to eagerly listen when elders talk. But there was one moment when reading a book on bird signs would have saved me a lot of trouble. Due to some dramatic circumstances, I had hastily put down the first month's rent on a house that I hadn't looked at too carefully. I was in the middle of writing a book under deadline, and time was scarce. I figured any house with room for a writing desk would do. Everything looked to be in good shape, and the scenery was book inspiring. It was a perfect spring day as I was inspecting the property and negotiating terms. As we stood outside on the lawn of my new digs, a large pileated woodpecker came and buried his head deep in a stump. He was rooting out grubs with a concerted effort and remarkable thoroughness. Not sure what it meant, I committed the scene to memory. My elders always said woodpeckers were good. It was not until one year later that I finally read parts of Ted Andrew's book *Animal-Speak* about woodpeckers and found what the message was. The woodpecker was a sign that I needed to pay attention to details and thoroughly inspect my new surroundings before committing to them.

Andrews wrote, "If a woodpecker has drummed out a song for you, then you should ask yourself some specific questions. Are you looking at aspects of your life rationally? Are others around you not discriminating in their activities? Are you? Are you or others in your life just jumping into situations with little or no analysis?"[64] I had to laugh when I read it. The answer to the last questions was yes! I missed the message and had to move out within six months. The charming place had no Certificate of Occupancy for a good reason. It was full of bugs—electrical, structural, and plumbing ones. So sometimes it pays to read a book. A small, downy woodpecker lives near my current dwelling, so I continue to look for details and "knock on wood" that nothing goes wrong with the house.

HEALING
(AND HUMOROUS) BIRDS

There are a number of vital traditions still practiced today among Native American healers that might be mistaken for faith healing. Many Natives have told me they studied the Japanese healing art called Reiki because "it's what we've all been doin' for years now anyway, eh?" Some Native healing methods involve energy transference without touching, like Reiki, while some involve a laying on of hands, like in Pentecostal churches, or even adjustments. Others involve healing through inner transference, or inner journeys.

These are passed on in secret, but birds seem to know all about them. There are many stories told about how birds have helped heal humans and in a variety of ways. Appearing in our dreams is a common method birds use to get our attention and heal us. But some birds use more hands-on methods.

Nuthatch Saves Injured Girl

The nuthatch is associated with faith in spirit and putting that into action. (See color insert, plate 18.) Apparently this bird is a faith healer as well. My sister Lynn, who has a special relationship with birds, spoke of a time when she had a pain below her left shoulder blade and was in need of attention. She was standing outside her door on a beautiful May Day morning (Beltaine, if you're Irish) and noticed a red-breasted nuthatch looking at her from a low branch. It said, "Beep beep!" She answered, "Good morning" in Mi'kmaq. Then she said, "You look exceptionally bright and handsome today!," and in fact, the bird seemed to have a bright light around it. Suddenly, the bird bolted forward and thumped her in that spot, making the pain disappear. Even though the nuthatch cannot fly backward like its friend the hummingbird, this one managed to bounce off, recover, and continue flying upward. The pain never came back. When she told Grandfather Turtle, he said, "That was one of your ancestors helping you!"

A Grouse with a Heart

An Anishinabi elder whose teachings I love to listen to is Eddy Stevenson. He has various climes he calls home, including an Anishinabi reserve in Canada. But one of the more remarkable bird encounters happened outside his home in Putnam County, not fifty miles from New York City, while he was doing chores. Eddy was sitting on a stone wall outside his house, and as his wife, Bobbie, was leaving in the family car, a grouse came up to Eddy and stood in front of him. The grouse stared Eddy in the eyes. Eddy greeted the grouse.

The bird jumped up onto the stone wall and walked over to Eddy. He jumped up and stood on Eddy's left shoulder. He stretched his neck out and stared into Eddy's left eye. Eddy just stared back. They were eyeball to eyeball. The bird was getting his attention, that was clear enough. Then the bird jumped down, walked to Eddy's other side, jumped onto his other shoulder, then stared into Eddy's right eye, again at a close distance. Eddy was still not getting the message, so the bird jumped up on top of Eddy's long silver head of hair and began kneading his head like dough, sort of like a feathered cat. He gave Eddy a scalp massage for a few painful minutes, then Eddy took the bird off his head and placed it on the ground. He looked at the bird and said, "I have work to do, so if you'll excuse me, I have to go."

Eddy's wife Bobbie had asked him to put some boxes high up on a shelf outside. Eddy already had the ladder ready and was eager to go to work. He walked over to the ladder, grasped the rails, and began to climb up, when the same grouse bit him on the leg. Eddy got back down and stooped a bit before the bird, explaining that there was a lot of work to do and he didn't have time for all this play. He walked around doing various things, but the grouse followed him everywhere he went, as if trying to get in his way and slow him down. Eddy went back to the ladder and started to climb again, but the grouse ran over and bit his other leg, really hard this time. Eddy thought it might be bleeding, so he sat down on the stone wall to take a look. He couldn't seem to get this bird to understand anything about being a human. The bird jumped on the wall and started poking Eddy hard in the chest, near his heart. Eddy shooed him away.

Eddy's wife came home and got out of the car, puzzled. Normally, Eddy would have had all the chores done long before. "Why aren't the chores done?" she asked.

"I had a visitor!" He explained to his wife everything that had happened, and she answered, "You need to ask your uncle Arthur. He knows all about animals and birds."

Eddy went to visit his Indian uncle up north, and the uncle heard the story and said, "You're sick!"

Could it have been that simple? Eddy went to the doctor, and the doctor stared in his left eye, then stared in his right eye, and then thumped his chest, and then told him he had a heart condition and that it could be serious. The doctor said Eddy would have to "slow down, take off work for a while, and for God's sake, don't climb any ladders!"

That was the second opinion. Eddy went back to the grouse and explained all about the heart condition and the doctor visit and thanked the bird for his help. The grouse flew up in the air and disappeared and was never seen again. In fact, it was the only grouse anyone had ever seen in that part of town. In the Native world, birds are some of the best healers. They don't charge much, and they make house calls.[65]

The Grouse That Saved Me

Suburban dwellers often take the grouse for granted, but many Plains Indians dance the spiraling grouse dance to honor the grouse, a sacred animal.[66] These dances are accompanied by drumming, in part to honor the "drumming" sound the grouse makes with its wings in the spring during its mating season. The drum is a musical instrument associated with shamanic healing, and the grouse is an expert healer. The sound of the drum is also a bridge to the spirit world.

There are many grouse stories. This is mine. It is a "change of plans" story more than a healing story. I was driving very fast along a winding mountain road, too fast, in fact, but I needed to get to a sound studio for a live radio broadcast at eight in the morning and was running terribly late. I was imagining all the horrible things the host would say about me on the air if I wasn't there on time. In the passenger seat was a very special woman who was also going to be interviewed on the air, a woman who lived close to nature, in an intimate relationship with birds and other creatures, observing the ways of plants, birds, and animals in the same single-focused way my Mi'kmaq mentor, my great aunt Helen, used to when I was growing up. Her knowledge was considerable, and although she was shy, I wanted to bring her on the air to share her understanding with the listening audience, whoever they may be. Her hair was a rusty red, something like a grouse, and could occasionally "grouse" (British slang for complaining) if she was ticked off. She had a way of stalling if she was unsure of what she was being asked to do, or when the shyness was setting in. Halfway down the road, an airborne ruffed grouse came hurtling toward us. It seemed to be coming at the window, but at the last moment, darted downward and smashed directly in the grillwork of the car. We both screamed unintentionally as the horrible thud reverberated throughout the car. I slammed on the brakes. My guest jumped out of the car and did veterinary medicine on the wounded bird, which lay in a heap in front of the car.

"Why don't you watch where you're going?" she said to me. "I couldn't stop." I answered. "You were driving too fast!" she retorted. I explained that we were late for the show and now would be even later.

"We're not going anywhere until we see what we can do for this bird!" She knelt by the bird and felt its heart beat. She moved and straightened the wings; she massaged its extremities. She talked to it as if it was a wounded president, meanwhile I was apparently not worth talking to any more. She picked up the bird and carefully carried it to the side of the road. She made a makeshift nest in the tall grass and laid the bird in the nest to rest. After a long time, the bird began to regain consciousness, but it was not clear if it would live or die. She encouraged the bird to fly again, but I could see she had her doubts. I said, "Well, the radio show is basically over now. I guess we can go and explain what happened, so that I have at least some chance of getting asked back."

We got back in the car and drove toward town, this time a little slower. I turned a sharp corner, and there was the answer to the riddle. A huge 18-wheeler had jackknifed on a turn and smashed into a telephone pole. The pole was across the road and the wires were down or hanging low. It was a mess, and it looked as if the wires were live. At the speed I was going, I would have smashed into the wires, the pole, and the truck before braking. In fact, the accident had just happened several minutes earlier, about the time the grouse threw itself in front of my car to slow me down. That bird saved my life and that of my passenger! He prevented us from hitting the truck, which would have truly changed our plans for the day. *Migwetch* to the grouse!

Partridge/Family

Although the grouse may look like a female partridge, its temperament is different. Natives often think of the partridge person as one who is rather concerned with his or her appearance and with clothing. The partridge is a poor cousin to the pheasant, whose feathers are considered very beautiful and have been used by the Creek and other peoples to decorate the finest hats and cloaks. In some cases, the partridge can tell us that we need to spend more attention on this area, perhaps in order to attract a mate so that we can raise a family, but for the most part, the Native teaching heads in another direction. One person in my

Native community told me that deer and other birds and animals are not afraid of humans, they are afraid of humans with clothes on. Those who own their own piece of God's country and wish to return to God's original decorum (as was good enough for Adam and Eve) and that of their ancestors, in the privacy of their own property, sometimes find that creatures we think of as timid are no longer afraid and become quite friendly. My main source for this important information may wish to remain anonymous, but it is known that it was common for deer hunters to hunt with very little, if anything, on in the summer. Rumor has it that Adam had more trouble hunting after he left the garden; someone should have told him to ditch his city slicker suits for the real thing when Eve wasn't around.

Aunt Helen's husband, John Perley, probably a Maliseet, we're not sure, was camping with Helen on their honeymoon. He was trying to make a good impression on his new wife, but that morning he had on only a shirt and his BVDs, when he saw a partridge through the window of the lodge. Bringing home a partridge dinner would surely impress the young lady, but he knew they must be hunted at close range, with a shot through the head. He thrust his feet into some rubber boots and grabbed his rifle and went off trying to get close. According to her biographer, "The partridge is a wily bird, teasing the hunter by moving ever so innocently just out of range. That morning John stalked the partridge as it made its way deeper and deeper into the forest. Caught up with the excitement of the chase, he had at first not noticed any discomfort, but in the deep woods it was colder. John shivered, decided that the elusive partridge wasn't worth the trouble, and started back to camp. But where was camp?"[67]

By the end of the day, he was still wandering lost in the wilderness without any pants on, still no partridge, and no sign of human habitation. He knew Helen knew the rules of the road about hunting. He gave up on making a good impression. If he was going to live, he'd have to let Helen see him with his pants down. He shot off his one bullet as a call for help, and she responded with an answering shot that told him of her whereabouts. Apparently, she was looking for him as well. Their reunion must have been interesting!

In Native bird lore, the partridge was telling him that all the primping and posturing that makes for good courtship can lead us astray when it comes to a long-term relationship. Once the marriage vows are made, it is good to let our guard down, to show our real hopes and fears, to communicate. Otherwise we might grow distant from each other, our love growing cold like my uncle's . . . well, never mind. The incident helped the two lovebirds get to know each other really well, and the marriage produced a nest of fine-feathered Perleys who are still among us today.

Helen was never the shrinking violet anyway. Not long afterward, Helen and John were living off the land on vacation in Texas and ran low on food. There were crabs in the river that flowed near the Alamo, but the store-bought bait wouldn't tempt them. Any time one of the fishing party got near them, they'd scuttle back into their holes. Helen wasn't going to miss breakfast over a fussy bunch of crabs. She marched into the brush and shot a turkey buzzard. She cleaned it and cut it up right there, stuck the buzzard meat on her hook, and soon had a crab feast the size of Texas.[68]

Pigeon Club

Many city dwellers develop a close relationship with the blue rock pigeon, even though they are not actually indigenous to this territory. One woman living in the Morningside Heights area of Manhattan has made friends with a pigeon couple, male and female, whom she has named Gregory Peck and Miss Hook, and lets them hang out on the kitchen windowsill. She enjoys talking to them and feeding them by hand.[69] As with my Aunt Helen's farm, the boundary between wild and tame sometimes becomes hard to find. Pigeons, by the way, are unique in that they can produce low-pitched infrasounds at nearly 0.5 Hz, even as they are cooing at a higher pitch.[70]

A Cherokee pipe carrier named Blessing Bird lived with a pet pigeon in the Baltimore area, one who neatly did its duty on a newspaper on top of a dresser in the house. One time she came home with a pizza treat for her animals and found Spike the miniature schnauzer, Pussywillow the cat, and Gonza the female pigeon, all in a puppy pile, staring at the TV. Gonza was sitting on top of Spike. They both looked at her with eyelids lowered for two seconds, the universal interspecies sign for "Don't touch that dial!" It must have been a wildlife show. Their eyes returned to the screen. When she showed them the pizza, they all began to eat at once, but turning their backs to her as if to say, "Don't touch *our* pizza!" They were a fun group. Some dogs bite cats, and some cats bite birds, but not these happy creatures. As Blessing Bird observed, "Sometimes the lion really does lie down with the lamb!"

One time while Blessing Bird was in the bathroom, the pigeon came in and started cooing repeatedly, dancing about in front of her, flying through the house to the screen door in the back, and then returning to repeat the gesture. After a while, Blessing Bird realized there was something wrong. She flew to the backdoor, paired with the pigeon, and immediately saw the problem; Spike's chain was lying in the yard, broken, and Spike was nowhere to be seen. Blessing Bird eventually found Spike, who had lost his way in the city, and returned him to his loving avian and feline friends.

As the three creatures played together, sometimes Gonza lay on her back, pigeon legs held limply in the air, and played dead, until Pussywillow came up to sniff her, and then she'd leap up and fly away, knowing kitty would be up for the chase. They had quite a time.

Many years ago, Blessing Bird was preparing to attend her first pow-wow and was assembling and donning the best regalia she could find, as the pigeon watched in fascination from atop the dresser. It was the first time the bird had seen a human exhibit this new behavior under her watch. She found one of Gonza's largest wing feathers lying in front of her and picked it up. It was a lefty. She wagged it in front of Gonza and said, "Isn't this one pretty? Shall I tie it into my left braid?" Receiving no complaints, Blessing Bird did as she promised, looking for a look of approval from Gonza. Gonza seized a matching feather from the right wing, which had been on top of the dresser mirror and held it firmly in her beak. She fluttered down to the floor and placed it at the feet of Blessing Bird, then turned her head to look up at the human to see if she understood. Blessing Bird took the righty feather and attached it to her right braid. Now she was ready to powwow with the best of them! The bird nodded and flew back up to its perch, glowing with greater respect for this intelligent animal before her.

Life Is Worth Living

A man named Featherhawk wrote to me, telling the following story:

It was the fourth day of my third detox and I was drawn to be outside. I was regaining my senses and felt the pull to the stand of evergreens nearby. Although I noticed the birds in the trees, I hadn't thought much of it. As I stood in the midst of five tall evergreens, I began to hear the birds chattering above me. I looked up to see about a dozen crows flitting about nervously. As I watched them, they flew from branch to branch until one sprig of pine dropped before my feet from their movements. Although there were many fallen branches, this one was fresh. I reached down for it and brought it up to my face, snapping the sprig in two pieces. I took in the deep scent, and again and again I smelled it. As I drank in its fragrance, the thought came into my mind that if I were to continue doing what I had been doing to myself I would never get the opportunity to enjoy such a blessing ever again. The crows then left with a flourish as I cried tears of joy for the first time in ages. It was at that moment I knew I must change the path my life was taking or be lost forever. The crows were telling me I still had a purpose here and that I must do everything I can to stay."[71]

PEACEMAKING
AND PATIENT BIRDS

The Peacemakers: Herons, Egrets, and Cranes

Herons are traditionally birds of peace, peacemakers. I have heard from elders from coast to coast that herons "make peace between other birds." The heron, *telaka* in Lenape, is a bird of brotherhood, which in Lenape is *waymachteniank*. This word has yet a deeper meaning than mere kin relationship; it implies a universal brotherhood that is invisible and yet cannot be broken. The suffix *teniank* means "a general state of things," so it is not the kind of brotherhood limited to those with the same mother, unless that mother is the Earth itself.

The Mi'kmaq call this bird *dum-gwal-ee-gun-idge*, which means "his neck is broken." This relates to the idea of "the wounded healer," the thought that many who are brave enough to dedicate themselves to the techniques of conflict resolution now called the way of the heron, are those whose "necks have been broken" already by the scourge of violence. Who else but those who have gone deep within to heal their wounds would give the matter a great deal of thought and come up with strategies for eliminating conflict? If you see a heron, it may be telling you that your anger may be misplaced and that it is not a time to fight with others. I remember at least one or two occasions where I was mistakenly angry with someone, thanks to misinformation and misunderstanding, and a heron made a visit to make me slow down and get better information. On the morning of 9/11, a great blue heron flew right over my head, a rare enough event that it stopped me in my tracks and inspired me to write and speak about employing the way of the heron even then.

Plate 1. Bald Eagle
An icon of strength and liberty, the bald eagle was a symbol of freedom to Native Americans long before George Washington chose it as the official symbol of the United States.

© Alan W. Wells

THE FOUR GATEKEEPERS

According to a widespread tradition among Eastern Algonquins, the eagle is the gatekeeper of the North, the red-tailed hawk is the gatekeeper of the East; the crow is the gatekeeper of the South, and the owl is the gatekeeper of the West. Here we see that Bird Medicine Wheel illustrated photographically, with North tilted somewhat to the right. (In the larger Medicine Wheel of all the animals, the entire Bird Medicine Wheel is in the South, and that larger animal wheel is, in turn, in the East of another wheel, and so on.) These four strong birds are constantly in relationship with each other, with the eagle and hawk considered pure messengers of enlightened states who bring good fortune, and the crow and owl considered shadow world messengers who may, as some argue, bring misfortune at times. All four are capable of bringing important messages of warning.

Plate 2. Barred Owl

Owls sit in the West of the Bird Medicine Wheel, the place of the setting sun and of night. Owl medicine is taken very seriously, as they often are bringers of tragic news, such as the death of a loved one. As nocturnal birds with moonlike eyes, they are associated with helping us make the transition into the unseen world of the unconscious. Owls can turn their heads 270 degrees, and their eyesight is eight times more powerful than humans.

Plate 3. American Crow

Crows are warning birds and produce a universal alert signal, which all species of animals can understand. Crows work in teams to eat meat because they don't have serrated beaks. Crows are highly intelligent and can make simple tools. So why do they gather in massive crow councils each year at the same spots, usually near former Native American village sites, and make noise? It must be important!

© Alan W. Wells

Plate 4. Bald Eagle

Next to the golden eagle, the bald eagle is the most noble of birds and changes its appearance through several phases of growth, just as we do. The bald eagle was a symbol of freedom to Native Americans long before George Washington's time. Although all eagles "sit in the north," there is a white eagle that can only be seen in the spirit world, and this is an infallible messenger for the Creator. According to most traditions, the bald eagle brings good luck (unless you are a small rodent!).

Plate 5. Red-Tailed Hawk

The red-tailed hawk sits in the East, as its red color reflects the rising sun. The red tail brings messages concerning our path in life—the big picture. Although birds of war, they are trusted defenders and protectors who often intercede on behalf of humans. Red tails are highly prone to albinism; hence, pale specimens like this one are called white hawks and are highly revered as divine messengers and protectors.

© Alan W. Wells

Plate 6. Red-Tailed Hawk

The red-tailed hawk will often try to get your attention; either by letting its shadow pass over you, by circling over your head, by saluting you, or by screaming at you. They can "ride shotgun," gliding directly over your car or directly past your side window. Many Native Americans see hawks as the most "human" of birds and consider them good role models overall, but what they are trying to say to us is sometimes hard to fathom. Like the owl, they seem to save their most dramatic entrances to announce the death of a loved one. A hawk deserves our respect as a "junior eagle."

Plate 7. White-Breasted Nuthatch

Native American tradition says this bird teaches about faith; faith in the power of nature and that things will fall together all by themselves as soon as we stop forcing. The nuthatch is also a faith healer, who guides us out of trouble and can heal our pain in many ways.

© Alan W. Wells

© Alan W. Wells

© Alan W. Wells

Plate 8. Barred Owl

As with most owls, the barred owl's facial feathers increase its acute hearing. The barred owl is clownish at times, sporting a maniacal laugh and saying "Who who who cooks for you? Who cooks for y'aaall?" Although they sit in the West of the wheel with other owls, they can be found year-round in east Texas!

Plate 9. Red-Headed Woodpecker

Woodpeckers are the home builders' union of the avian world, and their holes may be used by four or five other species of birds over the course of a few summers. They pick out bugs from fallen trees and so are associated with paying attention to detail. Among other warnings, they tell us to read the fine print on the wampum treaty. The red-headed woodpecker is now endangered in Connecticut.

Plate 10. Red-Bellied Woodpecker

The red mark on this woodpecker's belly is often hard to see; the most prominent feature is the patch of red on its head, "a little blanket of blood." The red-headed woodpecker, on the other hand, is red from the neck up.

Plate 11. Black-Throated Green Warbler

This bird says *ziseep* the Mi'kmaq word for wild bird and the basis of *ziseebem,* which means "my wild bird, my sweetheart." This bird is endangered by deforestation in Mexico, where it spends the winter, but their mating call can still be heard in the Maritimes in spring, calling, "Where is my wild bird? Where is my sweetheart?"—at least to Mi'kmaq ears.

© Alan W. Wells

© Alan W. Wells

Plate 12. Northern Harrier

The northern harrier sits on the border between a hawk and an owl, with features of both. It is the direct descendant of the Egyptian marsh hawk, an actual species of bird, associated with the Egyptian god Horus. They fly silently and observe, but do not like being observed.

Plate 13. Great Blue Heron

The heron is very patient; he stands still like a statue for hours until a fish comes by, and then he moves like lightning to grasp it. This is how purposeful we should be in conducting trade and conversation. The heron is said to "resolve conflicts between other birds," and so is the symbol of peacemaking and conflict resolution. The way of the heron is a body of ancient heron teachings at the core of eastern Algonquin life, which trains us in the art of speaking and extends into diplomacy, democratic procedures, and nonviolent protest, even civil disobedience. Henry David Thoreau learned these at the feet of two great Penobscot diplomats, Joseph Attien and Joseph Polis.

Plate 14. Snowy Egret

Years ago, my sister's canoe wandered into uncharted wetlands in Maryland's Eastern Shore region. As she held her breath, she witnessed one of nature's most amazing sights: about eighteen snowy egrets dancing in a circle, as a mated pair swam to the center from opposite sides of the circle. The romantic couple flapped their wings pushing against each other until they levitated into the air and then floated back down to return to their assigned spots, making room for the next mated pair to seal their oaths to one another.

It was a life-changing event. She became a birder! This photo by world-famous (and incredibly patient) wildlife photographer Jan Henriksen was taken just before such a spectacle and gives us at least a glimpse of what my sister experienced as a wide-eyed youth. The snowy egrets' close cousins, the reddish egrets, still nest each year at Green Island in the Gulf of Mexico, having survived the oil spill of 2010.

Plates 15–17. Brown Pelicans

One of the largest birds in North America, the brown pelican has a wing span of up to eight feet and can weigh up to twelve pounds. It is the state bird of Louisiana, but its habitat reaches from the Amazon to Maryland. Called *aruna* by the Taino, it is considered a sign of good fortune. Two of its main nesting areas are Dauphin Island and Petit Bois Island. The Taino hold special reverence for this bird, as do the Atakapa-Ishak people on the Gulf Coast's Grand Bayou. They and their neighbors, the Houma, are part of the Vessels of Opportunity program, using their fishing boats to help clean up the waters on which they and the birds depend, a process that will take years.

© Alan W. Wells

Plate 18. White-Breasted Nuthatch

The miraculous nuthatch can't walk on water but likes to stand upside-down to get a fresh perspective on life. This optimistic little bird helps us see things differently and brings us insights.

Plate 19. Hummingbird

Hummingbirds are warriors who can defeat Bear in battle, but are also the most delicate of creatures. They are bringers of beauty and enjoyers of sweetness, who can fly backward or stand still in the air. They are passionate lovers of freedom who die quickly in captivity. One hummingbird became trapped in my sister's room and panicked and started to destroy itself, but a wise nuthatch came to the window and, through the glass, made eye contact and got the suicidal little bird to calm down, take a breath, and think about what it was doing and how it got into this spot. The hummingbird then retraced its steps and flew out of the room to its freedom.

© Alan W. Wells

© Becky Spear

© Becky Spear

Plate 20. Seagull the Magician

Seagulls remember human faces for over ten years and often come back to repay good deeds and ill. A Native youth from Long Island used to treat his seagull friends to tropical shrimp, pocketed from his mother's Chinese fast-food restaurant. Years later, while at a nearby college, he unknowingly dropped the gold Cross ballpoint pen his uncle had given him onto the sidewalk. A seagull picked it up and flew over his head, dropping the pen so that it slid down his books and hit him in the chest. He thanked the seagull, recognizing his old friend. A sailor told me that the gull whose wing he'd bandaged and repaired on board his ship came back each fall, regardless of his location on the Atlantic. Another seagull dropped a fish at my feet as I walked across my grandfather's praying spot, a significant gift from a seagull's point of view.

© Alan W. Wells

Plate 21. Canada Goose

Canada geese, who mate for life and can live over twenty years, have been providing meals to Native Americans for a very long time: Butchered goose bones found in Alaska date back eleven thousand or more years. To this day, they play a very special role in Native American life, associated with the spirit of the shamanic healer. Their wing fluff is used sometimes as an offering, like tobacco. At this writing, many U.S. states and cities are at war with the overpopulating goose, exterminating them in gas chambers by the thousands. FIDO, a pro-pet organization based in Brooklyn is fighting, among others, to stop the gassing of geese in New York City.

Plate 22. Western Bluebird

Many Native American cultures consider the western bluebird to be sacred, including the Cochiti and the Navajo. At the Ye'iibicheii winter nightway ceremony, the Navajo sing the "Bluebird Song" on the final day at sunrise, saying, "Bluebird said to me, get up my grandchild, it is dawn."

Plate 23. Eastern Bluebird
The New York state bird, the eastern bluebird is a sign of good fortune, and although once decimated by DDT, I am happy to say this cheerful creature is making a big comeback in the state in recent years. Almost constantly in motion, this restless bird will nonetheless guide you to your heart's content if you follow where it leads you, so they say. Years ago, one literally jumped from post to post and led me along a dirt path to the site of one of my first sweat lodge experiences, a very happy experience indeed!

© Alan W. Wells

Plate 24.
American Robin
Many Native Americans recognize the robin as a bird that brings messages about relationships and family. Robins are role models who take good care of their children and their mates and live in close proximity to humans. They can also warn us of earthquakes, as an Ojibway friend of mine recently learned, by singing their "rain is coming" song rapidly and at a high pitch. One danger robins can't foresee is poison, and these birds are particularly susceptible to its various forms, such as DDT.

© Alan W. Wells

Plate 25. Northern Harrier

Northern harriers or marsh hawks, associated with Horus, began to show up around Ahngwet (a Mi'kmaq woman) the day her Egyptologist father passed away. The previous day, she had asked him to give her a sign if he could hear her from the other side. As she was driving home from the hospital for the last time, a harrier circled over her car in a downtown traffic jam, then perched on a sign to her left. That was the first of a series of startling encounters with a species of bird usually known to be quite reticent.

Plate 26. Mallard

The mallard has a number of courtship rituals that were adopted over time by Native Americans. The male's courtship dance and his preening, giving of gifts, "taking her out to dinner," and other rituals have been adopted by Native Americans and perhaps all societies on Earth.

Plate 27. Eastern Screech Owl, Red Phase (above left)
The eastern screech owl is a mysterious bird, who can sit and watch you for a long time. Many Native people believe that the owl is an oracle from the world of the dead. Just days after my friend Shoshana passed away, an eastern screech owl in a red phase came to perch in her favorite tree outside my window, looking out over the landscape she loved. Although it was broad daylight, it stayed for a long time. Was it sent by her spirit? Or was it a coincidence?

Plate 28. American Crow (above right)
Crows come together sometimes in great gatherings Native Americans call crow councils, such as this one at an auto repair shop in Middletown, New York, near the site of an ancient crossroads that no longer exists. This photo was taken on our leap day, but the gathering probably started around February 1, the old Ground Hog Day, a Native American holiday.

Plate 29. Red-Tailed Hawk   **Plate 30. Bald Eagle**

Sit calmly and discuss all sides of the issues before embarking on conflict—that is the way of the heron. (See color insert, plate 13.) One speech, called "Seven Tough Steps to World Peace," is still on the Internet, as I write these words. It simply describes the timeless techniques of diplomacy used by the Algonkin-ode people for thousands of years to maintain harmony in face-to-face communities and between neighboring tribes and nations. Henry David Thoreau learned some of these things from the Penobscots, namely his trail guides Joseph Attien and Joseph Polis; Dr. Martin Luther King Jr. used these same techniques in Atlanta and then Alabama. The key is to gather accurate information and to pray together for guidance and then to combine symbolic gesture with heightened speech to make one's views clear. Of course there is much more.

Egrets, like the herons, are peacemakers, and it is considered a good sign to see one when you are experiencing conflict.

Depsimana relates a story told to her by a Heron or Crane Clan grandmother of the Anishinabi, Keewaydinoquay. The grandmother took a bundle of crane bones to an Anishinabi medicine man and asked him to create some bone whistles from them. Whistles carved from the bones of a deceased bird can be used to call that bird forward, or certainly the spirit of that bird. People have been making flutes out of crane bones for least nine thousand years. Flutes made of crane bones have been found in Jiahu, China, dated to 7000 BCE.[72]

It was an unusual request. The crane, in the words of Depsimana, is the "international bird of peace." The old man agreed to bring forth the peaceful power of this bird with his carving skills. The elder would test the frequency of the bones as he labored to transform them into musical instruments and powerful spiritual tools, and the sound they made was so beautiful, that by the time the Crane Clan grandmother came back to pick up the flutes, everyone in the village was crying. It is said that crane bone flutes bring all creation to attention, not unlike Gabriel's horn,[73] and that when the Creator is present in our hearts, the people cry.

Herons and Longevity

Shawnee Elder Dark Rain Thom, author of *The Shawnee: Kokumthena's Grandchildren,* and her husband, noted author James Alexander Thom, with whom she wrote *Warrior Woman,* were married barefoot in the ceremonial arbor, beside a pond on her tribe's ground in Ohio. There were many Shawnee women present, friends of Dark Rain, and also some white people and those of various nations. As the ceremony was concluding, they both noticed a great number of herons and egrets on the opposite shore, but among their guests there was a difference of opinion. The Shawnee women all agreed there were old people standing across the water during the ceremony, whereas others just saw egrets. Eventually they figured out that they were speaking of the same thing, that the Shawnee were referring to the birds as "old people." No further explanation was offered.[74] This is interesting because the Chinese also associate the heron with longevity.

Heron Traffic

Aunt Helen Perley was a keen observer of bird behavior and was not shy about comparing their world to ours. To quote Helen from Johnson's biography of her, *Mrs. Perley's People*: "Did you ever notice, when it gets dark, how the trucks come out on the highways and the passenger cars disappear? It's like the birds on the marshes. When you sail downriver in the daytime, the great blue herons stand on the shore and the terns fly over your head. As the night falls, the black-crowned night herons take their places by the brackish pools. Sometimes, near the shore, bats fly over your head and owls go by on silent wings. People don't notice, but there is night traffic on the river just as there is on the highway. A river that runs to the sea is my kind of road."[75]

Herons and Cranes: Teachers of Patience

The herons and other cranes signify not only peacemaking and conflict resolution but infinite patience as well. They stand in the river on one foot without moving a muscle for hours, until an unwary fish comes by thinking that their foot is just a stick in the mud. The crane moves with lightning-swift efficiency, snares the fish in its bill, and then flies away.

Some herons are more clever than others, and some fashion fish lures that rival the tackle boxes of human anglers. If the green heron can get ahold of some bread crumbs, it will sprinkle them over the surface of the water, and then catch the fish that come up to eat the crumbs. If it has no crumbs, the green heron will pull out a small feather and let it float on the water as if it were fly-fishing. Again, when the fish come up to nibble at the fly, the green heron pounces.

As a symbol of patience, the heron tells us, "Quiet down!" In Mi'kmaq, we say it says, "*Tchai-nai!*" It will stand still for hours if it has to, to catch its breakfast. In *No Word for Time,* I described how restless and impatient I was to begin my fast. Grandfather Turtle went to his shelf and picked up two heron feathers and gave them to me, saying, "Here's two crane feathers to use in your smudging. It's not as strong as an eagle feather, but it's pretty good!" Then he said, "Look at the cranes by the river. They will teach you patience. He's showing you how to live *sah-be-u-wen,* the spiritual way of life. Wait as long as it takes for things to be ready, then act fast."[76]

The crane's reputation for vigilance is ancient and widespread. Beryl Rowland, in the book *Birds with Human Souls,* wrote:

The crane holding a pebble in its foot is an illustration of proverbial watchfulness and prudence. Flying in formation in a strong wind, the crane was said to pick up a stone. The bird used the stone as ballast or dropped it to find out by the noise it made whether the crossing was over sea or land. According to Aristotle and Pliny, when the crane acted as night sentinel during migration, it stood on one foot and held a pebble in the other. If the watcher fell asleep the noise of the falling pebble woke it; if danger threatened, the bird dropped the pebble toward the rest of the flock.[77]

The snowy egret, on the other hand, gets impatient. When fishing, the egret will stir the surface of the water with his yellow toes, just enough to create ripples, which will either lure the fish to the surface or scare them out of their hiding places.

Snowy Egret Dance

Many years ago, my sister Lynn and her best friend Sally were canoeing through some uncharted wetlands in the eastern shore region of Maryland, west of Ocean City, but far from the nearest roadway or even Indian Trail. There was a slow current, so they stopped paddling and just floated along silently, to see if they could spot some birds or other wildlife that the noises of their oars would otherwise scare away. Their canoe took them to a clearing where there was no brush or reeds, just shallow water. There the two seekers beheld a most amazing sight: sixteen to twenty large snowy egrets stood in a perfect circle, with equal space between each of the majestic birds. The birds were all looking at each other silently in anticipation, but for what, Lynn and Sally did not know. (See color insert, plate 14.*)

Two of the birds stepped forward, their feathers ruffed, and waded purposefully to the center of the circle. There, the pair pushed their chests against each other, long necks stretched back, and began to dance on their webbed feet. The other birds seemed to dance and sway imperceptibly along with the paired couple. The two birds began to flap their wings in synchronicity and rose up slowly into the air as if levitating by magic. The dancers reached a height, and then slowly came back to earth. They turned and went back to their places, and the next couple came forward to do the same thing. A third couple followed. The canoe drifted away, but Lynn never forgot that incredible spectacle, a formal dance ritual performed by snowy egrets, probably a mating dance, performed there for thousands of years and passed on through countless generations.

There is a square dance step that is quite similar, but I suspect that

---

*Lynn did not have her camera in hand, but wildlife photographer Jan Henriksen was able to document a similar group of egrets.

it was adapted from a Native American dance step that was in turn adapted from watching the snowy egrets, whose polite and formal ways of courtship could not be improved on. But I never saw square dance couples float up to the ceiling and then come back down to the center of the circle like that before. This would win the prize for best couple in any contest!

Rowland, again in *Birds with Human Souls*, describes a crane's dance as follows:

> Cranes dance; not hesitantly, as you might expect, but with all the aplomb of Scottish country dancers tackling "Marie's Wedding." Marjorie Kinnan Rawlings in her novel *The Yearling* thought that they danced a cotillion: "The cranes were dancing a cotillion as surely as it was danced at Volusia . . . In the heart of the circle several moved counterclockwise . . . The outer circle shuffled around and around. The group in the center attained a slow frenzy."
>
> The circular movement was important: to the ancients the ring dance associated the cranes with the sun. The cranes brought the spring and were surrogates of the resurgent sun god. Their dance epitomized both fertility and death rituals.[78]

Rowland goes on to quote several European sources describing this fluttering love dance as involving nine steps and a leap.[79]

These observations and beliefs about cranes from around the world are strikingly similar to Native American reports about these highly unusual and intelligent birds. In his book *Moving Within the Circle*, author Bryan Burton describes a Native American dance with obvious bird origins:

> The Women's Shawl Dance of the Nanticoke . . . is one of the few surviving original East Coast style dances, with dancers learning from other dancers, always referring to the Nanticoke as the source. Sometimes referred to as the Swan Dance, this dance features

beautiful shawls used to imitate the gracefulness of birds with movements mimicking soaring, gliding, and flying. The bowing of heads and lowering of shawls signifies humility before the Creator, while the movement of the dance honors the four directions.

In a typical performance of the Shawl Dance, women dancers follow a lead dancer into the circle with arms extended and shawls flowing to represent wings. The tilt of the arms with the shawl outspread shows various stages of flight. Dancers freely use motions of soaring, gliding, slow flapping, and graceful body movements to honor birds through imitation. At some point, the dancers form two rows and the lead pair weaves through the group—"soaring" and "gliding" with subsequent pairs beginning this movement as the point where the maneuver was initiated by the lead dancer. Eventually the dancers follow the lead dancer out of the dance circle. As with many Native American dances, the exact sequence of movements is flexible depending upon the lead dancer and creativity of individual dancers.[80]

The Cypress Swamp, where I believe my sister, Lynn, saw the snowy egret mating dance is twenty miles long and overlaps both Wicomico County, Maryland, and Sussex County, Delaware, which is where Burton witnessed the Nanticoke dance on many occasions at pow-wows held there each year. It would be more than reasonable to suggest that the "swans" so honored in the dance might actually be the snowy egrets who travel thousands of miles to mate each year in those remote wetland pools where few dare to paddle. That would mean that Lynn was not the first to see that remarkable sight, but that local Nanticokes had witnessed it as well, perhaps hundreds of years earlier, and were so moved that they created a dance in its honor.

Shorebirds and Synchronicity

Shorebirds, such as the plover, sandpiper, and other small birds, run, turn, and fly in perfect synchronicity as a group, perhaps we should say as a single organism, even though they have no leader. Science struggles to explain exactly how this happens, but I have seen a similar level of group cohesiveness among Algonquian-speaking people such as the Mi'kmaq. There are situations when everyone shows up at the same time even though no time has been specified, or leaves at the same moment without so much as a word from anyone, or even good-bye. I suspect that in the past, this remarkable quality was yet more pronounced. It also happens when a large group of people are closely related to each other. This level of synchronicity has to be instinctual, but is also considered a virtue among Native people, one that may have been learned by pointing to shorebirds as role models thousands of years ago, communicating with fellow humans in a language that existed before words.

Geese: Heralders of Spring and Adventure

Geese are very important to the Cree up north and to the Native peoples of Long Island, just to mention a few nations who honor this special migratory bird. (See color insert, plate 21.) While eagles and hawks can bring messages back and forth from the Creator, according to widespread Native American tradition, some believe that geese can bring our messages and prayers up to the Creator as well, via goose down, which is held sacred by the elders.

According to Nissequogue Raymundo Rodriguez, the Long Island Natives prize goose feathers for the white puffy down that appears at the base of the feather, a feature which no other bird's feather has, at least not in quite the same way. While some collect this down to stuff jackets and pillows for retail, the Nissequogue see it as a spiritual and ceremonial source of power. This small cloud of fluff is considered the equivalent of the smoke from the bowl of a sacred pipe or the smudge smoke from the smudging bowl. Held in the hand like tobacco while praying, when it is released, it floats upward on the wind like smoke, bringing our prayers skyward to the Creator. When it is found on the grass beside a lake, it is considered a blessing and is collected to be used in an outdoor ceremony. When it is seen floating slowly by someone's face as it travels on the wind, it may be a prayer made on that person's behalf, or a reminder that the Creator is present everywhere.

The return of the goose is a sign of spring, and the renewed greening of the Earth, but their honking in the fall is a call to adventure. Worldwide, they are associated with the vision quest and the shaman's journey into the spirit world. Geese are monogamous and mate for life.

The flight feathers of a goose are highly aerodynamic and draw a lot of air. If you are just learning to dance traditionally, take a large goose feather and dance with it. As you move it around, you will feel the pull of the air. If you let it, that quill will teach you how to fancy dance in the proper manner. Sometimes at traditional powwows, you can see women dancing while holding a goose feather, letting it dance around in the air with its own grace, as they dance with their shawls uplifted as if about to take off for the sky.[81]

PART 4

OTHER
BIRD ALLIES

HUMMINGBIRDS

Hummingbird, the Rainbow Bridge

The hummingbird is recognized by the Mi'kmaq for its rainbow colors and is associated therefore with the rainbow bridge, the sky road that arches through the twelve levels of clouds above us and also leads us into the heavenly worlds of the great light, and back again. (See color insert, plate 19.) The hummingbird is associated with joy. In Mayan teachings, it is associated with the fifth sun (also called the black sun, or the fifth world).[1] To Jamie Sams, a writer and artist of Seneca-Cherokee descent, the hummingbird brings love medicine to open the heart. She writes, "Because of their magical qualities, Hummingbird feathers have been used for millennium in the making of love charms. It is said that Hummingbird conjures love as no other medicine does, and that Hummingbird feathers open the heart. Without an open and loving heart, you can never taste the nectar and pure bliss of life. To Brother and Sister Hummingbird, life is a wonderland of delight—darting from one beautiful flower to another, tasting the essences, and radiating the colors."[2] Sams also goes on to say that hummingbirds quickly die if caged, caught or imprisoned.

One day, a hummingbird came into my sister Lynn's house in New Brunswick, Canada, through an open door, and frantically and repeatedly threw herself against the large front window in an attempt to free herself, without success. After almost exhausting herself from hitting the ceiling and the window, a nuthatch (very similar to the one that had helped Lynn years before) flew up to the other side of the window and hovered there, flying back and forth in front of the depleted hummingbird, as if to give her encouragement, support, and energy to keep going. Nuthatches may be another form of little helpers to the spirit when any fellow creature is in need. The hummer calmed down long enough for Lynn to grab a handful of branches and extend them high enough for the little bird to perch on and take it outside to freedom.

One woman I interviewed, "Marina," an anthropologist who works with indigenous populations around the world, found herself on two occasions, not far apart, ministering to hummingbirds that had crashed headfirst into a wall while trying to escape a closed room. She asked what the Algonquins would say that meant, and I answered that hummingbirds are messengers of joy and ecstasy, associated with music and art but also freedom. I asked her, a musician, if she felt that at that moment in her life she was beating her head against a wall, at a loss to find joy in her music. Her eyes lit up with surprise, and said, "Absolutely. That was a time when the red tape and hassles of academic life completely overwhelmed my joy in creating music. Right on target. I was beating my head against a monolithic wall of academia, and I felt imprisoned by it, unable to escape like the birds I had found indoors, half dead on the floor. Never again!"

Without realizing it, Marina had heeded the warning of the hummingbirds: We need to feel free in order to create. It reminds me of the New Hampshire slogan, "Live free or die." That's how hummingbirds are able to live miraculous existences.

Hummingbird: Guardian of Tobacco

Blessing Bird, a woman of Cherokee, Tuscarora, and Lenape descent, was a priest of the Good Medicine Society and a pipe carrier who worked with Native American war veterans in Perrypoint VA Medical Center in Perryville, Maryland, as well as prisoners in facilities like the state prisons in Jessup, Hagerstown, and Cumberland. Strongly identified with Cherokee traditions, she learned from her elder Grandfather Sings Alone and prayed with the wounded and dying from both a Christian and traditional perspective. It was a long and winding path to get her to that place where she felt she could perform these sacerdotal duties.

I asked her how she got her name, Blessing Bird, and was not disappointed when I heard the tale. When the time was right, she carved her pipe out of local soapstone given to her by an elder, and a pipe stem was carved for her by a man who was carving a staff for a bishop, using the same wood. This was appropriate given her Native Christian leanings, very common among Eastern Cherokee. She showed the pipe to her elder Grandfather Sings Alone, and he urged her to go on a vision quest to earn the right to carry the pipe and also to see if it was right for her to have a new name. She would have to look for signs in nature and for visitations from the spirit world as well. Not one to harbor possessions, she could not afford to go to Bear Butte or even Dreamer's Rock at Delaware Water Gap. Due to practical limitations, she had to stay inside the city and county of Baltimore. After all, that was where she hoped to be of service to her community.

Grandfather perched her on a huge rock on an island in Gwenn's Falls Creek, in the middle of Leakin' Park, a place where no one could get to her without a boat. She fasted and prayed for four days and nights with her pipe, smoking it each day. She looked high and low for a name, and although she saw eagles and hawks fly by, she knew that names like Eagle Woman or Hawk Priestess were totally inappropriate for her, a humble servant of the Great Spirit, whose greatest power was that of the "beginner's mind." On the fourth day, she stood and held her pipe out in a gesture of beseechment and asked for help from the Cherokee ancestors, crying out, "What is my *name?*"

She sat down again and placed the pipe in her lap, a pouch of tobacco next to it. At that moment, a tiny ruby-throated hummingbird buzzed by her ear. She thought it was a large bee, and thought to herself, "I certainly do not want the name bumblebee!" The hummingbird flitted around her, hovering over the new pipe, sticking its nose into the bowl several different times to check on her tobacco. She had never seen a hummingbird before except in close-up telephoto pictures and on TV. She had always assumed they were the size of parrots, or even larger. She didn't know what it was and thought she was dreaming. Surely no earthly bird could be that small! After the bird had stuck its head into her pipe bowl several times, it flew away, to her dismay. She called out, "If you want some water, I have some in my shell!" She held her abalone shell aloft, but the bird was gone. When she looked down next to the bowl, there was a tiny green iridescent hummingbird feather lying next to her pipe, a gift of great value among people of her culture, the color suggesting a message of love from the Great Mother Earth herself.

When she finished her fast, she told her story to Grandfather Sings Alone and asked him what it was. With amazement, he said it sounded like a hummingbird, but what would a hummingbird be doing in downtown Baltimore, Maryland? Then she showed him the feather! She had placed it in the beaded leather holder for her tamper. It was a hummingbird, all right!

He said it was a sacred bird with powerful medicine and told her a Cherokee story, a story from her ancestors: "The giants, powerful spiritual beings, had taken tobacco away from the Cherokee as a punishment for their bad behavior. Without tobacco, they could not pray any more, and it was a sad time for the people. Finally, one day, a Cherokee grandfather turned himself into a hummingbird to go to the giants and see if he could steal back some tobacco seeds, carrying them in his tiny beak. The raven, the crow, the eagle, and the hawk had all tried to sneak into the realm of the giants to steal back tobacco, but all had been caught and killed for their effrontery. The hummingbird grandfather zipped by unnoticed right under the noses of the giants and stole the tiny tobacco seeds and then flew back to the Cherokee people. They planted the seeds and, with a lot of sun and water and loving care, had many beautiful tobacco plants by summer. They began to pray all over again, this time with more humility and greater gratitude for the privilege. To this day, Hummingbird is called the tobacco guardian and is a sacred bird, and it is absolutely forbidden to harm him."

Blessing Bird had been smoking tobacco for three days, and although the bowl had been cleaned and had no seeds or leaves inside it to her knowledge, it still smelled of tobacco. Perhaps the hummingbird, as guardian of tobacco, was checking to see if the aspiring pipe carrier's bowl was carved right and if she was cleaning it properly. The bird apparently was well pleased, because that evening, while meditating in the shower, she who was not yet called Blessing Bird heard a voice from Spirit say she was the Giveaway Hummingbird and that she shall be called Blessing Bird. Recognizing that a miracle had happened, Grandfather Sings Alone recognized her new name and translated it into Cherokee for her, and that is the name she has been known by ever since—to everyone but the state and local authorities.[3]

As the hummingbird is associated among the Maya with fallen or injured warriors, it is interesting that Blessing Bird shared her hummingbird pipe with so many Native American war veterans, many of whom have lost brothers and friends in battle. Many of the prisoners she's worked with are Cherokee, who cannot properly perform sacred ceremony without her presence because the giants (that is, the Maryland State corrections wardens) have found their behavior wanting and wished to punish them by restricting their ceremonial activities.* Surely she helped Hummingbird return tobacco to the people. *Wado!*

A Bird of Blessing

Blessing Bird is now among the fallen warriors of the Cherokee. She passed away October 3, 2011, after a bout with cancer, survived by her best friend Running Deer and all those like myself who considered themselves part of her intentional family.[4] I was rushing off to work when I received the phone call from Running Deer, telling me of Blessing Bird's death from a fatal disease that she had held hidden from me and in some ways from herself. I had to sit for a while to compose myself before driving. Running Deer said it was among her last requests that her stories be included in *Bird Medicine*. Few elders have

---

*Tobacco is classified as contraband for all U.S. prisoners, so the use of it is strictly controlled. Blessing Bird, Eddy Stevenson, Grandfather Turtle, William Commanda, Tom Porter, and a number of others mentioned in this book have volunteered their services again and again as pipe carriers for incarcerated Native Americans so that they can still practice the sacraments of their faith while serving time.

the Bird Medicine like our young Blessing Bird had; she was truly one with them. Of course, her request has been granted, and a copy of this book will be donated to the memorial library and Native American resource center, which will be built in Jackson, West Virginia, in her honor. Having promised all that and more, I set out on my sorrowful journey to work, along the Taconic Parkway, thinking and wondering about Blessing Bird. Just north of Ossining, driving 55 miles per hour, I watched as a large female red-tailed hawk positioned herself right outside my driver's side window, which was closed. The end of her right wing tip was less than a foot from my window, and she was gliding effortlessly at the same speed I was traveling, navigating a narrow passage between a clifflike embankment to her left and me to her right. I had a car positioned to my right as well, as I was in the passing lane, but it was hard to keep my eyes on the road. Then the bird swooped down and sped along with me, gliding six inches to a foot off the ground so that I could see the somewhat symmetrical pattern of rust red and white triangles on her back and head up close. (See color insert, plate 29.) I felt as if I were flying with her. After what seemed like an eternity, she rose up again, flying beside me again at eye level but just to the fore, looking straight ahead. The cliff ended. She slowed down to let me catch up to her, and then suddenly turned her head directly toward me and stared at me from about two feet away. I went into a trance. In all my adventures with birds, I had never experienced anything like that before. I remembered I was driving a car but could not remember where I was going. I turned my eyes back to the road for a single second (everything was fine, but my exit was approaching) and when I looked back to the hawk again, she rose up and flexed one wing tip in the universal "bird salute" gesture, and then threw her head back in the "see you around" gesture, all of which flowed beautifully together as only a hawk can do, and then shot off into the woods. If that wasn't Blessing Bird traveling inside that bird to say hello from the spirit world, I'd like to hear a better explanation. I guess she really wanted to be in this book!

Hummingbird Taboos of the Kickapoo

Taboos are a complicated subject to explain to an American audience, and Americans tend to rebel against taboos more than any other society. However, the consequences of breaking the taboos of the nation one lives in or are visiting are considerable. The issue of taboos reached a heightened pitch when the English were colonizing the "third world" in the sixteenth and seventeenth centuries. I wrote about this problem in *Henry Hudson and the Algonquins of New York*, describing an incident when an English/Dutch crew killed and ate a sacred manta ray, oblivious of the serious taboo they were violating. And yet the British have their own taboos: while in England, if you tilt your bowl of soup toward you to spoon out the last drops or lift it to your lips, you will have violated a strict code of etiquette and will be frowned upon and corrected, if not shunned. Many of the more serious taboos of the world involve hunting sacred animals, and the punishment is serious. The violator is often told a story about someone who committed that violation and met a sad fate of some kind, but some societies don't wait for such slow justice.

Hummingbirds are widely considered sacred among the nations of Mexico, including the Maya. The Kickapoo are originally from the East Coast, but in the period from contact to the Civil War, were in the prairies states of the United States. When they moved to Mexico, they came into contact not only with Maya but with a great number of hummingbirds. It was probably at that time they adopted hummingbird taboos.

Felipe A. Latorre, coauthor of *The Mexican Kickapoo Indians*, writes, "One day a woman was sitting in our garden when a hummingbird appeared, flitting from flower to flower in search of nectar. The sight of the bird brought forth an account of an experience she had had as a child. One day, while cutting fire wood in the *monte*, she came upon the tiny nest of a hummingbird, in which lay a newly hatched bird. Elated over her find and wishing to make a present of it to her grandmother, she carefully took the nest and proudly carried it home. On seeing what the child had done, the grandmother cut off a switch and punished her until the blood ran from her legs. Crying with pain, she was directed to take the nest to the exact branch where she had found it and never again to molest this bird, as it was sacred to her clan."[5]

With climate change, hummingbirds seem to be appearing in greater numbers in the United States and are expanding northward like the tufted titmouse and several other songbirds.* Do Mayan rules apply everywhere? It depends, but I wouldn't take any chances.

Rainbow Warriors

All hummingbirds have coloration that is at least slightly reminiscent of the rainbow, some more than others. The ruby-throated hummingbird is almost unreal looking with its bright shimmering colors, as if it were molded out of rainbows rather than clay. While this has led to associations with joy, sensuality, and the visual arts, there is a profound shamanistic significance to the rainbow that the hummingbird shares as well.

Rainbows reference the uniting of the four races of humanity—red, yellow, black, and white, the so-called rainbow race. This was mentioned in ancient prophecies, which were made before the time of Christopher Columbus. It refers to a time when all the races of the world will intermarry on Turtle Island, that is North America, and their children will usher in the Eighth Fire, a time of peace and harmony with nature.

But a deeper meaning of the rainbow is that it is a bridge connecting earth and sky, the spiritual and material worlds. Those on the spiritual path are pledged to help creation continue, and to do this, they need to be at home in both worlds and also need to have a way to get back and forth between these two realms. In the classic text *Shamanism*, Mircea Eliade notes that a considerable number of cultures around the world see the rainbow as a bridge connecting earth and sky; the bridge of the Gods. He writes, "It is always by the way of the rainbow that mythical

---

*According to several sources, the tufted titmouse's original territory was as far north as New Jersey. Now it is found in Canada year-round.

heroes reach the sky. Thus for example, in Polynesia the Maori hero Tawhaki and his family, and the Hawaiian hero Aukelenuiaiku, regularly visit the upper regions by climbing the rainbow or by means of a kite, to deliver the souls of the dead, or to meet their spirit-wives. The same mythical function of the rainbow is found in Indonesia, Melanesia, and Japan."[6] Among Native Americans, there are similar stories to be found, and the tiny rainbow emblazoned across the chest of this little bird indicates that this is a spiritual hero from the highest realms.

The ribbon shirts, or prayer shirts, worn by elders of Algonkin-ode, Haudenosaunee, Cherokee, and sometimes Lakota nations, embody the prayers of the six and, of course, seven directions, with a rainbow of ribbons emblazoned across the chest, not unlike a hummingbird. They employ the colors of the rainbow because a prayer is the greatest bridge between heaven and earth. It is our rainbow to the sky. Of course, the rainbow also brings us back down to earth again.

Siberian shamans also use ribbons and call them rainbows, which in their Altaic language also means bridge because they represent the shaman's skyward journey. Rainbows are painted on their ceremonial drum, which is also called a bow, as its magic launches the shaman to the celestial realms like an arrow. In fact, the drum may be the rainbow, the celestial bridge, in some cases.[7] To me, seeing a hummingbird is like saying a thousand prayers to the rainbow spirit, the bridge to the spirit world.

SEAGULLS

Seagull the Magician

In Caribbean cultures such as the Taino, and other Native cultures as well, seagulls are considered ancestors, especially when they appear far inland. (See color insert, plate 20.) Seagulls are a lot like crows, but are bringers of good tidings, at least more often than crows. Seagulls talk to you, they tell stories and jokes, share teachings, offer gifts, and are among the most playful of birds. They can be there one minute, gone the next, appearing and vanishing at will. Seagulls stare into the fierce wind and laugh—*ha, ha, ha, ha, ha!* They steer you on the right path, but rarely scold like their brothers the crows.[8] They are remarkable fishermen, acrobats, and clowns.

The nations of Long Island Sound seem to have a genuine affection for seagulls, and good thing—there are so many to be found there. Raymundo Rodriguez, a Nissequogue from North Shore Long Island, always made it a habit to feed and talk to seagulls as he was growing up near the place where the Nissequogue River meets Long Island Sound. He fed them french fries, hamburger, bread, crackers, chicken feed, and, once in a while, real store-bought seafood he had boosted from the dinner table leftovers the night before to use as bait! The gulls, unfairly labeled bandits because they will speed by and grab a sandwich from the hand of someone they don't like, especially enjoyed the purloined delicacies from the sea. These included not only scallops and the highly prized gulf shrimp, but local rock shrimp, popcorn shrimp, and other seafood treats.

When he graduated from high school, Raymundo received a beautiful gold Cross ballpoint pen from his maternal uncle and namesake Raymond Wheeler, who later became tribal chief of the Nissequogue.

It became a treasured possession. In his first year at college, Raymundo was walking from his lab class in marine biology to his car at the other end of a large parking lot. Two friends were walking with him. Suddenly, the three boys heard a loud screaming and cawing behind them and spun around, looking up into the sky. Swooping down behind them were three seagulls in formation. The outside two birds were cawing as loud as they could, but the central figure had something sticking out of his mouth, the golden pen. The bird had the pen lodged carefully in his throat; he dropped his head and the pen hit Raymundo on the bridge of his nose and then fell into the cradle between his arms and his three-ring vinyl binder called a Trapper Keeper, a name that suddenly became more significant.

He had dropped the pen before entering the parking lot and was receiving a teaching to be more mindful of taking care of his things, a friendly reminder, delivered in elegant seagull style. He grabbed the pen and held it up to the sky, thanking the seagulls for their assistance.

In fact, seagulls have a remarkable memory for faces, and according to *The Sibley Guide to Bird Life and Behavior,* can recognize a human they have not seen in ten or more years.[9] These birds apparently remembered Raymundo from years ago when he fed them all that store-bought gulf shrimp as a child. Seagulls never forget.

I heard a story from a sailor who rescued an injured seagull once and nursed it back to health over a summer on the sea. During that time of rehabilitation, the seagull and sailor became quite close, and the gull would often perch on the man's right shoulder to get a better view of the sea. The seagull healed, and as the weather cooled, it flew away. But each autumn, that bird finds that sailor wherever he may be floating on the Atlantic Ocean and drops by to sit on his right shoulder. They watch the sea together, feed each other, and share recollections of old times.

Seagulls in the Interior

Raymundo continued to feed seagulls wherever he traveled and continued to find them his helpers. They would find him even far inland, where the presence of a seagull seems to take on special significance. Recently, while on a trip near Bancroft, a town north of Algonquin Park Ontario, thousands of miles from the sea, he had another strange experience with seagulls. He had been seeing loons and geese and ducks, but no gulls. He got up early the next morning to take a walk at sunrise. There were no birds in the motel parking lot, as he trudged across it on his way to take a walk in the nearby forest. When he returned an hour later, there were three gulls in the parking lot, and the lot was covered with seagull feathers. However the three gulls did not seem to be missing any. He stooped and picked up dozens of these feathers and brought them inside to show his chums. An hour and a half later, he brought his friends out to see the remaining feathers, to gawk and stare at the great numbers of feathers lying there, but they were all gone. There were no gulls left, and not a single seagull feather remained.

Tony Moon Hawk, an Unkechaug, also grew up on Long Island, near the Forge River, and remembers its seagulls fondly. Certain kinds of baitfish would come in toward shore in swarms; these fish were an important catch for the Unkechaug but were invisible from the shore. To catch them, the Unkechaug watch their allies, the seagulls. When they see the seagulls start diving for the small fish, the Unkechaug go out in their canoes and catch them from the same spot and have a good haul. They use the fish for bait but eat some of them as well. Tony recounts how seagulls would come into shore when there was a storm at sea. If he was in the city and saw seagulls, he knew a storm was probably approaching from the Atlantic.

Herring gulls are not particularly peaceful birds and have a kind of war dance of sorts. A gull establishing his territory will aim his beak at an opponent, the same posture the bird assumes when pecking another bird in an actual battle. Then the bird will strut several feet closer to the opposing bird in a threatening manner, sometimes even making pecking motions in the air aimed at the other bird.[10] This is a clear territorial signal that the opposing bird should back off. If the stranger does not want a fight, he knows what agonistic signals to make to show respect and even humility. In this way, the aggressive moves of the territorial bird actually prevent rather than instigate conflict. Native Americans, and other indigenous people, have used gestures in battle to show that their intentions are serious, hoping for either a surrender or perhaps a last-minute parley. Some war dances contain nonverbal references not only to human territorial signals, but bird signals as well. William Shakespeare's surname, whether a stage name, pseudonym, or actual surname, refers to an actor who uses this particular gesture, the shaking of a spear, in a mock battle scene, possibly to excess. It doesn't take a genius to see the connection between the seagull's battle pose and the actor's, only the herring gull is usually a better actor.

The average seagull has about ten different kinds of calls, something for every occasion, including a random unpleasant encounter with another bird down at the "raw oyster bar."

Seagulls and Deception

Mi'kmaq people do not believe in tricksters and do not ignore lying and deception. This is one reason why seagulls do not get a blanket approval from Mi'kmaq people, because some are trickier than others. The idea that some birds and certain animals use their signals deceptively has been well established by dozens of ornithologists/zoologists, and yet it is still considered within the realm of theory. Examples of deceptive signals are issuing a food call when there is no food in order to bring a mate closer; issuing a warning call when there is no danger, so that the signaler can have the food for himself; and giving a predator call when being pursued by a member of the same species, so that the other stops and looks around, giving the caller time to escape. Another is the mimicking of poisonous species to scare off attackers. What is interesting from a Native American point of view is that deception is punished in birds and animals by their peers if they themselves have been deceived. According to ornithologist Gisela Kaplan, "Deception is perhaps the most complex form of communication. It can occur only when a communication system is firmly in place and usually functions in a consistent and reliable (referred to as 'honest') fashion. Individuals who are detected signaling dishonestly are punished or their signals are ignored. Deception is a risky form of communication. Its existence suggests the intentionality of communication."[11] She is speaking of birds and animals, but the same could be said of many First Nations communities today in Canada. Although there were no courts and jails in traditional society, there was no need; people who broke the rules were dealt with immediately and in a constructive manner, which sometimes involved what could be called punishment. The perpetrator pays a price in a way that helps restore some measure of dignity to the victim and also teaches skills, values, and trust to the perpetrator. This is now called "restorative justice," very popular among the First Nations of Canada today. The balance of justice is reset, and everyone moves forward.

Seagull and the Fish

I spent each of my childhood summers in Old Orchard Beach, Maine, learning from my great aunt Helen about birds and other highly intelligent beings. I used to walk along the beach alone, pacing the edge of the waves, feeling the sun on my shoulders and the power of the wind in my long hair. Seagulls were everywhere, and I always enjoyed watching them as a boy.

One day, I was walking along, deep in meditation on spiritual matters, and a seagull flew over me and dropped a large fish at my feet, in fact, where I was about to step. Good thing he didn't miss his target! I stopped, of course, and pondered the meaning of this gift, so valuable to the seagulls—the gift of food. It is the gift of life. I picked it up and thanked the seagull, who was already flying in the distance ahead. I asked myself if I was hungry enough to carry the big twisting fish home for supper, but I was not hungry. I decided to save the life of the fish and, walking waist high into the water, threw the creature back into the Atlantic Ocean where it swam away unharmed. I have often wondered what the seagull was thinking, but it was clearly an honor, and I changed my spirit name to Seagull, which is Goeland in French, Gwylan in Welsh, and Glochundeeaitch(eh) in Mi'kmaq. I later learned that some Mi'kmaq lore says that seagulls take food away from other birds, but I know one seagull who was very generous indeed.

I undertook a path of meditation after that, composing poetry as a way of keeping my focus on the spirit world, using Seagull as a pen name. I wrote many poems and songs about seagulls. Needless to say, I was amazed when, the following year, the book *Jonathan Livingston Seagull* came out, first in hardback and then in paperback. As millions of readers did, I found numerous similarities between myself and Jonathan. I continued to look to seagulls for signs, which were many. I wrote a letter to Richard Bach, the author of *Jonathan Livingston Seagull*, explaining some of the coincidences I found in his book. Eventually, I received a charming note, which said, "Thanks for the kind words for Jonathan. Keep flying!" I kept that note in the book, and still have it today . . . somewhere.

One day, while in a sad state, and walking along that same stretch of beach to lift my spirits, I found a dead seagull, rolling at the edge of the tide. I was growing up, learning that nothing lasts forever and that endings can bring sorrow to those who are attached to that which passes away. I buried the dead bird in the sand. At thirty-four, I was given the name Chipmunk, Abachbahametch, by a Mi'kmaq elder and was told to let go of Seagull, which does not rank as a bird of power in Mi'kmaq tradition. I let it go, but the power I have seen in seagulls is not forgotten, nor have I forgotten the seagull's precious gift, a big fish!

Just recently I told the story of the generous seagull to a Maine relative and described the exact spot where the fish landed. After forty years of wondering, the missing puzzle piece appeared at last. In response to my story, I was told that my Mi'kmaq grandfather, whom I never knew, used to walk to that same spot early each morning and toss a pinch of tobacco into the Atlantic Ocean as an offering to the Great Spirit. That was his special spot, his power spot, his secret place.* Now I wonder if that seagull was guided by him to come back to say hello.

---

*Anthropologists talk about shamans identifying power spots, but Forrest Carter in the book *The Education of Little Tree* writes about the importance of having a *secret place* (see Carter, p. 203) and talks of being made clean there by the presence of birds. Most of the seagull photos included in this book were taken near my grandfather's secret place, by his great-granddaughter Becky, who was named after his mother-in-law.

SPARROWS

The Faith of the Sparrow

Some urban dwellers mistakenly think that birds aren't aware that humans hang bird feeders and so they never realize where the food comes from. According to a half-dozen people I interviewed, nothing could be further from the truth; just try *not* filling the bird feeder and see what happens! Grandmother White Wolf has a long kitchen window that looks out over an evergreen hedge. Early in the spring, she takes dime-size pieces of bread and, reaching deep into the branches of the hedge, squeezes the bread into the Y of the branches, well hidden inside the hedge. The first time she did it, she wondered if the sparrows, common visitors to her window, would ever find the hidden treasure, or if they found it, would enjoy eating it.

She hid the bread several times, then stopped doing her job, thinking, perhaps, it wasn't making a difference. She looked out her window one snowy morning, and there was a whole line of hungry faces, a row of sparrows sitting on top of the hedge, staring into the kitchen window, right at her! The expression on their little faces was clear; their body language was speaking volumes, sitting perfectly still with a purposeful intensity, concentrating their eyes on hers. She wasn't doing her job! They had eaten all those hidden provisions and wanted more. It struck her how they were able to convey their concerns to her, even though she wasn't a bird. She promised to start over, this time with some leftover hot dog buns.

Dark Rain Thom, a Shawnee elder, and her husband, noted frontier author James Alexander Thom, have also seen birds lined up, staring at the window, when the bird feeder runs dry of seed.

I have a bird feeder outside my window that is filled with thistle

192

seeds, which attracts gold finches. There are six golden finches that swarm around the feeder every morning. The feeder has only three feeding stations or perches most of the time, so the birds take turns. Three have breakfast, while three sit on nearby tree limbs. After a while, one will swoop down and tap one of the diners on the shoulder; that one jumps up, and like lightning, the other takes his place and starts chowing down, until he, too, is tapped and returns to his limb. All six replace each other in endless combinations, similar to a musical composition that never quite repeats. This aerobatic square dance can go on for hours, but the swapping of positions happens quicker than the eye can see, somewhat like the switching of positions of electrons in an atomic ring. Their dance reveals something about the nature of the universe, but exactly what I haven't a clue. It is only my job to replace the thistle seed when it gets down to empty, which doesn't take that long, and observe the fluttering of golden wings with admiration. When I fail to fill the feeder, the goldfinches know who to blame! There are over three hundred types of finches, so they symbolize variety.

Sparrows, especially house sparrows, are very common birds, but that is no reason to ignore the recent concern over cell transmitters and their effects on house sparrows. Because of their light construction and size and the fact that they are "high nesters" (they prefer to build their nests in the eaves of houses) the radiation from cell transmitters causes them to die or disappear from the area in greater numbers than other species. This happened recently in Scotland, where a major disappearance of house sparrows forced the nation to remove or redesign all cell towers in suburban and urban regions. The sparrows then returned. A Native American friend named Geneviva told me that when she found a dead sparrow at a gas station, she got a message from the Great Spirit to pick it up, take it home, and give it a full burial. Spirit told her, "It is noble to be ordinary." It was a timely message, as the studies done in Scotland and elsewhere in Europe have not been widely discussed in North America, where there is a yet greater density of such towers.

Water Wings

Many birds love washing themselves in creative ways. My friend Janet has reported two recent sightings of birds cleansing themselves in imaginative ways. A rain shower had created a deep pool of water on top of an unused section of vinyl roofing that was sitting in her yard, curved in a way to create a basin. A hawk landed and spontaneously began bathing in the accidental pool that was created. He was ducking his head under the water and splashing the water under his wings and over his back. Without seeing his tail, it was impossible for Janet to tell if it was a Cooper's hawk or a sharp-shinned hawk, but it was unusual behavior for a hawk, even on a hot day.

Yet more recently, on the second of two 100-plus-degree afternoons, she was watering a garden with a spray nozzle, creating long arcing flumes of water across the yard. Three house sparrows flying in close formation flew through the center of the spray at high speed, causing a splash in midair that helped hose down the sprayer as well as the sprayed. Delighted with their free hose down, they made a U-turn, whipped around, and went through the spray again, and then several more times for good measure. All the while, the sparrows were twittering excitedly, making a lot of noise like giggling children making the most of an open fire hydrant. It was a playful moment in interspecies history.

Some small birds are quite clever. One news report described house sparrows hovering in front of the electric eye sensors at the entrances to grocery stores, cafés, and other places where food might lie unguarded, causing the automatic doors to open and close so that they could steal food. I have also heard that black-capped chickadees and red-breasted nuthatches can tell if a sunflower seed is empty or full solely by weight.

LOONS

The Songs of the Loon

There is a story about a Native American mother who took her two sons to swim in a deep lake. One of the sons ventured too far out into the middle of the lake, while she wasn't watching, and disappeared from view. The mother called and called, but the son didn't return. She and her other son went out in a canoe to look for him, but he was gone. Twilight came, and still the son did not return. The mother's calls for him to come back became filled with mournful longing and sorrow. Finally, she turned into a loon so that she could look down on the waters from above and continues to cry out to him, even though she knows by now he is drowned.

The loon has a large vocabulary, and twelve registered cries, most of them filled with mournful longing. Mother loons also carry their children on their backs, between their wings while swimming. This piggyback style helps create a strong bond between parent and child and helps the tiny baby loon get a broader perspective on life on the lake, while remaining safe from harm. The mother loon won't take any chances after losing her first mythical son in the drowning incident mentioned in the story.

The Canadian dollar is called a loonie because there is a picture of a loon in flight engraved on each one. Canada takes great pride in its mournful loons. Loons are the oldest species of birds in North America and have been here millions of years. The Ojibway teachings say that the loon was the first creature to come here after the waters receded. The first sound in creation was the call of the loon. That's why it touches our hearts and our souls. It is our grandfather. When the rains stopped and the clouds first parted, the sun reflected off the waters. The dappled light reflected onto the body of the loon, giving its feathers a dappled look, which is still there to this day, so that we always remember the bird who saw the beginnings of the world as we know it.[12] On or about December 1, loons fly straight over Lake Ontario for New York. Lake Ontario has become home to thousands of cormerands, which are fierce birds (as described in both Shakespeare and Corinthians) who were introduced to Canada in the 1920s and are not indigenous. They are natural predators of and competitors with the gentle loons and tend to gang up on them. This fact makes it necessary for the loons to travel nonstop over Lake Ontario each winter, on their way south.

There are numerous dangers to Canada's official bird both in the United States and in Canada itself, but it is not too late. Grandfather William Commanda was outspoken in the defense of this ancient creature until his passing in 2011, but to this day there are no loon protection societies in Canada. There is a legend that England will never fall as long as there are ravens in the Tower of London. Those ravens are very well tended, for that reason. Maybe someone should spread similar rumors about Canada and its loons.

Loon Society

A long time ago, a male elder sat beside a beautiful lake, watching a fire he was keeping for a visiting group of clan mothers from the far north, who were conducting a private ceremony at the top of the hill. All of a sudden, a group of nine loons began to dance in the air in front of him, calling out their mysterious loon songs as they soared and dived. They did not tire, or leave to do other loon things, but kept dancing for an extraordinarily long time.

The clan mothers were there to initiate a young woman into their clan, a coming-of-age ceremony for her, but the fire tender did not know more than that. The loons finally left. A moment later, the head clan mother came down the hill, her work finally finished. As she thanked him, he told her that he had seen nine loons dancing and gave her a look, as if to ask, "Does that mean anything to you?"

The distinguished clan mother simply smiled and said, "We're Loon Clan!"

Loons at Risk

This important notice was posted on a Department of Environmental Conservation (DEC) sign at Meacham Lake, in the Adirondack Mountains of New York state:

> Please keep your distance from nesting loons or loons with chicks. Motorboats, personal watercraft, canoes, and kayaks can flood loons from their nests, leaving eggs vulnerable to predators, chilling, overheating, or abandonment. Loon nests are right on the water's edge and can be flooded by boatwash. Boats and other watercraft can disrupt parental care and feeding of young. Please enjoy and respect this symbol of wilderness by staying as far away as possible, leaving them more room if they vocalize or show signs of fear.
>
> Loons are a Species of Special Concern in New York State. Loons, their chicks, and nest sites are fully protected by state and federal laws. If you observe a loon being harassed or injured, please contact the DEC.
>
> Please use alternatives to lead fishing sinkers and jigs. Loons and other water birds swallow pebbles to help grind up and digest food. Unfortunately, they can also swallow lead tackle among stones on the lake bottom, or that is attached to a fish that has broken free from an angler's line. Swallowing a single lead sinker or jig can kill a loon or other water bird. Please use caution.

You do not have to see a loon to be a danger to one, so even if you don't notice them, be mindful of their presence. They are ancient allies.

PARROTS

Parrots are a bird to be reckoned with. One person I know says they are the crown of creation, outranking humans. After all, some live longer than most of us, they can speak foreign languages (such as English and other human tongues), and are intelligent enough to have a measurable IQ by human standards. The wild parrots of Telegraph Hill in San Francisco have been featured in films, but many other parrot communities exist all over the United States. Etaoqua, a Mohican woman, and a few other Natives from New York have stated that before the coming of the white man, parrots and other flamboyant birds were common in the state. Etaoqua says the Pennacook (conventionally translated as "at the bottom of the hill") of the Merrimack River valley in New Hampshire and Massachusetts are also called the bird tribe of the Mohicannuk (traditional name of the Mohican) Confederacy, because, while *pen* means "hill," *pin* means "bird" in Mohican. Algonquian place and tribal names often have many layers of meaning; the language lends itself to word play and ambiguity, which is a great source of pride and enjoyment for these highly verbal people. There is a legend that they are called the bird tribe because they "come from another planet"; however, this has yet to be confirmed by anthropologists and historians.

Table Talk

Parrots are among the most sensitive of birds, and according to Native Americans from many eastern nations, they were originally North American as well as South American citizens. Parrots love freedom and only pull out their own feathers when in captivity. Etaoqua says that the Mohican have stories and legends about parrots and were familiar with multicolored birds before contact with Europeans. The Nissequogue say the same thing. Parrots can also ruff their feathers to an almost horizontal position when they are on the defensive. This can make them appear twice their normal size, in order to discourage predators.[13]

A down-to-earth woman I know named Victoria loves animals and birds. She has lived with a lilac-crowned Amazon parrot for twenty-eight years. The parrot was not restricted to a cage, but sometimes sat on a perch, a piece of furniture, or Victoria's shoulder. One day after a death in the family, Victoria was sitting at the table crying. The parrot was perched on the other end of the table. The parrot walked across the table and placed her foot [hand?] on top of Victoria's hand and held it there for a while. The parrot had a lot to say most of the time, but this was the first time Victoria had cried in the presence of the bird, and the first time the parrot had made this universal inter-species gesture of "I understand" and moved to console the human. At times like these, no words need to be spoken—even between parrots and people.

Parrots Are Our Friends (Perry the Parrot)

Lindsay, who has long been a part of Ottawa's Native community, recently lost a friend of almost twenty-five years. He was a parrot named Perry, a mitred conure from Peru. Lindsay and his wife, Sandy, rescued the bird in the fall of 1985 from a careless owner, who had mistreated him more out of ignorance than malice.

For the first month, Perry wouldn't allow anyone to get close, until Lindsay reached into the cage one day and touched him on the nose. It would have been hard to guess who was more surprised. The bird then decided that Lindsay was all right, and a friendship blossomed.

Perry adopted Lindsay as family and would regurgitate half-digested food for him, as a mother bird would do for a chick. Lindsay appreciated the thought, but didn't really wish to accept the honor. Perry figured this out, and then just went through the motions, eating the birdie porridge himself.

Perry was smart and had a sense of humor, a sense of the fun, funny, and incongruous. He was very playful; he would stick his head into Lindsay's mouth like a lion tamer and pull it out again, bobbing with amusement.

Lindsay gradually learned Perry's language and behavior. In the last two years of his life, the bird decided that he wanted to know more about his person. He would sit on Lindsay's knee, studying him intently. Lindsay would affectionately grasp Perry's beak between his thumb and forefinger. Perry ultimately returned the gesture by holding Lindsay's nose with his foot.

Perry even taught himself to laugh: When Lindsay was reading something humorous or watching a television comedy and would chuckle, Perry would join in with his own little "cluck-cluck-cluck." This was just imitation at first. However, he soon understood the context. He would do something on his own that he regarded as funny and accompany it with a happy "cluck-cluck-cluck."

Perry was so much more than this. In the end, the bird and the man had become inseparable and could "read" each other completely.

Perry passed into the spirit world on July 31, 2010, and left an empty space in the family. The teaching that comes from such special friends is that we are not that different from each other, whether we are a human being, bird, or any of the Creator's creatures.

Parrot Liberation

Parrots, parakeets, and cockatiels are freedom-loving birds, but they are rarely free of captivity in North America. Almost all of them are store-bought. They try to escape even the best of masters and occasionally succeed. When they do, they tend to find each other and congregate in secret communities in suburban or even urban parks. There is such a park in Bed-Stuy in Brooklyn (and at Brooklyn College, where the monk parakeet has become an unofficial mascot) surprisingly enough. There is also one in Edgewater, New Jersey, where there is an extraordinarily high population of monk parakeets, or Quaker parrots; at least two hundred of them live free of cages but are also forced to find their own food. Members of the family are highly social creatures who groom and preen each other and are accustomed to much physical contact and prolonged attention from each other. The so-called lovebird is a member of the parrot family, so it is not surprising they congregate in such large numbers. As it turns out, kissing is yet another courtship ritual that humans learned from birds, something parrots do in many enthusiastic styles and positions. They share this need for cuddling with their human captors and yet need to break free as well, so by the time they reach Edgewater, they are also watching out for their former owners, who may be lurking in the bushes with butterfly nets, trying to rewin their lost feathered loves. There is some evidence to support a theory that parrots were once indigenous to New York state and the Eastern Seaboard in general. If so, these birds are simply returning to the land their ancestors roamed before the era of pet stores and bird feed.

Alison Evans-Fragale is not only a board member of the Brooklyn Parrot Society but is also the founder of the Edgewater Parrots organization. For the last several years, she has been spearheading a movement to remove the monk parakeet from the New Jersey Potentially Dangerous Species list, a smear on the character of these birds, which have been on the books since the 1970s. On May 22, 2006, Bill A1237 was unanimously passed to remove the name monk parakeet (Quaker parrot) from New Jersey's most-wanted list, with a vote of 77 to 0, thanks in part to Alison's grassroots work in getting petitions signed.*

---

*According to an article in *City Parrots: Urban Parrot Conservation*, dated December 12th, 2012, titled "Volutneers Work to Provide Temporary Nests for Edgewater Parakeets," nearly half of the two hundred parakeets in Edgewater will need shelter as many of the trees they live in are being cut down for various reasons. I visited Veteran's Memorial Park on December 16th, 2012, and the nests had all been removed. Volunteers are now creating makeshift shelters elsewhere. (http://cityparrots.org/journal/2012/12/12/volunteers-work-to-provide-temporary-nests-for-edgewater-mon.html.)

The Edgewater parrots live in large nests that range in size from that of a basketball to that of a living-room sofa, the latter of which can accommodate dozens of birds. In the winter, the birds favor nests built around transformer boxes. The state knocks those nests down, saying that they are fire hazards; however, the birds do seem to have trouble with Jersey's winter weather, which can be harsh, without the warming glow of a transformer box to keep them comfy. Evans-Fragale insists that the nests do not cause transformer fires. At least one such fire was proven to be the result of sabotage; a lit cigarette had been placed in the nest, and monk parakeets are strict nonsmokers. These parrots need clay drawn from cliffs to assist in the digestion of food, and Edgewater is near Cliffside and the Palisades cliffs, which provide plenty of clay.

One cockatiel owner describes how her captive bird likes to hook claws onto a giant rotating fan in her living room and hang upside down, with its chest against the front of the wire mesh of the faceguard. When the fan is on full blast, the small, lightweight bird can lift its wings and start to fly like an eagle without actually going anywhere, except left to right to left, as the great wind machine rotates. The cockatiel can continue with this fantasy for some time, at least until someone unplugs the fan.

Parrots and cockatiels can be cocky, however. One parrot owner, Tina Powell, tells me that her parrot will imitate her voice calling the dog, saying, "Here, Blue! Here puppy!" The puppy comes, and the parrot bites his nose so hard the dog goes running to its owner yelping. Ten minutes later, the same thing will occur again; the dog hears Tina's voice calling him by name, and the perky puppy, forgetting all about what happened last time, falls into the trap yet again.

Parrots have sensitive lungs and cannot deal with the airborne household toxins we take for granted. Burning an empty Teflon pan on the range breaks down the Teflon and creates a gas that can kill a parrot. The same is true with the Teflon coating on microwave popcorn bags. If you overheat them and burn the popcorn, the Teflon will emit gasses that can kill parrots. Scented candles are also a life-threatening hazard to a parrot. As the candle wax burns, the oils break down to emit the scent, but also other gasses as well, some of which are very harmful to parrots. Chocolate, avocado, and other common foods can be deadly to parrots as well. So before sharing a candlelit dinner of Chinese stir-fry with salad and after-dinner mints followed by popcorn and a movie with your parrot, please consult with your veterinarian.

TURKEYS

Recent studies led by archaeologist Camilla Speller have revealed that the Aztecs were the first to domesticate the turkey—about 2,000 years ago.

As Native Americans have long known, turkeys are good birds for food. They are very efficient, with mostly meat and little fat, and they have very little waste in proportion to their body weight. When you feed them, you're feeding yourself. They tend not to migrate, which is why, according to Heckewelder, the Lenape called the Unalatchtigo the "turkey clan" because they stayed in one place. The Lenape honored the turkey because it "stayed with them and about them."[14]

Turkeys like chestnut trees, and this was one of the reasons Native Americans cultivated this tree as one of the sacred groundnut trees. Unfortunately, most of them have died of blight. There is a type of chestnut tree that is immune to the blight called a *chinkapin*. It sheds thousands of small sweet chestnuts, which turkeys like just as much. If you have one in your yard, and you are in a rural area, you will attract wild turkeys. Turkeys also eat clover, acorns, nuts, grasshoppers, ticks, and other bugs. Moths and butterflies with eyelike *ocelli* patterns on their wings are more likely to survive a gaggle of hungry turkeys; as the turkeys approach, the moth or butterfly turns its back and spreads its wings, revealing a "face" to the turkey. The turkey will be drawn to the moth's "eyes" and end up with a mouthful of wing and no moth. It may even look enough like another raptor, such as an owl, to scare away the predator. It is one of nature's more clever defense weapons, one the moth has no control over making, but one which it wields masterfully.[15]

Turkeys are called ground eagles, because they rarely fly. But this ground eagle can run, and it uses its wings for gliding in between runs. It can glide ten or fifteen feet down a slope after building up some speed. Rainbow Weaver, a Mohawk ceremonial elder, says that the Creator made the "ground eagle" as a lesson to the American eagle, saying, "You may think you're the most powerful bird on the planet, and can fly high as you want to. But I want you to remember that sooner or later, you will have to come back to Earth to eat and to rest. Every living thing needs that connection with Mother Earth, and that includes you. So don't get so full of yourself that you forget to take care of the Earth, or I will turn you into a ground eagle!"

The turkey is also called the giveaway bird, because it provides so much food with little resistance to the hungry. Natives may associate the turkey with the Apache people, because the most famous turkey story by far is from the Apache. Here is a version of it. As you will see, it shows the turkey to be the most generous of birds, providing food for all—symbolically, at least.

An Apache Legend

Long ago when all the animals talked like people, Turkey overheard a boy begging his sister for food. "What does your younger brother want?" he asked the girl.

"He's hungry, but we have nothing to eat," she said.

When Turkey heard this, he shook himself all over. Many kinds of fruits and wild food dropped out of his feathers, and the brother and sister ate these up. Turkey shook himself again, and a variety of large corn dropped out. He shook himself a third time and yellow corn fell—and then a fourth time, which revealed white corn.

Turkey said to the boy and girl, "I have four kinds of corn seeds here for you, and this is a good place to plant them."

The sister and brother cut digging sticks and made holes with them. In the holes they planted the corn seeds. The next day the corn had already come up and was about a foot and a half high.

The brother and sister were inspired to be generous, just like the turkey, and gave away some of their seeds to other people. Today we see this spirit of generosity in the giveaway ceremony that takes place at every powwow.

THUNDERBIRDS

As mentioned before, Sitting Bull gained power from his dreams about the thunderbird and wrote several songs about them. No collection of Native American stories about birds would be complete without discussing these mythopoetic creatures. Much of the teachings about these multidimensional creatures are kept secret, but the basic story is well known. It is their wings that create thunder, according to children's tales. But there is also a story about a young man who was filled with virtue and never told a lie. He was so popular among the people that some of the leaders feared him as a threat to their power and captured him and tied him up to a tree, and then burned him alive. They left him there to die, leaving a big pile of ashes. After the ashes had cooled, a giant thunderbird rose from the ashes and flew around, helping the people and answering their prayers. There are many variations on this story, but some will say that the thunderbird is the Native American avatar, or even Jesus in another form. It is a story so old that thousands of variations have been created over the years as teaching tales. It is not only the Thor-like god of thunder, but also the one who has risen from the dead.

In the book *Dreamers without Power: The Menominee,* an interviewed elder says, after recalling that the sun was the first to be created:

> The Great Spirit saw the Indians, his people; he did not like what was happening; the Indian being killed [by bad spirits and animals]. The Great Spirit thought it over . . . "Well, instead I will make some ones to watch over these, my children . . ." Then he probably made the Thunderbirds. He put them over here; he put them everywhere. He put the Thunderbirds, large birds, to watch over these

Indians. They would speak to them and feed them, in order that the Thunderbirds should look after them carefully, so that they might be allowed to live well; that everything would grow abundantly here for them to eat, that the Thunderbirds would water [everything] with the water they carry—that it would rain properly so that everything would be wet—that is what the old people probably would pray for.[16]

A Menominee man interviewed by Alanson Skinner in 1921 said, "Beneath the Supreme Being, in descending order . . . are three tiers of bird-like deities. First . . . come the Thunderbirds, gods of war."[17]

Elsewhere, Menominee elders said that they thought of the universe as divided into strata, of which Earth is only one, with various deities in relationship with each other. According to the book, Dreamers without Power, "The residents of the upper strata . . . were friendly to man, or at least could be placated by him. The Thunderers, in the level just before Me-c-awe-tok, the supreme force in the universe, were especially friendly to man, and waged unceasing war against the horned serpents, who were man's most consistent persecutors."[18]

In this same book is a diagram of an old birch-bark scroll collected by Alanson Skinner in 1913. The bottom strip, read from right to left, depicts, first, the village of the thunderbirds in the sky, then their leader Wickano and the powerful wind and clouds he controls. Then we see Wickano resting, then the rain that belongs to the thunderers, then Wickano again, near a tornado, the clouds behind which the thunderbirds stalk their prey, and finally a thunderer pouncing on an evil serpent from the underworld. Apparently, songs were sung to punctuate the stories on the birch bark as they were told.[19]

PART 5

FLEDGLING
THOUGHTS

GATHERING FEATHERS

It is well known that Native Americans have many traditions about the use of found feathers, but as I stated earlier, the significance of the feather is all about the significance of the bird. But now that we have discussed a number of living birds, we can enjoy a few handfuls of stories about their feathers.

The Miami and Mascoutens used a ceremonial calumet, or pipe, decorated and enhanced with feathers, when they welcomed Nicholas Perrot to their village near Green Bay, Wisconsin in 1670. This account is by Bacqueville de La Potherie, a late seventeenth-century French historian of the New World:*

The old man held in his hand a calumet of red stone, with a long stick at the end; this was ornamented in its whole length with the heads of birds, flame-colored, and had in the middle a bunch of feathers colored a bright red, which resembled a great fan. As soon as he espied the leader of the Frenchmen, he presented to him the calumet, on the side next to the sun; and uttered words which were apparently addressed to all the spirits whom those people adore. The old man held it sometimes toward the east, and sometimes toward the west; then toward the sun; now he would stick the end in the ground, and then he would turn the calumet around him looking at it as if he were trying to point out the whole earth, with expressions which gave the Frenchman to understand that he had compassion

---

*Full name, Claude Charles le Roy Bacqueville de la Potherie, he wrote *History of the Savage Peoples Who are Allies of New France,* published in Paris in 1716, and quoted throughout Kinietz's *Indians of the Western Great Lakes, 1615–1760.* La Potherie relied on the accounts of French explorers and missionaries such as Perrot.

on [for] all men. Then he rubbed with his hand Perrot's head, back, legs, and feet, and sometimes his own body. This welcome lasted a long time, during which the old man made a harangue, after the fashion of a prayer, all to assure the Frenchman of the joy which all in the village felt at his arrival.[1]

Kinietz quotes Colonel Christopher Gist, who explored Ohio between 1750–51 and was among the first to note the names of the six divisions of the Miami. He describes the warrior's feather dance, as performed by three dancing masters, whose bodies were painted various colors. The dancers held long sticks in their hands, on the ends of which were fastened long feathers of swans and other birds, neatly woven into the general shape of bird wings. Gist reports that

[i]n this Disguise they performed many antick Tricks, waving their Sticks and Feathers about with great Skill to imitate the flying and fluttering of Birds, keeping exact time with their Musick; while they are dancing, some of the Warriors strike a Post, upon which the Musick and Dancers cease, and the Warrior gives an Account of his Achievements in War, and when he has done, throws down some Goods as a Recompense to the Performers and Musicians; after which they proceed in their Dance as before till another Warrior strikes ye Post, and so on as long as the Company think fit.[2]

I had the good fortune of seeing, at age fifteen, a Lakota-style war bonnet, modeled by my great aunt Helen. Aunt Helen grew up close to the family of a Native American trapper called John Rolfe. His wife made young Helen a full suit of buckskin with a beaded fringe shirt, which she showed me in the 1960s when I was a child. The Rolfes also made her the Lakota-style headdress (popular among Mi'kmaqs then), which trailed below her knees, made from the feathers of the great blue heron. When Aunt Helen put that colorful war bonnet on her head and asked me, "How do I look?," I was speechless.

My great aunt Helen, after graduating from high school, had to take a job in a country store, catering to tourists. She soon created a series of oil paintings of the five tribes of Maine that depicted chiefs wearing headdresses fashioned from sparrow feathers and sold them for fifty cents apiece. Today, the use of feathers in Native American craftwork has become quite diversified.

FEATHERS IN ARROWS, FANS, AND BADGES

Each species of bird has its own qualities, and this extends to the feathers it leaves behind. In fact, it extends to the crafting of arrows, whose fletching is made from feathers. As regards the Yuchi, Frank G. Speck, an American anthropologist who specialized in the Algonquian, Iroquoian, and other First Nations peoples, commented, in his *Ethnology of the Yuchi Indians* (1909):

> The arrows are feathered preferably with hawk feathers, as the Indians believe the hawk to be swift and sure in its flight.... Turkey tail feathers are much used also. The split plumes, two in number, are bound to the shaft at both ends with sinew. One side of the feather is shaved clean of ribs up to within an inch of the outer end. The lower or base end of the quill is then lashed on flat. The outer end is turned down and the turned down length is lashed on. In this way an ingenious twist is given to the feather, which causes the arrow to revolve in its flight, acting on the principle of the rifle bullet.[3]

Among the Creek, eagle feathers were made into fans and used in ceremonies. Breechcloths were ornamented with eagle talons and claws. Eagle feathers were used, but in Virginia, a whole hawk skin was stuffed and buzzard wings were used to embellish a headdress.[4] In traditional times, the Creek used specific feathers as badges of accomplishment or group recognition. A doctor or medicine man might use a vulture or buzzard feather to show that he dressed bullet wounds (as the feather was used to clean them). An owl feather would indicate good night vision. An eagle feather badge was a sign of a great accomplishment, perhaps bravery.[5] Turkey feathers were widely used to make feather cloaks and mantles but were also used to decorate the moccasins of Chickasaw high priests. Swan feathers were worn to show that one was a successful warrior, while crane feathers were used to make head-dresses for certain clans. Pheasant feathers were worn for their orna-mental beauty, and in one case at least, a headdress was made entirely of pheasant feathers—the latter documented in 1705 by Robert Beverley Jr., a historian of early colonial Virginia.[6] Sometimes the Creek would place a single red feather of a cardinal in a headdress, presumably to show authority within local hierarchy. An owl skin could be used as a badge or carried as a symbol of the Creek medicine man or priest. Interestingly, women tended not to wear bird feathers as much as men in Creek culture,[7] much the reverse of mainstream American culture. Creeks also wore bird claws in their ears, something you don't see very often these days.

I know a woman named Phyllis who follows the Red Road. She played viola in the National Arts Centre Orchestra in Ottawa, Ontario, and other groups. Her favorite bird is the loon, whose song is so plaintive—so like the sound of the viola. One day in February, in the National Arts Centre on Rideau Street in downtown Ottawa, she was sitting on the stage during a rehearsal, talking to a colleague, lamenting the fate of music and musicians in the then-twentieth cen-tury. She spoke sadly of the various intrigues that surrounded some of the players and the struggles all musicians have to endure. She looked down, and there was a feather sitting between her feet. As a loon lover, it didn't take her long to recognize what bird it was from. It was a loon badge, the one that honors singers and musicians. More obvi-ously, the badge honors those who lament and sigh about injustice. But how did it get inside the National Arts Centre in the middle of winter? To this day, Phyllis does not have an answer. But clearly, the loons were proud of her as a fellow musician and as a master of the art of lamentation as well.

BIRDS AND COLORS

Birds communicate by sound but are also sensitive to color and visual patterns. The Australian scientist Gisela Kaplan noticed this and conducted an experiment. For thirty days, she wore the same exact clothing when she went into the bird area of her lab in Australia to feed and talk to the birds. The birds recognized and welcomed her. On the thirty-first day, Kaplan wore strikingly different colors and designs, and the birds became upset. She described the reaction of the birds as one of visible fear. No other factors changed: her chatter to the birds was the same. On the thirty-second day, she wore the new clothes again to the bird area, and it brought the same reaction—fear. Then she changed, in front of the birds, from the unfamiliar outfit that had caused such a scandal back to the old familiar one, and the avian controversy disappeared. Trust was restored, and the birds went back to their regular feeding habits, without fear of any particular pattern or color.[8]

One wonders if birds' inability to change the color of their own plumage has made them uncomfortable with our tendency to constantly change ours. I further wonder if some bird shamans, following certain Native American traditions, tend to wear the same colors year after year, or even generation after generation, in order to gain greater acceptance among their avian allies. This is a subject for further discussion and research. Along the same line, one might also wonder what birds think of the various *kastoweh** worn by the People of the Longhouse or Haudenosaunee Confederacy. Kastoweh are

---

*Mohawk speaker Kevin Deer, mentioned earlier, is from Kahnawake, a reserve on the south shore of the St. Lawrence River, opposite Montreal. He spells the word *kastowah*, while John Fadden, a Mohawk speaker from Ahkwesashne, situated on the banks of the St. Lawrence at the junction of the St. Regis and Racquette rivers, spells the same word *kastoweh*. Some other communities spell it *gustoweh*.

traditional fitted hats made of strips of wood covered with feathers. The word *kastoweh* means "flowing/drifting feather" and is based on the Mohawk word *ostosareh,* meaning "feathers." This word is used only for these traditional hats. The generic word for hat in Mohawk would be *isah-nun-wah-re.*

Eagle feathers are always used in these hats, except in the case of the Tuscarora Nation, whose hats sometimes might feature an upright hawk or turkey feather, not an eagle's. The crown of the hat is covered with body feathers, usually the split feathers of turkey and others, and some small wing feathers as well (see facing page, far left drawing). For generations, the Seneca have been wearing kastowehs with a single standing or "skyward" feather. During these same centuries, the Mohawk have worn hats with three standing feathers, (far right drawing) while the Oneida (second from right drawing) have worn similar three-feathered hats, but with one feather pointed downward. The Onondaga wear two feathers, but one is pointed downward (third from right drawing). The Cayuga wear one feather like the Seneca, but it is standing at a 45-degree angle (the feather slants straight back and down; the drawing gives a false impression of pointing to the side). The Tuscarora (fifth from right drawing) arrived last, and either did not adopt a standing feather or featured a hawk or other feather. Yet even in the case of the Tuscarora, the hat is still covered with split body and small wing feathers like the others of the Longhouse.[9]

It is often said that the wearing of these kastoweh makes it easier for the various nations to recognize each other at gatherings. But if Gisela Kaplan's experiment is any indication, there might be more to the story. Birds react strongly to visual patterns and would, over time, be able to identify any hatted Seneca in ceremony from any Mohawk or Onondaga. The next question is, "What would their reaction be?" If birds pass down familiarity with humans intergenerationally as the Longhouse People pass down their kastoweh, would the modern-day hat wearers benefit from the rapport their ancestors had with the winged ones? Those traditional hats might be an invitation for birds to

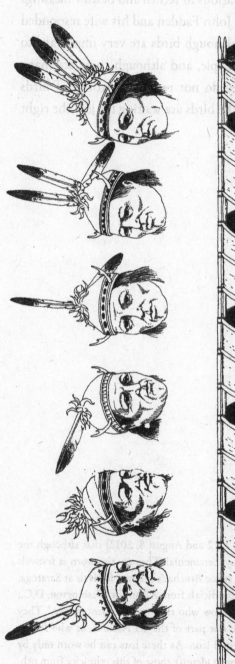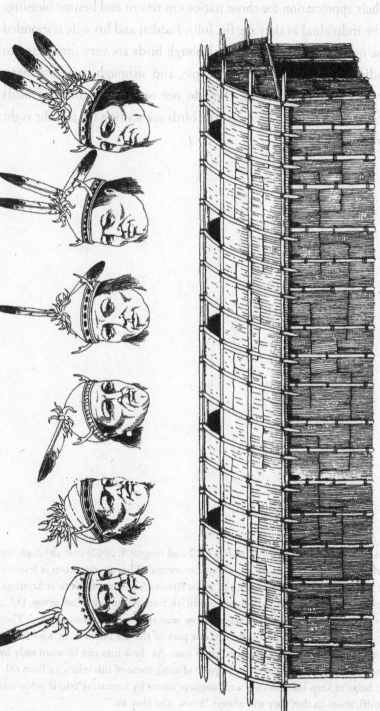

Kastoweh drawing by John Kahionhes Fadden, ©1994

show their appreciation for those nations in return and bestow blessings upon the individual as they see fit. John Fadden and his wife responded to these questions by saying that although birds are very important to the traditions of the Longhouse People, and although there are many bird stories still being retold, they do not recall any stories of birds reacting to the kastoweh. Perhaps the birds are waiting for just the right moment!*

---

*Fadden added in e-mails to me (April 9, 2012 and August 8, 2012) that although the kastoweh are traditional, they are not always ceremonial. They are also worn at festivals that are meant for entertainment, such as at Joe Bruchac's summer festivals at Saratoga, or as a political symbol when meeting with officials from Albany or Washington, D.C.; they are worn to show that the wearers "know who they are, Haudenosaunee." They are also worn by other Iroquois (who are not part of the Six Nations, or who follow a different form of government) as a cultural icon. As these hats can be worn only by Haudenosaunee, the wearing of them helps to identify those of this ethnicity from others, and helps to keep their culture and language intact by increasing ethnic pride and self-identification, so that they will always "know who they are!"

BIRD TOTEMS
FOR WARRIORS

A French explorer of the 1600s named Diliette made the following description of the ritual preparations of a war party of the Miami, an Algonquian-speaking nation of the Wakashan (or "Prairie") Confederacy. It is certainly unusual, so I will insert explanations where necessary in brackets.

"It is ordinarily in February that they prepare to go to war. [The chiefs] invite [as many as fifty men] to a feast and tell them that the time is approaching to go in search of men; so it is well to pay homage, according to their custom, to their birds so that these may be favorable."[10]

My understanding is that each warrior has a protector bird that helps him in battle, and that each warrior therefore has what the Munsee—their close relatives—call an *oot-sik-a-li-kan*, a carved replica of the protector or totem animal, made from wood or stone or possibly ceramic clay. I carried a wooden one in the image of a chipmunk for twenty years. In this case, the effigies were all of birds.

Diliette continues, "They all answer with a loud Ho! And after eating with great appetite they all go to get their mats and spread out their birds on a skin stretched in the middle of the cabin and with the *chichicoyas* they sing a whole night, saying: stone falcon, or crow, I pray to you that when I pursue the enemy I may go with the same speed in running as you do in flying, in order that I may be admired by my comrades and feared by our enemies. At break of day they bring back their birds."[11]

By birds, again he doesn't mean birds that are alive as Westerners think of it. They were again *oot-sik-a-li-kans*, carved into the images of living birds and carrying the spirits of those birds.

Diliette continues and later writes, "I have forgotten to say that the commander carries his mat, into which all of his men have put their birds, along with a good stock of herbs for healing the wounded. As soon as they stop, the chief takes out the birds and, after offering a short prayer to them, sends out three or four of the most active and brave to reconnoiter for the enemy."[12]

The Miami then hide near the enemy and then running at them with astonishing yells. According to Diliette, "they give the same cry as their birds in running after them."

It seems likely that the chief was also using the totemic figures to make sure none of the warriors lost patience with the slow protocol of diplomacy that precedes a war and that they didn't dare go out on a raid without his say so and without their protective bird spirit. If Tecumseh had his brother Tunskwatawa's bird *oot-sik-a-li-kan,* his hummingbird medicine, or his eagle feather in his pouch while he was away looking for his sister, would his brother have prematurely attacked General Harrison at Tippecanoe, thereby losing the war for the Ohio Valley Confederacy? I don't think so!

Diliette was a Jesuit missionary, and wrote of the Illinois, "This nation, as well as the Miami, has no religion. Some have the buffalo, the bear, others the cat, the buck, the lynx, for their [m]anitou. . . . Besides the animals I have already mentioned as *manitous,* they have also several birds which they use when they go to war and to which they cherish much superstition. They use the skins of stone falcons, crows, carrion crows, turtledoves, ducks, swallows, martins, parrots, and many others that I do not name."[13]*

Some of these birds may not have been carvings, but the remains of real birds wrapped in buckskin. Diliette is not clear. The Kickapoo of Mexico today, close relatives of the Miami of the Ohio Valley, still carry clan bundles, approximately two feet in length and six inches in thick-

---

*Though carefully observant of details, Diliette was disrespectful toward indigenous spirituality as he encountered it, and wrote of it seldom. This is alluded to in this passage, which speaks of the nation's "superstition."

ness, and store them in the rafters of their house. These bundles contain a sack of tobacco, a smoking pipe wrapped in cattail mats wrapped in the skin of a fawn, and clay paints, as well as Solomon's seal, also known as sweet medicine. According to the Latorres, these bundles also often include "desiccated parts of . . . birds, humming birds, owls, and feathers of the golden eagle and the sparrow hawk—all of these items containing magical powers and kept in finely tanned fawn skins, tied with thongs of the same material."[14]

It is interesting that birds play such important roles for adult warriors, as many of them were first trained by shooting at birds. According to the Latorres, when a Kickapoo boy is four years old, he is presented with a crude little bow and four bluntly pointed arrows by his father, uncle (his mother's brother, more often than not), or brother. He practices on a rolling metal hoop then tries his hand at birds and other game.

The Latorres continue, "When he kills his first bird with his bow and arrow, he takes it to his father or other male relative with whom he makes his home. The relative hangs the bird from the rafters of the house for safekeeping and goes to kill a deer to hold a feast and ceremony for the young hunter. Returning with a deer, the father speaks with the boy's clan leader." The leader fetes the young man and asks who has killed the bird, and the youngster answers, "I did!" As the Latorres describe, "After the leader and old people each eat a small bite of the bird, the leader prays again, announcing to Kitzihiat that the boy has killed his first game and asking that he be granted health, a long life, and continuous success in the hunt."[15]

THE EAGLE BONE FLUTE

The following story shows the importance of the eagle bone flute to the Omaha people. Its power is recognized far and wide among Native Americans even today. This story, which appears in Fletcher and La Flesche's *Omaha Nation,* was sent to me by Dennis Hastings.

The Te' ithaethe (literally, "buffalo to show compassion," meaning those to whom the buffalo has shown compassion by coming to them in a vision and giving power) society was committed to the knowledge of medicines for the curing of wounds. Membership was accorded to persons of both sexes to whom the buffalo appeared in dreams. The roots of wild anise (*Foeniculum vulgare*), hop (*Humulus lupulus*), and starhair groundcherry (*Physalis viscora*) were used for healing. Bits of these roots were ground between the teeth, then water was taken into the mouth, and the medicated liquid was blown with force into the wound.

The following account . . . details a scene witnessed in [author La Flesche's] boyhood when one of his playmates was accidentally shot by a young man who, with some companions, was firing a pistol at a mark.

After the shooting the excitement was intense, and above all the noise could be heard the heartrending wails of the unfortunate man who had wounded the boy in the head. The relatives of the lad were preparing to avenge his death, and those of the man to defend him. I made my way through the crowd, and peering over the shoulders of another boy, I saw on the ground a little form that I recognized.

Blood was oozing from a wound in the back of the boy's head and from one under the right eye near the nose. A man ordered the women to stop wailing and bade the people to stand back. Soon through an opening in the crowd I saw a tall man wrapped in a buffalo robe come up the hill and pass through the space to where the boy lay. He stooped over the child, felt of his wrist, and then of his heart. "He is alive," the man said. "set up a tent and take him in." The little body was lifted on a robe and carried by two men into a large tent that had been hastily erected. Meanwhile, a young man had been sent in all haste to call the buffalo doctors. Soon they were seen galloping over the hill on their horses, one or two at a time, their long hair flowing over their naked backs. They dismounted, and one by one entered the tent, where they joined the buffalo doctor who lived nearby and had already been called. A short consultation was held. The sides of the tent were drawn up to let in the fresh air and to permit the people to witness the operation.

All the buffalo medicine men sat around the boy, their eyes gleaming over their wrinkled faces. Then one of the men began in a low voice to tell how in a vision he had seen the buffalo which had revealed to him the secret of the medicine and taught him the song he must sing when using it. At the end of every sentence, the boy's father thanked him in terms of relationship. Then he compounded the roots he had taken from his skin pouch and started his song at the top of his voice. The other doctors, some twenty or more, joined in, and sang it in unison with a volume that could be heard a mile away. The song was accompanied by *a bone whistle imitating the cry of the eagle.*

After the doctor had started the song he put the bits of roots into his mouth, ground them with his teeth, and taking a mouthful of water, he approached the boy, bellowing and pawing the earth like an angry buffalo at bay. When near the boy he drew in a long breath, and with a whizzing noise forced the water from his mouth into the wound. The boy spread out his hands and winced as though he had been struck. The man uttered a series of short exclamations:

"Hi! hi! hi!" Then the father and the man who had wounded the boy lifted their outspread hands toward the doctor to signify their thanks. During the administration of the medicine all the men and two women doctors sang with energy the following song, which had been started by the operator:

(Sung in octave unison)

Literal translation: ni u^{n}shka xe (*nia*, part of me, hurt; *u^n*, me, you; *shkaxe*, make-you hurt me); *ego^n*, then; *thethu*, here; *ton*, from; *theathe*, I send; *kombtha*, I want or desire—from here I desire to send it.

A second doctor now repeated the treatment and started his song, all the others joining in the singing as before, while he administered the remedy.

At the completion of the song a third doctor made ready to give his application, starting his song, and all the other doctors joining as before in the singing.

At the end of the song the fourth doctor began to compound the roots, and when he was ready he began the following song, which was taken up by all the others and sung with forceful energy:

Literal translation: *ni*, water; *thu^n*, round; *thade*, to designate; *ama*, they; *uhekethe*, to yield to him; *itheama*, they say.

This song conveys to the Omaha mind a picture of the prairie, the round wallow standing like a pool with water, and the wounded buffalo being healed near it by its companions. There is a belief among the Omaha that the buffalo cure their wounds with their saliva; therefore the doctors prepare the herbs in the mouth and blow the water into the wound.

The doctors remained all night, applying their medicine and dressing the wound.

Four days the boy was treated in this manner. On the evening of the third day the doctors said the lad was out of danger, and that in the morning he would be made to stand and meet the rising sun, and so greet the return of life.

I went to bed early, so as to be up in time to see the ceremony. I was awakened by the sound of the singing, and hurried to the tent. Already a crowd had gathered. There was a mist in the air, as the doctors had foretold there would be, but as the dawn drew nearer the fog slowly disappeared, as if to unveil the great red sun that was just visible on the horizon. Slowly it grew larger and larger. The boy was gently lifted by two strong men, and when on his feet was told to take four steps toward the east, while the doctors sang the mystery song which belonged to this stage of the cure. The two men began to count as the boy feebly attempted to walk—one, two, three. The steps grew slower, and it did not seem as if he could make the fourth, but he dragged his foot and made the fourth. "Four!" cried the men; "It is done." Then the doctors sang the song of triumph.

The fees were then distributed. These were horses, robes, bear-claw necklaces, eagle feathers, embroidered leggings, and other articles of value. Toward these the relatives of the man who shot the boy contributed largely. One or two doctors remained with the boy for a time. In a month or so he was back among us, ready to play or to watch another pistol practice by the young men.[16]

TWELVE BIRDS

Here is a personal story, which illustrates the way birds can guide us spiritually in unexpected ways. On January 8, 2009, I was walking in the snowbound woods at night somewhere in Canada, and I placed tobacco on the snow and asked for guidance from the Great Spirit. I knew that it would be hard to get back to Canada, the land of my ancestors, for a while, and was grateful to be on this northern land again. I said a prayer for all my Canadian friends that I would no longer be able to see due to my intensified schedule in the United States.

While in meditation, I had what I would call a dreamlike experience, and it put me in an altered state, the residue of which stayed with me for the rest of the night and the following day. Looking toward a lake, a water manitou showed me that I would need to place myself in service to spirit in a different way, to use the Internet to send messages to my friends via e-mails.

I learned that I would be given messages and that I should share this with my fellow travelers around the United States and Canada. Then I was presented with twelve statements that were not worded as commandments but were simply called "Things to Remember" to help inspire those on the path of Manitou, or path of the spirit. Out of respect I did not try to write them down immediately, but kept on walking, letting them sink in. I got back in the car and drove toward Ottawa. At dawn, I saw a road sign, and it was the road where my teacher lived, Odjigwano, a ninety-five-year-old elder who held wampum belts of prophecy. I did not know I was close to his house. I drove into his guest parking space and sat there and meditated some more.

The wording of the twelve statements became vividly clear. I found a notepad and wrote them down one after another without revision. I

226

sat there about ten minutes. I realized I was there to share them with my elder, and to ask him if they were any good or if there were any mistakes. I understood there would be more reminders to come, but now was the time to call on Odjigwano.

It was early in the morning, but I knocked on the door, and they brought me right in. Both he and his *kijekwe* (significant other) Romola, were very excited about something and very glad to see me, even so early in the morning unannounced. Ten years earlier I had met him by the Lake at Maniwaki early in the morning and gave him *No Word for Time*, but this was the first time I had called on him this way after ten years of working together.

They told me that ten minutes earlier a dozen golden birds came to his window all at once. He knew it was a sign and called to his better half to come and see. It was a small windowsill and only eight birds could fit on it at once. The other four stood nearby, so there were twelve. Then another twelve came and perhaps one more. All in all there were as many as twenty-five birds.

Romola was going to get her camera, when I knocked on the door, and they flew away for a moment. Odjigwano said he knew it meant someone was coming to bring a message but did not know what the number twelve meant or twenty-five. I sat down with my writing pad in hand and read him the twelve reminders. After each one, he exclaimed in joy, saying, "That's right!" or a similar exclamation. It was a happy moment. I asked what the words for *things to remember* would be in his Native Algonquin (Mamawinini) language and he said it would be *mamaytonay nen demawin.*

We agreed it was a good time to send out messages such as this to remind people that by whatever name we use, the Great Spirit is in all things and loves us as we are a part of it. I decided to call these reminders "The Twelve Birds." He brought me to the window, and a few of the birds were still there. They were like mourning doves, but of a strange golden color. There were blue circles around their eyes. He said they looked like angels, and he felt very blessed.

All his life he had looked upon the presence of these doves as a blessing because they are so peaceful, and also because they are so shy that they don't come near humans that often unless they feel moved by spirit. He had sometimes seen one in his window, sometimes two, and once he saw three, but this morning as I knocked, there were twenty-five and he was amazed.

The story is often told of a small songbird that came to his window in 1961 when he had cancer and doctors had given him less than four months to live. He was an angry man then, drinking the white man's spirit water, and both were killing him. He asked the bird to tell Manitou that he was willing to give himself over to spirit to be a tool of the Creator for the rest of his life, however long it might last, or to take his life otherwise. The bird brought a message to him to help bring peace between the four races of the world.

Within six months he was back on his job. Doctors found him to be perfectly healthy, much to their amazement. Soon he was presented with the responsibility of carrying three wampum belts of prophecy. Thirty-five years later, his work for peace was so admired that he was asked to welcome the Dalai Lama to Canada. He had received the Order of Canada and showed me the letter that morning. He passed away on August 3, 2011, after ninety-seven years working for peace and understanding, but no sign of cancer had ever returned in those forty-nine years. An African entourage was sent to speak at William Commanda's funeral by Nelson Mandela.

It is often said among Algonkin-ode people that birds pray at dawn and that their prayers are heard by the Great Spirit. So let us not dismiss the arrival of these golden birds of the dawn as coincidence, but wait and see what will happen.

Here then are the twelve birds just as I read them to him and Romola on that beautiful snowy morning.

The Twelve Birds

If you wish to journey on the path of Manitou, follow these twelve birds or things to remember—*mamaytohnay nen demawin.*

1. Love and serve the Great Spirit in all you do.
2. Honor Earth in your thoughts, words, and actions.
3. Have fun, enjoy life, play; but be a responsible citizen of Earth.
4. Honor and respect all spiritual traditions rooted in the great harmony.
5. Speak from the heart but keep an open mind.
6. Remember to learn and then learn to remember.
7. Meditate often, on the silence, or on the voice of the wind. Tranquility is the crossing place to the other side.
8. Pray not for things but that you become closer to Manitou.
9. Trust God by entrusting yourself with the freedom to be as God made you.
10. Ever hone yourself as a better tool of the Creator.
11. Humble yourself before the Creator does it for you.
12. Speak truthfully but with kindness, as we are one spirit.

BLUEBIRDS OF HAPPINESS

The "bluebird of happiness" is a stale old American phrase—the blue-bird signifying good health, happiness, and renewal. I'm not sure where the phrase originated, but it certainly has stuck. Indigenous people around the world consider the bluebird a sign of hope and happiness, and many Native American cultures consider the bluebird to be sacred, including the Cochiti and the Navajo. At the Ye'iibicheii winter night-way ceremony, the Navajo sing the "Bluebird Song" on the final day at sunrise. The lyrics are usually translated as, "Bluebird said to me/Get up my grandchild, it is dawn/it said to me." (See color insert, plates 22 and 23.)

In *Tales of the Cochiti Indians,* Ruth Benedict shares the story "The Sun's Children," in which Sun impregnates a Cochiti girl who didn't want to marry. He then brings her back to where he found her and tells her that he will always come back to check on her. After four days he came back again and during those days her baby was born. They named him Bluebird (Culutiwa). Bluebird was later given a brother named Turquoise. As the boys grew up they began to wonder who was their father (as people told them they had none), so their mother sent them to meet their father Sun. He said to Bluebird:

> When it is time for the first day break, put this downy feather on your forehead. When it is time for it to get lighter, take it off and tie on this parrot-tail feather. Then start to come up. As you get halfway to noon, stop for a while and wait to see if anybody gives you sacred meal and pollen in Cochiti. As soon as you receive your sacred meal and pollen, go on again and wait again at noon for somebody to come and give you food. When you receive your sacred

meal and pollen, start again. When you come to setting, stop again and wait for food. As soon as you have stopped for a while, start off again and when you are getting near where Sun goes down, you will see two great monsters with long teeth lying low down (on the horizon). Don't be afraid. Go right down.[17]

The tiny bluebird has an orange sunlike area on his chest, surrounded by sky blue feathers, so he should not be surprised that he is "the son of the sun." This story is similar to the universal tale in which the beggar turns out to be a prince who has lost his way. The spiritual teaching is that we are all God's children with an inheritance in heaven, but that we stumble around in ignorance, not showing our light to anyone. Humble little Bluebird learns his true nature as a future solar being, and is trained to take his father's place someday—just as a young Cochiti boy hearing this story would be trained to take his father's place in the world. The downy feather is the first wisps of light in the morning. The parrot tail is the flare of red light that rises from the sun at dawn on the desert. In Native spirituality from coast to coast it is important for the people to feel responsible for bringing the sun up each day with ceremony and offering. In this teaching tale, we gather that unless we offer sacred meal and pollen every few hours, the sun will not continue to rise, as it was instructed to wait for us by its father. In the story, Bluebird ultimately has to face his fears and enter the underworld at sunset. He is told to be unafraid of the people he meets there. He too will someday come back each day to check up on his loved ones.

On the morning of December 17, 2010, I began to take bluebirds more seriously. I was speaking on the phone with my "grandfather" William Commanda, chief advisor of The Center for Algonquin Culture, and Romola, his longtime companion, telling them that President Barack Obama had just announced that he would sign the UN Declaration on the Rights of Indigenous Peoples. This was an issue that William had been fighting for his entire ninety-seven years. His historic speech at the UN Cry of the Earth Summit in 1993 was a landmark in the development of the United Nation's decision to begin to address the rights of indigenous peoples and nations, not just those colonial nations that held exclusive membership in the UN clubhouse.

That same day, his longtime friend Thomas Banyaka had also spoken and said that until the United Nations recognizes the rights of the world's indigenous peoples, the future of our species would be uncertain. Two years later, the United Nations announced the International Decade of the World's Indigenous People, and then member nations began to sign the Declaration on the Rights of Indigenous Peoples. William had taken an active role in getting Canadians to sign petitions requesting that the Canadian government endorse the declaration. You might say he "followed it like a hawk."

After many years of petitions, Canadian prime minister Stephen Harper finally signed the statement on November 12, 2010, leaving the United States the only country in the world to fail to do so. Harper's decision reaped immediate benefits, as the City of Ottawa government, a body politic independent of Harper, announced soon afterward a renewed interest in recognizing Victoria Island (Asinabka) as indigenous territory and encouraging fundraising for a Native center at that location, organized in part by Commanda. Now a U.S. president was promising to sign the same UN declaration, giving it the force of a treaty, leading perhaps to similar breakthroughs in the United States.

Both William and Romola were overjoyed at the surprising news. As the two of them were in Ottawa speaking on the phone with me in New York, two bluebirds (our New York state bird) appeared on the branch in front of my picture window. I had not seen a single bluebird in that location before. When I told them, Romola's voice became excited with emotion. "Bluebirds of happiness!" she said. "Put it in your book!" We interpreted it as a sign that the happiness we all felt was real and justified. The two birds stayed the rest of the day. Maybe there is something to that old phrase after all.

PART 6

THREATS
TO OUR BIRD ALLIES

THE CAUTIONARY TALE
OF THE PASSENGER PIGEON

When Henry Hudson visited what is now called the Hudson Valley Region in 1609, he found passenger pigeons in great abundance. His ship's mate Robert Juet wrote that at the north end of their journey upstream, a group of Natives feasted on them and brought them to the crew members. Juet called them pigeons, but these birds would not have been the European blue rock pigeon, now so dominant in New York, but the now-extinct passenger variety, *Ectopistes migratorius*. Hudson wrote: "[T]wo men were also dispatched at once with bows and arrows in quest of game, who soon after brought in a pair of pigeons which they had shot."[1] The Natives were trying to impress the sailors with their hunting skills. Dropping a pigeon in flight with a bow and arrow is not that easy, because the birds are fleet, and as they are overhead targets, the pull of gravity must be taken into consideration. Due to their great plentitude, they were probably not the most expensive item on the menu, but a welcome meal nonetheless for the weary travelers.

A Sand Hill band member and elder interviewed for this book said that passenger pigeons "were killed usually using a blowgun. There was a certain time of year when the pigeons were plentiful and could be killed easily."[2] There did not seem to be a sense among the Native people that passenger pigeons were especially sacred or spiritual, but they were great game birds.

Alsop writes of how plentiful these pigeons once were: "John James Audubon described migrating flocks [of passenger pigeons] that stretched for miles in the sky and took three days to pass over, and which he estimated to contain over a billion birds."[3] The Munsee also have preserved in their old stories and oral traditions of a time in *Wundjiyahkun,* their "old homeland back east," when the sky would become so blackened with the flocks of passenger pigeons that it would seem as if night had descended on the Munsee people in broad daylight.[4]

Few alive today have ever seen a passenger pigeon, but Natives of 1609 would have known them well. The male passenger pigeon had a reddish or tawny-colored breast and blue-gray head and a long, wedge-shaped tail. The female had a brownish-gray breast, more like a mourning dove in appearance. These tasty birds were logically a main source of food for Algonkin-ode hunters of the 1600s.

In line with the Algonkin-ode cultural rule of never harvesting the last of any group of plants or animals, the river peoples must have felt that the passenger was a gift from Father Sky and were confident that these plentiful creatures could never be wiped out, at least not in their lifetime. Alsop estimates that in Hudson's era, passenger pigeons may have made up an astounding one-quarter of the North American bird population. According to Alsop, "they nested in large groups . . . from Virginia and Kentucky, northward into southern Canada."[5]

Native Americans not only hunted the passenger pigeon, they also ate their eggs, as did numerous Americans of various stripes before 1898.* A monogamous pair of passenger pigeons will create two to three white eggs in a season (much less prolific than chickens), feeding their featherless young after hatching with "pigeon milk," a liquid secreted from their crops.[6] These eggs, too, gradually became too easy to find, a very short-lived blessing for the less perspicacious hunters of the 1800s.

Passenger pigeon songs were not very uplifting or musical—one was a loud, grating sound, another a croaking or chattering—but they were capable of short clucking notes as well.[7] Although passenger pigeons

---

*This can be surmised, as the common folk from around the world eat pigeon eggs. An Asian man shared his pigeon egg lunch with me on a bus while crossing the Malaysian jungle northward to Thailand. As the chicken is not an indigenous bird, and raptor eggs were not eaten (at least not by Algonkin-ode), the eggs of pigeons were probably the best available kind in the Hudson Valley in 1609.

were North American birds exclusively, Juet would have recognized them as similar to the English racing pigeon (various species, related to the blue rock). All pigeons around the world, including postal carrier or homing pigeons used in Baghdad in 1150 CE, are descendants of the blue rock pigeon of ancient times, presumably the kind used by the pharaohs of Egypt in 3000 BCE. Racing pigeons were particularly popular in Belgium, whose popularity would have overflowed into Holland with great ease.[8] Although Juet was English, at least eleven of the fifteen remaining sailors on Hudson's ship were Dutch or Flemish.

As the deciduous forests were cut down by the Europeans and replaced by farms, the "gregarious" passenger pigeon had nowhere to hide. Alsop comments that their demise coincided with the disappearance of their thickly forested Eastern Woodland habitat. In addition to this was the introduction of the feral rock pigeons, their competitors who thrived in cities and towns. After thousands of years of prolific expansion, the passenger pigeons were doomed by forces beyond their control.

It is ironically noted that this indigenous form of the species, fetched for Hudson's men by the Algonkin-ode that day, was completely replaced by the gray-suited European form within a few hundred years, helping to drive this once-predominant Eastern Woodlands bird into extinction. The last of the passenger pigeons was named Martha, and she died of old age at twenty-nine in the Cincinnati Zoo in 1914.[9] How the descendants of these same Algonkin-ode peoples have avoided extinction over these last centuries is a remarkable tale of courage and persistence, perhaps best told elsewhere.

BIRDS FACE
MULTIPLE HAZARDS

My sister Lynn lives near the Sunny Corners–Red Bank area of New Brunswick, Canada, and every winter at Christmas all the amateur naturalists (including many Mi'kmaq) participate in what is called the Christmas count. The word goes out from the Naturalist's Club of New Brunswick for everyone to count all the birds they see, of various types, between December 15 and January 5, and report back.

Lynn lives at the edge of a large forest, and so counting birds is usually easy to do, there are so many of them. Just before Christmas of 2009, she went out to count birds and found very few. She was very disappointed. It was the lowest count she'd ever reported: just a few migratory birds from farther north and a meager number of blue jays, cardinals, finches, chickadees, mourning doves, and crows. Were they avoiding her? Head bent low, she went in to report her humble numbers to the tribal representative in charge of the Christmas count, only to find that everyone else had low numbers this year, too. What was the problem? Where were all the birds? No one knows for sure, but it was a bad sign, not just for the coming year but for Earth.

What could have affected so many birds? No one knows, but recent articles have shown that global-warming trends have affected bird populations. As spring arrives earlier, birds' eggs hatch earlier as well, but the caterpillars that usually hatch at the same time, providing food for the chicks, are no longer on the same schedule, so there is nothing for the chicks to eat. In some cases, it is believed that these chicks starve to death from lack of food.

Radiation from cell phone towers has been shown in European

studies to decrease the number of eggs in high nesting species in just a few generations, but in this area of New Brunswick, cell towers are not as numerous as they are in the states, and some of the low count birds are coming from even higher latitudes where cell towers are even less plentiful. The cause of the drop in the Christmas count is unknown, but it is a cause for concern.[10]

The multiple hazards facing birds today include wildlife trafficking; the encroachment of our technology into the sky, such as an increase in lighted towers and electromagnetic transmissions; global warming; and environmental disasters such as the BP oil spill. By becoming more aware of these hazards, perhaps we can do something to mitigate them.

Wildlife Trafficking

In 2009, an article in *Smithsonian Magazine* revealed the sheer amount of illegal poaching and trafficking of birds worldwide—an illicit trade surpassed only by drugs and weapons. The article stated:

> Wildlife trafficking is thought to be the third most valuable illicit commerce in the world, after drugs and weapons, worth an estimated $10 billion a year, according to the U.S. State Department. Birds are the most common contraband; the State Department estimates that two million to five million wild birds, from hummingbirds to parrots to harpy eagles, are traded illegally worldwide every year. . . .
> In the United States, the Wild Bird Conservation Act of 1992 outlawed the importation of most wild-caught birds. (Unless you are at a flea market on the southern border, any parrot you see for sale in the United States was almost certainly bred in captivity.) In 2007, the European Union banned the importation of all wild birds; Ecuador and all but a few other South American countries ban the commercial harvesting and export of wild-caught parrots.
> Latin America is vulnerable to wildlife trafficking because of its

extraordinary biodiversity. Ecuador—about the size of Colorado—has about 1,600 species of birds; the entire continental United States has about 900.[11]

Charles Bergman, the author of the Smithsonian article, described seeing a nest tree of a macaw pair lying on the ground: "The tree lay on the ground, smashed and wet. There were no chicks. All that remained were a few wet and mangled feathers near the nest hole. We stood around the tree, speechless, as if by a coffin."[12] He goes on to note that "this illicit trade . . . destroys not only wild parrots but also the trees that serve as nest sites year after year. Thus trafficking harms future generations, too," and that "a recent study in Peru found that 48 percent of all blue-and-yellow macaws die when their trees are felled."[13]

Dangerous Migrations

Most populations of migratory birds are in serious decline, a trend that should certainly be alarming to those who watch birds for signs from ancestral guardians.[14] Although much migration happens at night, geese and raptors migrate during the day, usually in groups. Scientists like to do a migration census when the moon is somewhat full; they can get proportional numbers by counting the number and types of birds that cross the moon on a given night.

According to the Balmori reports from Spain, birds tend to hit into lighted towers at night. Some towers can kill thousands of birds in a single night. Other dangers are toxins, bad weather, wind towers,[15] predators, and noise. Studies show that global warming has also endangered the lives of migratory birds.[16]

Birds are definitely attracted to light as they fly along the coast at night in broadly scattered groups.[17] In the Northeast of the United States, 70 percent fly through cities on their way to Canada.[18] The light confuses them, but they tend to stay close to lit spots where there is sky glow and glare and often fly into obstacles, such as tall buildings and communication towers.[19] Many cities are turning off their skyscraper lights at night to save energy and find that they are saving birds as well. For several years, the Empire State Building has been turning off the lights on stories above the fortieth floor, and the bird collision rate has dropped 80 percent. Chicago turns off building lights after 11 p.m. Other cities that have organized bird curfews include Toronto, Denver, Boston, Washington, D.C., Minneapolis, Houston, San Francisco, Portland, Detroit, and Indianapolis.[20]

Sound is also a serious threat to night migrations. If there is too much noise at the vocal frequency of birds, they can't hear each other to communicate about their flight plans. Birds seem to find this confusing; the noise causes them stress, which could affect their reproduction in the long run. Jackson Heights, New York, is one example of how low-pitched ambient noise, can be a problem for these birds. Scientific measurements have shown that the amplitude of the noise at Jackson Heights has increased one decibel every year.[21]

Global warming is also affecting migration, causing the territorial ranges of many birds to change and move northward. The Christianized Eeyou Itschee Cree of James Bay's Île de Fort George Island eat goose every day and are protective of their birds.* The Canada goose is in many ways a symbol of their people and a role model for group activity, however unconscious.[22] Although it is still very cold where they live, the sudden change in geese flight patterns is a threat to their way of life. If the geese stopped flying over their island, it would spell disaster. Natives are also reporting many more hummingbirds in higher and higher latitudes and also farther into the Northeast. The Mi'kmaq are seeing more and more turkeys every year and turkey eggs as well, and they are being visited by the large sandhill crane for the first time, while eagles are foraging closer and closer to human development, feeling the squeeze in the sky that humans feel on the land.[23]

---

*Île de Fort George is on the northeastern shore of James Bay with a beachhead crossing over into Nunavut. Chisasibi is the nearest major Cree community.

Geese Exterminations

The Mamawinini (Algonquin Nation) hunters are also reporting that migrations of Canada geese have been greatly affected. These geese are not only coming and going at different times than in the past but are confederating together in larger and larger groups, so large that they can cause sanitation problems when they roost. Some municipalities are rounding up hundreds of these beautiful birds at a time, just to kill them and throw their bodies in the dumpster. According to Anishinabi elders, this is not right. There are other solutions available. A device that could "harvest" goose droppings quickly could yield economic benefits for the fertilizer industry. Meanwhile, many Native Americans on reservations cannot find a single goose or gander to harvest for their supper, and goose is a delicacy. Something is disrupting the migratory instincts of the Canada goose, perhaps irregular rainfall patterns caused by climate change, and it is causing disruptions for Native Americans as well.

Meanwhile, New York state has been busy exterminating two-thirds of its Canada geese population, reducing their numbers from 250,000 to 85,000 in the last three years. Over 400 geese were killed in Prospect Park in July of 2010. One would think that the Canadian government would have to approve of the killing of so many Canada geese; according to the Migratory Bird Act, essentially a treaty, the United States cannot harm birds that also live in Canada without permission. The *New York Times*'s Isolde Raftery quoted a "high-level official" as saying that the current goose population of 20,000 to 25,000 birds was "five times the amount that most people would find socially acceptable," suggesting the number would be reduced to about 4,000.[24]

Native Americans should find the high-level official's words "five times the amount that most people would find socially acceptable" totally unacceptable. Native people are taught that Earth does not belong to us, we belong to Earth. What society feels about birds does not justify killing them. In addition, the vague logic of this argument is just the kind that English teachers flunk students for concocting, quantifying a feeling with a specific number just to sound like a fact. An anonymous source close to the action told me that the city was in fact killing *all* the geese, including those at the Jamaica Bay Wildlife Refuge. Apparently zero has become the new socially acceptable number.

"New York is leading the way," he [the high-level official] said, speaking on condition of anonymity because he was presumably not authorized to speak to the press. Plans for other areas, he said, "do not include all the scientific background."[25] If he was such a high-level official, why isn't he authorized to speak to the press and who is censoring his "expertise"? And why are plans being made without all the scientific background in place?

According to a report prepared by several city, state, and federal agencies: "The captured geese are placed alive in commercial turkey crates. The geese would be brought to a secure location and euthanized with methods approved by the American Veterinary Medical Association. Euthanized geese would be buried."[26]

FIDO (Fellowship in the Interest of Dogs and their Owners) is a Brooklyn-based organization originally established to protect the rights of pets in New York City, but which immediately came to the defense of the geese when the bad news was announced about their extermination.

In a lengthy letter addressed to Tupper Thomas, president of the Prospect Park Alliance, on July 20, 2010, Anthony Chiappelloni, president of FIDO, chastises the alliance for giving the U.S. Department of Agriculture Wildlife Services permission to go into Prospect Park and slaughter the geese.[27] Concerns about geese had come to the forefront when it was determined that the crash of US Airways Flight 1549 into the Hudson River in January 2009 was caused by migratory Canada geese, who were sucked into the airplane's engines. The letter points out that the geese of Prospect Park were nonmigratory. Originally introduced to the park in the 1930s, they had been peaceful residents of the park for the previous eighty years and posed no threat to aircraft. Furthermore, the letter notes that culling of geese is only allowed within a seven-mile radius of an airport, and the Prospect Park geese were located nine miles from the nearest airport. The letter notes how no effort was made to relocate the geese. Geese were rounded up after midnight on July 8, 2010, during their molting phase, when they were unable to fly away and so were vulnerable and defenseless. With what the letter calls "military precision," the geese were crammed into boxes, transported to a warehouse, and gassed. Chiappelloni ends his letter with a call from FIDO for accountability, requesting that those who gave permission to the USDA to own up to what they did, explain why, and express regret.

FIDO's manifesto is very much in agreement with the views of thousands of New York City's Native Americans and their descendants and those of Native people around North America who are concerned about the welfare of Canada geese. The city and state have acted without recognizing several key ingredients to the Native American (unwritten) code of honor:

1. Respecting animals and birds
2. Understanding animal behavior
3. Getting consensus from involved parties
4. Acting with compassion and not fear
5. Dealing honestly with those involved
6. Taking individual responsibility
7. Asking for spiritual guidance before acting, and seeking permission from wild creatures before hunting them, and only for food.

In this circumstance in particular, it is clear that New York City has lost the earth-based spiritual path, which the Wappingers, Munsee, Canarsie, and Mohican once established on Manhattan island. Indigenous people around the world are aware of what is going on in New York City and are displeased. The wild gander was regarded by almost all ancient peoples as sacred. The ancestors of the Matouac of Long Island regarded the goose as a divine teacher. In ancient Asia and the Indian subcontinent (and presumably the Sunda Shelf people) the wild gander was the bird of creation, leaving the great egg from which Brahma was born. Why are they being killed, and how can we approve such cruel methods that are so reminiscent of Nazi war stories? This does not sound like the only solution.

Deepwater Horizon Oil Spill of 2010

When *Deepwater Horizon,* the British Petroleum (BP) oil derrick, exploded in the Gulf of Mexico on April 20, 2010, it triggered the second largest unintentional oil spill in marine history. The oil gushed unabated for three months.

Melanie Driscoll, Director of Bird Conservation for the Gulf Coast Conservation/Mississippi Flyway sector of the National Audubon Society, was present when the oil finally hit Louisiana's shores late in April, when its fatal tide finally became real to us. She posted a number of blogs that reveal, phase by phase and with uncommon candor the horrors and heartbreaks experienced by those on the front lines of bird rescue battles. On August 13th, 2010, she posted:

Just three months ago, I visited islands and a beach in southeastern Louisiana. Brightly colored orange and yellow booms were anchored around important pelican, gull, heron, and tern nesting colonies. It seemed the world awaited, with bated breath, the approach of oil that had been gushing from the Macondo well for over a week. Pelicans were carrying sticks, building nests, preparing to lay eggs. . . . The first tarballs, the size of my thumbnail, were washing up on our beaches. Fishing closures were starting. The press, eager to break the story, were scurrying about on boats, encroaching on nesting islands to get that coveted first shot of an oiled egg, peering off the dock in Venice looking for tidal waves of oil to wash ashore.[28]

The brown pelican, one of the larger birds of the Gulf Coast, weighing in at twelve pounds, with a wingspan of eight feet, was hardest hit by the oil spill whose initials are the same as its own, BP. (See color insert, plates 15, 16, and 17.) The brown pelican was endangered by industry around 1900, but revived by the 1960s. Then it was hard hit by the use of DDT and again became endangered, as the poison made its eggshells too thin to protect life. Thanks to Rachel Carson and others, DDT was banned, and the brown pelican came back. On November 11, 2009, the brown pelican count reached 659,000, and after one hundred years of struggle, this bird of plenty was finally taken off the endangered species list. Five months later, the Gulf oil spill placed this prehistoric bird once again on the top of the list of environmental concerns.

The pelican's eastern territory is from Virginia and Maryland to the mouth of the Amazon, but it nests on shoreside islands in the Gulf of Mexico, namely Dauphin Island and Petit Bois Island. Like the egret, the pelican is a sign of good fishing to come. The Taino call it *aruna*, and consider it a very sacred bird, a good luck sign, and a symbol of buoyancy, unselfishness, and abundance. Whatever good luck the ever-buoyant state of Louisiana was counting on from its state bird took a big setback. Nonetheless, through many dangers, toils, and snares, and thanks also to the heroic efforts of countless bird lovers of every race imaginable, the brown pelican emerged somewhat fortunate if not victorious.

Melanie Driscoll blogged, both joyfully and with regrets:

Last Friday, I watched the Louisiana Department of Wildlife and Fisheries release 45 rehabilitated young Brown Pelicans onto an island in southwest Louisiana. These pelicans have come so far. Laid in unoiled nests, hatched from fairly clean eggs, incubated by dedicated parents, fed as nestlings fish from waters that may be clean, or may be full of oil and dispersants. Oiled, at some point, by parents' breast feathers or by moving through oiled habitats. Captured, transported, stabilized, transported, cleaned, rehabilitated, transported again.

Freed! Some flew immediately out into Gulf waters, others stood on shore and stretched, then swam and ate fish provided by the state biologists. With a numbered red band on one leg and the upper bill painted green for identification, the gangly youngsters made one more step toward independence.

I thought I should feel joy, but mostly I felt apprehension. These birds will be guided largely by instinct, and they can follow adult pelicans that are nesting in numbers on that island. But the Gulf is so big, and they are so young. And we don't know what is out there. Merely one-quarter of one of the world's largest oil spills is still a lot of oil. Nearly two million gallons of chemical dispersant is an immense and terrifying experiment.

On my return trip home, I stopped at Rutherford Beach. A Sanderling fed near gulls and other shorebirds at the surf's edge, running jauntily, undaunted, in and out of the wave's feathered edges. Such a short time for such a small bird to have flown north, found a mate, defended a territory, raised young, and flown back to Louisiana beaches, through so many hazards, and this, just one more.

The press are largely gone because the oil is capped. Some people have already declared this over, and overblown—not even a disaster. I know that we cannot understand the impact of this spill on birds for many more months, perhaps years. For many creatures, we will never know.[29]

Two years after the first oil started leaking into the gulf, 2,263 birds out of 7,258 collected had been found dead with oil stains. At that point 826 of those collected were Brown Pelicans, a staggering number of them dead.[30] Using algorithmic models, multipliers, and additional studies, it will take many years to determine what the effects were both on birds local to the gulf and other long-distance flying populations who were harmed merely by flying over the area during the fires.[31] A recent study, for example, showed that petroleum traceable back to BP was found inside 20 of the first 22 American white pelican eggs analyzed in Minnesota in 2012, with an additional 14 of the first 18 eggs analyzed contaminated with dispersant.[32]

This is clearly a cautionary tale such as those shared around Native American winter fires for a hundred generations, and an illustration of the age-old expression, "We are all related; all creatures are our brothers and sisters," now summed up by the sound-bite-size label, "the butterfly effect." We must pay attention to these warning signs.

To those humans involved in the rescue operations, such as the Houma and the National Audubon Society, the cost is weighed not only in human property or lifeless black birds lying in the sand but in the heart as well. For scientists, the complex calculus involved in entering an ecosystem where humans don't normally belong in order to save it becomes a deeply troubling equation. Melanie Driscoll wrote:

> There is a difference between survival of individual birds and survival of a species. Decisions have been made to stay out of colonies, knowing that individuals were dying, because those same colonies were producing a new generation of pelicans, gulls, terns, herons, egrets, and spoonbills. Decisions were made to not move through fragile marshes weighed down with oil in an effort to preserve the homes to which surviving birds can return next year. Those have been heartbreaking decisions for everyone concerned. I will not second-guess them. Painful as they were and filled with unseen cost, they were protecting a new generation and the hope for the future.
>
> Remember, next year. Remember, when decisions are made about energy use. Remember, because, once this oil began to flow, it was already too late to save all of the birds. We must decide more wisely in the future. Because we must never let this happen again.[33]

What must we do to see that such things don't happen again? Better regulation of offshore drilling? In terms of strengthening the coastal ecosystems themselves, I can do no better than to quote from Melanie Driscoll's briefing for congressional staffers on the second anniversary of the gulf oil spill:

We must use all the tools at our disposal, including sediment diversions to reconnect the Mississippi River to the delta, to begin to halt and reverse decades-long marsh loss.

We must assess and mitigate other threats in this system, to provide the greatest chance for full recovery.

We thank you for your work to date to pass the Restore Act, and implore you to pass the final legislation with all due haste;

And we ask that you continue to prioritize this national treasure in the future, whether that means legislation to protect it or appropriations to restore the Gulf.[34]

One can only hope they were listening!

CELL PHONE TOWERS:
THE NEW DDT

One of the greatest threats our endangered allies ever faced was from DDT (dichlorodiphenyltrichloroethane). But it seems that cell phone towers may transmit an even greater threat, one that is equally invisible as DDT was in 1962.

Dr. Joseph Bruchac,* an Abenaki with an undergraduate degree in wildlife conservation from Cornell University, is well aware of the newest threats to bird welfare in developed countries, which now include cell towers, along with oil spills and global warming. Bruchac, who has authored more than 142 books, including *Rachel Carson: Preserving a Sense of Wonder*, a picture book for children, made these observations about the threat cell phone towers pose today:

> When Rachel Carson first revealed her research on DDT, she was described as a "dangerous radical," "the most dangerous woman in America," and "a threat to the American way of life." That was forty-five years ago. Now she is called a saint . . . Cell phone towers and the dangers brought to light in her book *Silent Spring* are comparable. In both cases, new technology was rushed in because of the good it could do. In its day DDT was regarded as a miracle chemical, and everyone began to use it everywhere. Then people began to

---

*In addition to his book on Rachel Carson, Bruchac is coauthor of the bestseller *Keepers of the Earth: Native American Stories and Environmental Activities for Children*, with Michael Kaduto. He has a deep personal involvement in Native American traditions and lifeways, and as author of *The Native American Sweat Lodge*, he was a national spokesperson for Native American culture in the aftermath of the Sedona sweat lodge deaths of 2009.

see the dead bodies of whole flocks of robins and other birds strewn across their lawns, and realized that the benefits of DDT were outweighed by the damages.

We are now in a comparable situation. We have rushed to act on building cell towers worldwide and birds are paying the price. Much competent scientific evidence is emerging to indicate that we have gone too far too fast and need to take a closer look before we proceed any further.

We need to make decisions based not on the expediency of the moment, but on the needs of future generations. After *Silent Spring* was published, DDT was banned, as other chemicals were discovered that did a better job without such devastation to the natural world. Electromagnetic radiation affects everything around it, and is in a way more pervasive. You have to ingest DDT to get sick. You don't have to eat electromagnetism to be affected by it, and it's everywhere.

Most store-bought apples in Rachel Carson's time had DDT. Industry claimed that if it stopped using DDT, bugs would destroy all food, that pests would "take over," and all food would die. We'd all be eating acorns! "DDT is our first and only defense," they said. The book Carson wrote while dying of cancer herself, was scholarly and carefully worded, and well researched. It was not sensationalistic. We need to take a similar look at cell phone towers and their effects on ourselves and our planet.[35]

If cell tower transmissions become ubiquitous, it will be difficult for Native Americans to find a place to build a sweat lodge where birds and other wildlife will not be deterred. Bruchac felt that the existence of such transmissions in a sacred ceremonial area would be counterproductive:

The sweat lodge is not just for the benefit of humans, it is done for all our relations. As one enters and leaves the lodge, one says, "all my relations" for this reason. It is a terrible sacrilege, therefore, to place a cell phone tower in a place of healing where it may cause disruptions in the lives of so many living things. The lodge is a place of healing for all, where we all can go to seek balance. There is a proper way to conduct a sweat lodge so as to create this balance. When you destroy the environment around you, you clearly destroy that healing place, and that balance.[36]

There are a number of little-known studies that indicate that cell tower transmissions have a serious effect on birds. Based on the lab reports I've read, cell towers harm migratory and other birds in ten significant ways.

1. They are driven away when the towers are erected.
2. They are forced to seek refuge in tiny holes in buildings and other nooks and crannies to protect themselves from the cell tower radiation.
3. They lose direction, get permanently lost, and are unable to return to their nests.
4. They become confused; for example, white storks in Spain are unable to build their nests near a cell tower. They drop sticks, can't remember how to build the nest, and start fighting with each other. Without a nest, the eggs drop to the ground and smash on the pavement. Storks are tenacious nesters, but they eventually give up and go away.
5. They have smaller hatchings; fewer eggs are deposited with each laying period, and embryos are less and less likely to be fertile.
6. They become crippled; legs become limp, and wings function less well.
7. They die; birds are often found dead near cell towers.
8. They lose mice as a source of food; mice are born deformed and produce increasingly smaller litters with each generation until reproduction ceases.

9. They lose insects as a source of food; insects lose over half of their reproductive power after a single exposure to a cell tower.

10. Their coloration changes; birds experience albinism (feathers turning white) or melanoma (darkening of feathers) after periods of radiation.

How the Storks Forgot How to Build Their Nests

Although the following sounds like a medicine story gone awry, it is based on a field study by scientists, including Alfonso Balmori, a biologist living in Valladolid, Spain.[37] This study suggests that things are quite out of balance in the bird kingdom these days.

In the town of Valladolid, twenty stork nests were built on the roofs of churches and on chimneys, all lying within 100 meters of several cell antennae. Between February 2003 and June 2004, scientists visited these stork nests between ten and fifteen times to see how they were doing in this new environment. Other storks living between 100 to 200 and from 200 to 300 meters away from the towers were also monitored separately. They found that stork couples living less than 300 meters from a tower had half the offspring of those lying beyond this mark. Twelve nests (40 percent) located within 200 meters of the towers had no offspring at all, but outside the 300-meter mark, almost all (with one exception) of the couples had chicks. Within 100 meters, chicks would often die of unknown causes. To quote Balmori, "Also, within this distance, couples frequently fought over the nest construction sticks and failed to advance the constructions of the nests. (Sticks fell to the ground while the couple tried to build the nest). Some nests were never completed and the storks remained passively in front of the cell site antennae."[38] Normally, they are tenacious nesters.

Mention the word *stork* and people think of the baby in the diaper hanging from the stork's mouth. They are fanatical nesters, and yet when confused and irritated by cell transmissions, these peaceful birds squabble and fight and in some cases never actually build a nest. The eggs are coming, the babies are on the way, but the two can't agree on anything and can't even hold onto the sticks. Without a nest to lay the eggs in, the mother-to-be delivers them into space, they drop to the ground and are smashed to bits. In other words, with the introduction of cell towers, these worldwide symbols of good parenthood become as dysfunctional as the Bickersons in need of relationship therapy. We're not supposed to imagine what cell towers are doing to human relationships.

Balmori explains, "Birds are especially sensitive to the magnetic fields. The white stork (*Ciconia ciconia*) build their nests on pinnacles and other very high places with high electromagnetic contamination (exposed to the microwaves). Also, they usually live inside the urban environment, where the electromagnetic contamination is higher, and remain in the nest a lot of the time, for this reason the decrease on the brood can be a good biological indicator to detect the effects of these radiations."[39] Balmori adds that many couples never even built nests, and several dead offspring were found. The remarkable faithfulness of the white stork to its family and nesting location actually increases the damage caused to them by the microwaves. In one comment worthy of note, Balmori states, "Smaller organisms (children, birds, small mammals, etc.) are especially vulnerable, as absorption of microwaves of the frequency used in mobile telephones is greater as a consequence of the thinner skull of a bird, the penetration of the radiation into the brain is greater."[40]

A Danger to Migration

Balmori also noted how cell phone towers present a danger to migrating birds: "Several million birds of 230 species die annually from collisions with the masts of telecommunication facilities in the United States during migration. The cause of the accidents has yet to be proven, although one knows that they mainly take place during the night, in fog, or bad weather. The birds use several orientation systems: the stars, the sun, the site-specific recognition and the geomagnetic field. The illumination of the towers probably attracts the birds in the darkness, but it is possible that the accidents take place in circumstances of little visibility, because at the time, other navigational tools are not available."[41]

In one study, scientists found that the effects of a pulsed radio frequency signal on the brains of zebra finches were similar to those produced by cell towers, specifically a 900 MHz signal modulated at 217 Hz.[42] This study showed that the stimulation produced by these electromagnetic blasts produced significant change in more than half the brain cells. Up to 76 percent of the cells increased their firing by 3.5 fold, while other cells decreased accordingly and some were not affected. Fifty-two percent of the cells were excited, 17 percent responded with inhibition, and 31 percent remained neutral. My understanding is that both the stimulated and destimulated cells would decrease in functionality during that time. The study also stated boldly, "Such responses indicate potential effects on humans using hand-held cellular phones." These are called nonthermal effects, as they do not actually heat up the brain.

A study published in *Nature* magazine stressed the importance of a magnetically sensitive chemical reaction in the eyes of birds in the process of navigation over the older magnetite theory, which simply assists in forward direction. The study, a joint effort written by experts from all over the world, states that "oscillating magnetic fields disrupt the magnetic orientation behavior of migratory birds. Robins were disoriented when exposed to a vertically aligned broadband (0.1–10 MHz) or single-frequency (7 MHz) field in addition to the geomagnetic field. Moreover, in the 7 MHz oscillating field, this effect depended on the angle between the oscillating and the geomagnetic fields. The birds exhibited seasonally appropriate migratory orientation when the oscillating field was parallel to the geomagnetic field, but were disoriented when it was presented at a 24 to 48 degree angle."[43]

In other words, all a migratory bird would have to do would be to cross over the invisible field in front of a cell tower at an angle of 24 to 48 degrees, and he or she would become totally lost and go miles off course. Some I have spoken to paint a picture of a lone migratory bird after such an invisible encounter, spending the rest of its life on a barren mountaintop, unable to find the rest of its flock. It may or may not be that severe.

Recently, in mid-January, I was walking with a friend around Vassar College in Poughkeepsie, a quiet scene, as school was still in recess, and from beyond the great castle known as Vassar Library, we heard a din like a storm of noise approaching and realized that a large flock of Canada geese was coming down from the northeast. As they first appeared over the parapets, it seemed that everything was in order, flying in several V-shaped fleets at once, but suddenly some started turning to the west while others continued south. Then another group came in and started going in all directions, and then the first group came back from the south looking for the others, and after quite a while of reorganizing, it seemed the larger part of the group headed west. Although far from a scientific study, it was the kind of behavior I had never seen before in Canada geese. They looked totally confused. Could it be there was some food source to the west? Or were they confused by the high density of cell phone transmissions in that area? This is a subject for further study, but the sight of such master navigators wandering lost over Poughkeepsie gave me cause to worry about the state of the planet and the effect of cell transmitters on migratory birds.

Other Effects of Electromagnetic Transmissions on Birds

Perhaps the most significant work in the field of cell towers and their effects on birds comes from a series of reports by Alfonso Balmori, called "The Balmori Reports." Of these, the most shocking is "The Effects of Microwave Radiation on the Wildlife: Preliminary Results."[44] This report has five sections:

1. *Population monitoring of house sparrows in Valladolid, Spain:* This section shows that in streets containing high levels of electromagnetic (EM) contamination due to cell tower transmission, the sparrow population disappeared. Over time,

they gradually left all contaminated areas, moving to uncontaminated areas. An important part of this study shows that, within the contaminated areas, sparrows seek refuge in naturally screened areas, some of them hardly larger than the bird itself. This forces the sparrow into self-imprisonment in these niches. As these EM streams are fairly constant, it would seem to me that this alone could cause the bird to starve to death. Balmori also found specimens in the affected area that had albinism (a pale discoloration) in their feathers and couldn't fly properly. He also linked EM contamination to the sudden decrease of sparrows in England. Balmori stated in this section that EM radiation could affect reproduction, the circulatory and nervous system, and the overall health and well-being of birds.

2. *Population Monitoring in Winter Sleeping Places:* This section showed that central group sleeping places were abandoned when contaminated, causing starlings to sleep in small groups, sometimes in places they would not normally sleep.

3. *Other Comments on Wildlife and Electromagnetic Fields:* This study showed the disappearance of kestrels; the disappearance of white stork nests near cell towers; the finding of dead rock doves near phone masts; the loss of carrier pigeons; plumage deterioration, bone problems, discoloration, and an unwillingness to fly above a few feet in magpies; and the displacement of collared doves, who left the entire city to avoid cell tower radiation. The study also found . . . infertility in eggs of many species and a general dulling, discoloration, and damage to the plumage of all birds—a sign of illness. Among other animal species, the study noted a decrease in bat populations so severe that tagging could no longer be continued; an almost complete elimination of insect life near the cell towers over several (insect) generations, resulting in starvation for the birds; and "frequent death" of hamsters and guinea pigs near cell towers. The study also

mentioned that the tops of trees in the path of a cell tower dry up and suggested that plants in the range of a cell tower would become dull and unhealthy, grow more slowly, and would tend to acquire diseases.

4. *Monitoring the Wild Birds Nesting in Campo Grande and Urban Park in Valladolid, Spain:* This large-scale study, involving contact with over five hundred birds of fifteen species, was conducted in 1996, 1997, and 1998, with two to four visits per year. Then in 2002, a more exhaustive study was completed, with four samplings in April 2002 alone. In that time, blackbirds decreased from 8 to 5 couples, the great tit decreased from 4 to 1 couple; the serin went from 5 to 1 couple; the greenfinch went from 7 couples to 1; the coal tit was reduced from 2 to 1 couple; the wren was reduced from 5 couples to 1; and the collared dove was reduced by 50 percent. During that time, "silence areas" were discovered, where breeding couples totally disappeared, which had, in the past, been noisy with birdsong. The study showed that "67% of the birds in Campo Grande have suffered important population decrease or have totally disappeared between 1998 and 2002."[45] During this time, conventional air pollution levels dropped; however, five base stations for cell towers were placed during this time at less than 100 meters from the park.

5. *Population monitoring of house sparrows in the United Kingdom:* Evidence of a connection between sparrow decline in the United Kingdom and the introduction of phone mast GSM (global system for mobile communication) shows a close correlation between the introduction of cell towers in the UK and the disappearance of English house sparrows. It shows how the concentration of towers in cities resulted in sparrows abandoning cities and moving to small towns. Cell towers are installed in high places, and their signal fields are therefore high and affect birds whose breeding, singing, feeding, and nesting locations are of

high elevation, such as the house sparrow, the starling, and the magpie. At the end of this study, Balmori writes, quoting Paul Kelbie, a Scottish correspondent, writing for *The Independent* (London): "In November 1999, in Scotland, over one third of all Scottish Local Planning Authorities adopted or publically committed themselves to adopting precautionary policies as a direct result, by choosing to keep transmitter masts away from schools and residential areas. Two years later, the demise of the House Sparrows appears to have been reversed in Scotland."[46]

On this happy note, we will wind up our discussion of the studies on cell towers and their effects on birds. These are, for the most part, European studies because funding for cell towers and their effects on birds is being allocated in Europe. One can be sure that the situation is the same or worse in the United States, which is where cell phone use per capita is highest in the world.

WHAT CAN WE DO?

There have been a number of issues discussed in this book regarding threats to various species of birds in the United States and Canada. The question is, What can we do? Obviously, I hope that you feel passionately about our avian allies and will want to learn more about them, possibly even acting on their behalf where they have no voice. What you do with your emotion and devotion is up to you. This is meant to be a book about living more closely with spirit, and the spiritual elders often say, "Don't get messed up in politics." And yet other elders say that our true purpose is to help creation continue and that we need to walk our talk and put our spiritual energies into action to make that happen.

The reading of bird signs as omens is one of the few truly global shamanic traditions that is still practiced in most countries, so one thing you can do is to learn more about the bird omen reading practices of your own ancestors and your own ethnicity, do more research on birds, and try to share this book with others. It's a great experience to communicate with birds—through thoughts, through prayer, through nonverbal gestures, through speaking to them. You never know what will happen, or what they will do.

The Audubon Society was placed in charge of the rescue of birds on the Gulf Coast. This process will be an ongoing challenge for years to come. One thing an activist can do is donate money to the Audubon Society, with a letter requesting the funds be used toward rescuing brown pelicans, snowy egrets, and other birds specifically harmed by the BP oil spill and for restoring their habitats. The letter can also make a plea for an account of how the money is spent and what the society is actually doing in response to the situation. Please note the Coast Guard is keeping tallies of the numbers of bird fatalities, and this information is also publicly available. On the other hand, some have chosen to buy gas at stations not crowned by the pretty green sign with the sunburst design and the letters BP in white.

In regard to the damage to migratory birds from cell phone transmitter towers, that is a different story. While boycotting might have worked ten years ago, it will not work now. We need our cell phones to call our congressmen and women, the editors of major newspapers, and each other. Corded land lines create the least radiation, but new equipment is often better insulated than old units.

Speaking as a concerned citizen, one of the major problems with cell phone towers is the violation of poorly worded agreements between local citing councils and the giant multinational cell tower corporations involved. Cell companies should not be able to change the amplitude, wattage, modality, or any other aspect of the agreed-upon cell tower, without a chance for every citizen to vote on it. State legislatures must plug all loopholes in current agreements and licenses so that cell tower companies will reduce their wattages to that which the citing councils intended. This is a complex process and is only the first step of many. Laws could be written to penalize noncompliant phone companies after a certain date. That money would go toward funding research on better ways to transmit cell phone messages altogether, with no harm to birds. Satellite technology might actually be safer for birds than towers. Miniantennae and minitransmitters on cars, in homes, and in stores might be a safer solution. Cell phones could be developed with greater receptivity without posing a greater risk to the user. These could be sold in conjunction with an actual decrease in the power levels of the cell tower transmissions and fewer towers.

Funds should be made available through various channels for the cell tower companies to redesign their transmission systems. The FCC should encourage such change. With the current cell tower design, birds within 100 meters of the towers are clearly in harm's way, no less so than humans. But all other factors being equal, the amount of damage in this danger zone depends, apparently, on the amount of power going through the tower, and this information (regarding wattage, etc.) is currently not being made public. Congress could require all cell companies to publish monthly reports as to the strength of their signals at each tower, broken down on a daily and hourly basis, if necessary. The FCC would be required to monitor the accuracy of the reports and enforce compliance with the most conservative interpretation of the license agreement. We might begin to see a moratorium on all new cell tower constructions, as soon as the information concerning the damage to birds living, or even flying, near transmitters is made public. Some might want to find new ways to protect these birds.

Cell companies and some of their customers may fear going back to an earlier state of existence where not every dog and cat has twenty-four-hour-a-day cell phone reception, even on top of Mount Shasta. If this unlikely scenario happens, it will be temporary at worst. But necessity is the mother of invention, and such a step backward will inspire inventors to think up new technologies that won't kill hundreds of thousands of birds each year, while providing the excellent phone service cell phone customers have come to rely on. With new funding will come new companies that are not tied down to dead-end obsolete technologies that solve one problem only to create another. Meanwhile, it is always good to be involved with bird rehabilitation centers, volunteering as a worker and giving your financial support, to make sure that any of the thousands of birds that are injured each year by cell towers and other threats have a chance to start over. It's time for a change, because in the end, it's not just about the birds, it's about us, our children, and our future.

AFTERWORD

Experiences with birds and the messages from spirit keep occurring, and though I feel finished with the book, the book is not necessarily finished with me. It was April 14, 2012, and I had just submitted the first draft to Inner Traditions and was working on taxes. I went outside into the mid-April sunshine to sit at a table in my yard and relax. A strange golden bird jumped onto the lowest branch of a tree, just a few feet above me and to my left, and began to "talk" to me in a language I could not understand. This bird had a black face (not head!) and was a bright golden color like a male goldfinch, but it was more than twice the size of a one. It seemed to be saying "So there you are," over and over. He stayed there for at least twenty minutes, looking at me and "talking." I got a good look at the feathered visitor but had no idea what it was. My first thought was that it was a Baltimore oriole, but the song seemed too flutelike and twittery. (They are more orange than yellow in my region and sound more like a thrush.)

The bird made me think of my father, who had passed on in 2007, and who therefore never knew about the bird book. Although my mother is Mi'kmaq and very knowledgeable about Native American bird lore, my father was a proud Welshman and not at all unfamiliar with Druidic and Brythonic shamanism. Maybe I was thinking about him because I had just been reading his unpublished book "Eye of the Horizon." Maybe I was thinking about him because I had gotten a message that same morning from the raptor center about a harrier to be named in my honor, a bird I associated with him, and another message from a woman named Lila Pritchard. His spirit was in the air—literally.

Two days later, I described the bird to my friend, Janet, and she responded that it was a meadowlark. I looked up both the eastern and western meadowlark, and the western was the bird with the closest physical and musical resemblance to this bright bird. Then I thought of *The Lark Ascending: Romance for Violin and Orchestsra*, the symphonic piece by Welshman Ralph Vaughan Williams that my father used to listen to over and over when I was in music school. He would sit transfixed when it would come on the radio, and we knew all talking would have to stop. I learned that Vaughan Williams was inspired by a poem by the same name by George Meredith, and that the poem and symphonic piece were both associated with an old traditional Welsh harp tune called "The Rising of the Lark" by Elizabeth Grant. This song is associated with Owain Glyndyr's War Song, and the same words are sung to it. Owen Glendower, as Shakespeare called him, the last independent Prince of Wales, was associated with the lark. He is the George Washington of Wales (some say a "King Arthur"), a direct descendant of Prince Llewelyn the Great and a man who united Wales in 1400 and established the Welsh parliament in Machynlleth shortly thereafter. It was said that under Glendower's rule, "the sky was never so dull and cold that no lark sang."[1] Then it all came back to me; a magical trip to Wales with my father when I was thirteen years old to explore the castles that old Owen Glendower had liberated from English rule. I sat in the windowsills of several of them, Shrewsbury, Aberstwyth, Caerleon, Raglan, and most memorably, Carmarthen, about which I wrote a poem (included in *Before the Heart Fell Open*). Young and impressionable, I imagined myself to be the reincarnation of one of the sons of Owen Glendower. Dad thought that Owen Glendower might have been an ancestor of ours, as his people were from the Severn and Wye valleys where some of Owen's ancestors were from. Besides encouraging me to explore my mother's Mi'kmaq people and their history,

Dad's invitation to study the history of our ancestors in Wales first-hand with him was one of the greatest gifts he ever gave me. This bird, the metaphysical symbol of Owen Glendower, and therefore of Wales, had come to remind me that Europe once had a great tradition of Bird Medicine and that it was important to mention this so that it would never be forgotten. Had my father returned from the spirit world with the help of the western meadowlark, a bird rarely if ever seen in eastern New York? If so, that lark was descending not only to say hello but to remind me of my Welsh heritage and to help me finish my book as well. And my Welsh father would agree wholeheartedly with Sitting Bull, who said, "Let us teach our boys to be kind to all the birds, especially to our meadowlark friends that speak to us in our language."[2]

NOTES

PART 1. WHAT IS BIRD MEDICINE?

1. Kaplan and Rogers, *Songs, Roars, and Rituals,* 86.
2. Telephone conversation, July 20, 2010.
3. Conversation with Raymundo Rodriguez, January 18, 2010.
4. Conversation with Tina Powell, August 17, 2010.
5. Conversation with Debbie Bahune, Saco, Maine, March 26, 2012.
6. Kaplan and Rogers, *Songs, Roars, and Rituals,* 70–71.
7. "Broken Mammoth Archaeology Project," Office of History and Archaeology.
8. Correspondence from Charles Holmes, August 8, 2012.
9. Holmes, "The Beringian and Transitional Periods in Alaska."
10. Potter et al., "A Terminal Pleistocene Child Cremation and Residential Structure from Eastern Beringia."
11. Mails, Evehema, and Cheshire, *Hote Villa,* 44–46.
12. Rowland, *Birds with Human Souls,* xiv.
13. Eliade, *Shamanism,* 131.
14. Swamp, *Thanksgiving Address.*
15. Telephone conversation with Betsy Stang, December 30, 2009.
16. Telephone conversation with Eugene Blackbear Sr., January 4, 2010.
17. Crowley, "Turtle and BP: Brown Pelican."
18. Thumbadoo, *Learning from a Kindergarten Dropout,* 26.
19. E-mail letter from Kenneth Cohen, January 13, 2010.

20. Latorre and Latorre, *The Mexican Kickapoo Indians,* 348.

21. Larsen, *Shaman's Doorway,* 66.

22. Telephone interview with Manitou Ikwe, January 2, 2010.

PART 2. THE FOUR GATEKEEPERS

1. Interview with Robert Young Eagle, Pine Hill, New York, August 14, 2010.

2. Conversation with Raymundo Rodriguez, August 18, 2010, in response to information from Robert Young Eagle, per conversation of August 14, 2010.

3. Emerson, *Indian Myths,* 421–22.

4. Adapted from Emerson, *Indian Myths.*

5. Interview with William Commanda, January 2, 2010.

6. Telephone conversation with Margery Coffey, January 18, 2010.

7. Telephone interview with White Deer of Autumn, January 3, 2010.

8. Rowland, *Birds with Human Souls,* xiv.

9. See Bruchac, *Native American Stories of the Sacred.*

10. Pritchard, *No Word for Time,* 46.

11. Powell, *The Cheyenne, Ma'heo'o's People,* 65.

12. Telephone conversation, May 25, 2010.

13. E-mail exchange, February 25, 2012.

14. Interview with Robin Youngblood, Maniwaki, Quebec, Spiritual Elder's Gathering, August 7, 2010.

15. Interview with and subsequent e-mail from Manna Jo Greene, January 1, 2012.

16. Conversations with Judy Abbott, including one at Big Indian, New York, finalized via letter, August 14, 2012.

17. Strachey quoted in Swanton, *The Indians of the Southeastern United States,* 702.

18. Adair quoted in ibid., 706.

19. Hawkins quoted in ibid., 702.

20. Sibley, *The Sibley Guide to Bird Life and Behavior,* 213.

21. Royal BC Museum, www.cityview.bc.ca/Victoria/royalbcmuseum4.html (page now defunct; accessed August 31, 2010).

22. Conversation with Kevin Deer, Kanatsiohareke Strawberry Festival, June 30, 2012, and subsequent e-mails and phone conversations, finalized on August 13, 2012.

23. Conversation with Tony Moonhawk and Marcey Tree-in-the-Wind Langhorn, August 2010.

24. Etaoqua, unpublished manuscript. Used by permission of the author.

25. Johnson, *Mrs. Perley's People*, 151.

26. Telephone conversation with David Fescier, January 13, 2010.

27. Brown, "Distress Call Not Keeping Crows Away."

28. Castaneda, *The Eagle's Gift*, 54.

29. Telephone conversation with Margery Coffey, quoting Dennis Hastings, January 18, 2010.

30. Telephone conversation with Margery Coffey, January 18, 2010.

31. Kacelnik, Weir, and Campbell, "Shaping of Hooks in New Caledonian Crows," 981. Used by permission.

32. Sibley, *The Sibley Guide to Bird Life and Behavior*, 37.

33. Conversation with Debbie Bahune, Saco, Maine, March 26, 2012.

34. Heinrich, *Ravens in Winter*, 12.

35. Telephone interview with Heather Wiggs, June 26, 2010.

36. Telephone interview with Grandmother White Wolf, May 26, 2010.

37. Johnson, *Mrs. Perley's People*, 115.

38. Pritchard, *Native American Stories of the Sacred*.

39. Sams and Carson, *Medicine Cards*, 121.

40. Ibid.

41. Eliade, *Shamanism*, 103.

42. Ibid, 104–5.

43. Interview with Dark Rain Thom, Bloomington, Indiana, June 18, 2010.

44. Johnson, *Mrs. Perley's People*, 100.

45. Interview with Manna Jo Greene, confirmed by Lisa Petagumskum, January 22, 2012, via Facebook.

46. Sams and Carson, *Medicine Cards*, 121.

PART 3. MENTORS AND MESSENGERS

1. E-mailed letter from Kenneth Cohen, January 13, 2010.

2. Telephone interview with Bente Hansen, July, 2010, finalized March 14, 2012.

3. Conversation with Elaine Henwood, Manhattan, July 2010; interview, February 10, finalized, March 13, 2012.

4. Told to me by Fred Gassler, close friend of the late Ed Loos, May 29, 2010.

5. Conversation with Kevin Deer, Kanatsiohareke Strawberry Festival, June 30, 2012, and subsequent e-mails and phone conversations, finalized on August 13, 2012.

6. Based on telephone conversations with Ken Gale and Valeria Kondratiev, March 12, 2012.

7. Telephone conversation with Barbel Haynes, December 2010.

8. Zoey Wood-Salomon, printed promotional material.

9. Telephone conversation with Kenneth Cohen, January 14, 2010.

10. Cohen, *Honoring the Medicine*, 85.

11. Telephone conversation with Eddy Stevenson, January 15, 2010.

12. William Commanda told me this story himself a half-dozen times; see also Thumbadoo, *Learning from a Kindergarten Dropout*.

13. Knapp quoted in Foreman, *Sequoyah*, 21–22.

14. Kaplan and Rogers, *Songs, Roars, and Rituals*, 70.

15. Hastings and Coffey, "Grandfather Remembers."

16. Telephone interview with Dr. Margery Coffey, January 18, 2010.

17. For more information, see Sibley, *The Sibley Guide to Bird Life and Behavior*, 36.

18. See Kroodsma, *Backyard Birdsong Guide*, digital recordings.

19. Interview with Lynn Pritchard, August 13, 2010.

20. Telephone conversation, January 15, 2010.

21. Edward Benton-Banai, *The Mishomis Book*, 58.

22. Kroodsma, *The Backyard Birdsong Guide*, 126–27.

23. See Willie, "Mystery of the Missing Migrants," 84.

24. Ibid., 83.

25. Ibid., 82.

26. Kaplan, "The Native Melodies."

27. Johnson, *Mrs. Perley's People*, 40–41.

28. Ibid., 50.

29. Tanner, *The Falcon*, 306.

30. Michael Gillen per e-mail August 26, 2010.

31. Utley, *The Lance and the Shield*, 30.

32. Ibid.

33. Ibid.

34. Ibid., 29.

35. Ibid.

36. Ibid.

37. Kinietz, *Indians of the Western Great Lakes, 1615–1760*, 129.

38. Ibid., 132.

39. Ibid., 251.

40. Interview with Lynn Pritchard, August 13, 2010.

41. Pritchard, "Magpies with a Message."

42. Telephone interview with Monique Renaud, August 28, 2010.

43. Oannes Pritzker interviewed January 3, 2010, shortly before he passed into the spirit world.

44. Latorre and Latorre, *The Mexican Kickapoo Indians*, 347.

45. Telephone conversation with White Deer of Autumn (Gabriel Horn), January 3, 2010.

46. According to former Sand Hill Band chief Sam Beeler, via telephone call with Cora Chandler, May 2010.

47. Steiger and Hansen, *Mysteries of Animal Intelligence*, 38.

48. Ibid., 56.

49. Ibid., 41.

50. Ibid.

51. Kaplan and Rogers, *Songs, Roars, and Rituals*, 192.

52. Clark et al., "Increasing Breeding Behaviors in a Captive Colony of Northern Bald Ibis Through Conspecific Acoustic Enrichment."

53. Interview with "Brenda," May 2010; finalized March 31, 2012.

54. Kaplan and Rogers, *Songs, Roars, and Rituals*, 19–20.

55. Swanton, *The Indians of the Southeastern United States*, 703.

56. Interview with L., Charbot Lake, Ontario, pointing to pairs of duck boxes while standing with me in a wetlands area.

57. Conversations with George Paul, Mi'kmaq storyteller, various occasions.

58. Swanton, *The Indians of the Southeastern United States*, 707.

59. Kaplan and Rogers, *Songs, Roars, and Rituals*, 19–20.

60. Rowland, *Birds with Human Souls*, xv.

61. Swanton, *The Indians of the Southeastern United States*, 702.

62. Pritchard, *Introductory Guide to Micmac Indian Words and Phrases*, 11.

63. Ibid., 10.

64. Andrews, *Animal-Speak*, 207.

65. Interview with Eddy Stevenson, March 8, 2010.

66. Sams and Carson, *Medicine Cards*, 173.

67. Johnson, *Mrs. Perley's People*, 55–56.

68. Ibid., 62.

69. Conversation, July 2010; subsequent e-mail August 12, 2012.

70. Kaplan and Rogers, *Songs, Roars, and Rituals*, 85.

71. Interview with Featherhawk, Middletown, New York, December 4, 2010.

72. This information provided by Dr. Michael Gillen, Pace University, October 20, 2010.

73. Telephone conversation with Depsimana, July 20, 2010.

74. Interview Thom residence, Bloomington, Indiana, June 18–19, 2010.

75. Johnson, *Mrs. Perley's People*, 63.

76. Pritchard, *No Word for Time*, 24–25.

77. Rowland, *Birds with Human Souls*, 33.

78. Ibid., 31.

79. Ibid., 31–32.

80. Burton, *Moving Within the Circle*, 103.

81. Interview with Raymundo Rodriguez, January 18, 2010.

PART 4. OTHER BIRD ALLIES

1. Sams and Carson, *Medicine Cards*, 213.

2. Ibid.

3. Telephone interview with Blessing Bird, April 2010.

4. Letter from Running Deer, March 8, 2012.

5. Latorre and Latorre, *The Mexican Kickapoo Indians*, 348.

6. Eliade, *Shamanism*, 132–33.

7. Ibid., 132–35.

8. Based on interview with Raymundo Rodriguez, January 18, 2010.

9. Sibley, *The Sibley Guide to Bird Life and Behavior*, 36.

10. Kaplan and Rogers, *Songs, Roars, and Rituals*, 17.

11. Ibid., 56.

12. Interview with anonymous Mohawk source, Ontario, 2010.

13. Kaplan and Rogers, *Songs, Roars, and Rituals*, 23.

14. Wallace, *Indians in Pennsylvania*, 83.

15. Kaplan and Rogers, *Songs, Roars, and Rituals*, 11–12, 76–77.

16. Menomini informant quoted in Spindler and Spindler, *Dreamers without Power*, 40–41.

17. Skinner quoted in Spindler and Spindler, *Dreamers without Power*, 41.

18. Spindler and Spindler, *Dreamers without Power*, 12.

19. Ibid., 12–13.

PART 5. FLEDGLING THOUGHTS

1. La Potherie quoted in Kinietz, *Indians of the Western Great Lakes, 1615–1760*, 193.

2. Gist quoted in Kinietz, *Indians of the Western Great Lakes, 1615–1760*, 196.

3. Speck quoted in Latorre and Latorre, *The Mexican Kickapoo Indians*, 574.

4. Ibid., 251, 442.

5. Ibid., 251.

6. Ibid.

7. Ibid., 253.

8. Kaplan and Rogers, *Songs, Roars, and Rituals*, 71.

9. Confirmed by John Fadden, per e-mail, April, 9, 2012.

10. Diliette quoted in Kinietz, *Indians of the Western Great Lakes, 1615–1760*, 197.

11. Ibid.

12. Ibid., 198–99.

13. Ibid., 213.

14. Latorre and Latorre, *The Mexican Kickapoo Indians,* 270–71.

15. Ibid., 337.

16. Fletcher and La Flesche, *Omaha Nation.*

17. Benedict, *Tales of the Cochiti Indians,* 24–25.

PART 6. THREATS TO OUR BIRD ALLIES

1. Pritchard, *Henry Hudson and the Algonquins of New York,* 185–86.

2. Interview with "David," a Sand Hill Band member and elder and medicine man of Cherokee descent, around Christmas of 2008, by Robin Hill-Chandler, a Sand Hill member of Munsee descent.

3. Alsop, *Birds of the Mid-Atlantic,* 38.

4. A confirmed source close to former Munseetown Delaware chief Mark Peters.

5. Alsop, *Birds of the Mid-Atlantic,* 38.

6. *Encyclopedia Britannica,* vol. 17 (1960 edition): 920–21.

7. Alsop, *Birds of the Mid-Atlantic,* 38.

8. *Encyclopedia Britannica,* vol. 17 (1960 edition): 920–21.

9. Alsop, *Birds of the Mid-Atlantic,* 38.

10. Telephone conversation with Ahngwet, January 11, 2010.

11. Bergman, "Wildlife Trafficking," 37.

12. Ibid., 40.

13. Ibid.

14. Robbins et al., "Population Declines in North American Birds That Migrate to the Neotropics." See also Faaborg et al., "Recent Advances in Understanding Migration Systems of New World Land Birds" and Mickleburgh, Hutson, and Racey, "A Review of the Global Conservation Status of Bats."

15. Drewitt and Langston, "Collision Effects of Wind-Power Generators and Other Obstacles on Birds." See also Kunz et al., "Assessing Impacts of Wind-Energy Development on Nocturnally Active Birds and Bats."

16. Both et al., "Avian Population Consequences of Climate Change Are Most Severe for Long-distance Migrants in Seasonal Habitats." See also Saino et al., "Climate Warming, Ecological Mismatch at Arrival and Population Decline in Migratory Birds."

17. Deda, Elbertzhagen, and Klussmann, "Light Pollution and the Impacts on Biodiversity, Species and Their Habitats."

18. Evans-Ogden, *Collision Course.*

19. Gehring, Paul, and Albert, "Communication Towers, Lights, and Birds." See also Holker et al., "Light Pollution as a Biodiversity Threat"; Longcore and Rich, "Ecological Light Pollution"; and Kempernaers et al., "Artificial Night Lighting Affects Dawn Song, Extra-Pair Siring Success, and Lay Date in Songbirds."

20. Evans-Ogden, "Summary Report on the Bird Friendly Building Program." See also, J. Alan Clark slide show based on Evans-Ogden report and conversation with C. Sheppard.

21. See Barber, Crooks, and Fristrup, "The Costs of Chronic Noise Exposure for Terrestrial Organism"; Kight and Swaddle, "How and Why Dnvironmental Noise Impacts Animals: An Integrative Mechanistic Review"; Slabbekoorn and Ripmeester, "Birdsong and Anthropogenic Noise"; Francis, Ortega, and Cruz, "Noise Pollution Changes Avian Communities and Species Interactions"; Halfwerk et al., "Low-Frequency Songs Lose Their Potency in Noisy Urban Conditions"; and Farnsworth, "Flight Calls and Their Value for Future Ornithological Studies and Conservation Research."

22. Telephone conversation with Manitou Ikwe, firsthand report, August 15, 2012.

23. Interview with Lynn Pritchard, August 13, 2010.

24. Raftery, "Agencies Plan to Reduce Canada Geese Population by Two-Thirds."

25. Ibid.

26. Ibid.

27. www.fidobrooklyn.org/geese.html (accessed June 23, 2012) and finalized via phone conversation with Chiappelloni, August 13, 2012.

28. Driscoll, "Audubon Oil Spill Response Team Update: Thoughts on the Release of Young Rehabbed Pelicans," August 13, 2010.

29. Ibid.

30. Driscoll, "My Capitol Hill Briefing on the Second Anniversary of the Gulf Oil Spill," April 20, 2012.

31. Ibid.

32. *BirdWatching*, "BP Oil Found in Minnesota Pelican Eggs."

33. Driscoll, "Audubon Oil Spill Response Team Update: Awaiting Tropical Storm Bonnie," July 23, 2010.

34. Driscoll, "My Capitol Hill Briefing on the Second Anniversary of the Gulf Oil Spill," April 20, 2012.

35. Telephone interview with Joseph Bruchac, January 3, 2010.

36. Ibid.

37. Balmori, "Possible Effects of Electromagnetic Fields from Phone Masts on a Population of White Stork (*Ciconia ciconia*)."

38. Ibid., 113.

39. Ibid.

40. Ibid., 115.

41. Ibid.

42. Beason and Semm, "Responses of Neurons to an Amplitude Modulated Microwave Stimulus."

43. Ritz et al., "Resonance Effects Indicate a Radical-Pair Mechanism for Avian Magnetic Compass."

44. Balmori, "The Effects of Microwave Radiation on the Wildlife: Preliminary Results."

45. Ibid.

46. Kelbie quoted in ibid.

AFTERWORD

1. Edward, *Wales*, 289.

2. Utley, *The Lance and the Shield*, 30.

BIBLIOGRAPHY

ABC Action News. "Oil Spill May Effect Entire Generation of Brown Pelican." June 4, 2010.

Alsop, Fred J. III. *Birds of the Mid-Atlantic.* Washington, D.C.: Smithsonian Handbook, 2002.

Andrews, Ted. *Animal-Speak: The Spiritual and Magical Powers of Creatures Great and Small.* St. Paul, Minn.: Llewellyn Publications, 1993.

Balmori, Alfonso. "The Effects of Microwave Radiation on the Wildlife: Preliminary Results." Paper. "The Balmori Reports." February 2003.

——. "Possible Effects of Electromagnetic Fields from Phone Masts on a Population of White Stork." *Electromagnetic Biology and Medicine* 24 (2005): 109–19.

Barber, J. R., K. R. Crooks, and K. M. Fristrup. "The Costs of Chronic Noise Exposure for Terrestrial Organisms." *Trends in Ecology and Evolution* 25, no. 3 (2009): 180–89.

Beason, Robert C., and Peter Semm. "Responses of Neurons to an Amplitude Modulated Microwave Stimulus." *Neuroscience Letters* 333 (2002): 175–78.

Benedict, Ruth. *Tales of the Cochiti Indians.* D.C.: Bureau of American Ethnology, 1932.

Benton-Banai, Edward. *The Mishomis Book.* Hayward, Wis.: Indian Country Communications, 1988.

Bergman, Charles. "Wildlife Trafficking." *Smithsonian,* December 2009.

BirdWatching. "BP Oil Found in Minnesota Pelican Eggs: Oil, Dispersant Confirmed in Largest Colonies of American White Pelican." October 26, 2012. www.birdwatchingdaily.com.

Both, Christiaan, et al. "Avian Population Consequences of Climate Change Are Most Severe for Long-Distance Migrants in Seasonal Habitats." *Proceedings of the Royal Society B* 277 (2010): 1259–66.

"Broken Mammoth Archaeology Project." Office of History and Archaeology, Alaska Department of Natural Resources, Division of Parks and Outdoor Recreation. http://dnr.alaska.gov/parks/oha/mammoth/mammoth6.htm (accessed April 5, 2012).

Brown, Nathan. "Distress Call Not Keeping Crows Away: Middletown Looking at Different Control Options." Middletown *Times Herald-Record,* February 29, 2012.

Bruchac, Joseph. *The Native American Sweat Lodge: History and Legends.* Freedom, Caif.: Crossing Press, 1993.

———. *Rachel Carson: Preserving a Sense of Wonder.* Illustrated by Thomas Locker. Golden, Colo.: Fulcrum, 2004.

———. *The Wind Eagle and Other Abenaki Stories.* Greenfield, N.Y.: Greenfield Review Press, 1985.

Burton, Bryan. *Moving Within the Circle.* Wauwatosa, Wis.: Plank Road Publishing, 2009.

Cadutto, Michael J., and Joseph Bruchac. *Keepers of the Earth: Native American Stories and Environmental Activities for Children.* Golden, Colo.: Fulcrum, 1997.

Carter, Forrest. *The Education of Little Tree.* Albuquerque: University of New Mexico Press, 1976.

Castaneda, Carlos. *The Eagle's Gift.* New York: Ballantine Books, 1981.

Clark, J. A., et al. "Increasing Breeding Behaviors in a Captive Colony of Northern Bald Ibis Through Conspecific Acoustic Enrichment." *Zoo Biology* 30 (August 2, 2011): 1–11.

Cohen, Kenneth. *Honoring the Medicine: The Essential Guide to Native American Healing.* New York: Ballantine Books, 2003.

Crowley, Therese. "Turtle and BP: Brown Pelican." *The Alternative Press,* August 28, 2010. http://thealternativepress.com/articles/turtle-and-bp-brown-pelican.

Deda, P. I. Elbertzhagen, and M. Klussmann, "Light Pollution and the Impacts on Biodiversity, Species and Their Habitats." In *Starlight: A Common Heritage,* 133–39. Edited by C. Marin and J. Jafari. International

Conference in the Defence of the Quality of the Night Sky and the Right to Observe the Stars, April 19–20, 2007. Starlight Initiative, Instituto de Astrofisica de Canarias. La Palma, Spain: Unesco, 2007.

Densmore, Frances. *Teton Sioux Music*. New York: Da Capo Press, 1972. First published Bureau of American Ethnology, Bulletin 61. 1918. Washington, D.C.: Goverment Printing Office, 1918.

Drewitt, A. L., and R. H. W. Langston. "Collision Effects of Wind-Power Generators and Other Obstacles on Birds." *Annals of the New York Academy of Sciences* 1134 (2008): 233–66.

Driscoll, Melanie. "Audubon Oil Spill Response Team Update: Awaiting Tropical Storm Bonnie." July 23, 2010. http://magblog.audubon.org/audubon-oil-spill-response-team-update-awaiting-tropical-storm-bonnie.

———. "Audubon Oil Spill Response Team Update: Thoughts on the Release of Young Rehabbed Pelicans." August 13, 2010. http://magblog.audubon.org/audubon-oil-spill-response-team-update-thoughts-release-young-rehabbed-pelicans.

———. "My Capitol Hill Briefing on the Second Anniversary of the Gulf Oil Spill." April 20, 2012. http://magblog.audubon.org/my-capitol-hill-briefing-second-anniversary-gulf-oil-spill.

Edward, Owen Morgan. *Wales*. New York/London: C. P. Putnam's Sons/T. Fisher Unwin, 1902.

Eliade, Mircea. *Shamanism: Archaic Techniques of Ecstasy*. Bollingen Series LXXVI. Translated from the French by Willard R. Trask. Princeton, N.J.: Princeton University Press, 1964. First published as *Le Chamanisme et les techniques archaiques de l'extase*. Paris: Librairie Payot, 1951.

Emerson, Ellen Russell. *Indian Myths: Or Legends, Traditions, and Symbols of the Aborigines of America, Compared with Those of Other Countries, including Hindostan, Egypt, Persia, Assyria, and China*. Minneapolis: Ross & Haines, 1965. First published Boston: James R. Osgood and Company, 1884.

Evans-Ogden, Lesley J. *Collision Course: The Hazards of Lighted Structures and Windows to Migrating Birds*. Lincoln: University of Nebraska Press, 1996.

———. "Summary Report on the Bird Friendly Building Program: Effect of Light Reduction on Collision of Migratory Birds." Special Report for the Fatal Light Awareness Program, Toronto, Canada, 2002.

Faaborg, John et al. "Recent Advances in Understanding Migration Systems of New World Land Birds." *Ecological Monographs* 80, no. 1 (2010): 3–48.

Farnsworth, A. "Flight Calls and Their Value for Future Ornithological Studies and Conservation Research." *Auk* 122 (2005): 733–46.

Fletcher, Alice C., and Francis La Flesche. *Omaha Nation*. 2 vols. Lincoln: University of Nebraska Press, 1992. First published Twenty-Seventh Annual Report of the Bureau of American Ethnology to the Secretary of the Smithsonian Institution, 1905–1906. Washington, D.C.: Bureau of American Ethnology, 1911.

Forde, Cyril Daryll. *Ethnography of the Yuma Indians*. Berkeley: University of California Press, 1931.

Foreman, Grant. *Sequoyah*. Norman: University of Oklahoma Press, 1938.

Francis, C. D., C. P. Ortega, and A. Cruz. "Noise Pollution Changes Avian Communities and Species Interactions." *Current Biology* 19 (2009): 1415–19.

Gehring, J., K. Paul, and M. M. Albert. "Communication Towers, Lights, and Birds: Successful Methods of Reducing the Frequency of Avian Collisions." *Ecological Applications* 19 (209): 505–14 (2009).

Gist, Christopher. "Colonel Christopher Gist's Journal of a Tour through Ohio and Kentucky in 1751." With notes and sketch by J. Stoddard Johnson. *Filson Club Publications*, no. 13. Louisville, Ky.: J. P. Morton and Company, 1898.

Halfwerk, W. et al. "Low-Frequency Songs Lose Their Potency in Noisy Urban Conditions." *Proceedings of the National Academy of Sciences* 108, no. 35 (2011): 14549–54.

Hastings, Dennis, and Margery Coffey. "Grandfather Remembers—Broken Treaties/Stolen Land: The Omaha Land Theft." Ph.D. diss., 2009.

Heinrich, Bernd. *Ravens in Winter*. New York: Summit Books, 1989.

Heckewelder, John Gottlieb Ernestus. *History, Manners, and Customs of the Indian Nations*. Philadelphia: The Historical Society of Pennsylvania, 1876.

Higheagle, Robert P. "Twenty-five Songs Made by Sitting Bull." In *Teton Sioux Music* by Frances Densmore. Smithsonian Institution Bureau of American Ethnology, Bulletin 61. Washington, D.C.: Government Printing Office, 1918, 157–172.

Holker, F., C. Wolter, E. K. Perkin, and K. Tockner. "Light Pollution as a Biodiversity Threat." *Trends in Ecology & Evolution* 25 (2010): 681–82.

Holmes, Charles E. "The Beringian and Transitional Periods in Alaska: Technology of the East Beringian Tradition as Viewed from Swan Point." In *From the Yenisei to the Yukon: Interpreting Lithic Assemblage Variability in Late Pleistocene/Early Holocene Beringia,* 179–91. Edited by Ted Goebel and Ian Buvit. College Station, Tex.: Texas A & M University Press, 2011.

Johnson, Eleanor Noyes. *Mrs. Perley's People.* Illustrated by Robert L. Jefferson. Philadelphia: Westminster Press, 1970.

Kacelnik, Alex, Alex A. S. Weir, and Jackie Campbell. "Shaping of Hooks in New Caledonian Crows." *Science* 297 (August 9, 2002), 981.

Kaplan, Gisela. "The Native Melodies." *The Australian News,* March 6, 2008. http://blogs.theaustralian.news.com.au/giselakaplanblog (accessed July 27, 2010).

Kaplan, Gisela, and Lesley J. Rogers. *Songs, Roars, and Rituals: Communication in Birds, Mammals, and Other Animals.* Cambridge: Harvard University Press, 2000.

Kempernaers, B., et al. "Artificial Night Lighting Affects Dawn Song, Extra-Pair Siring Success, and Lay Date in Songbirds." *Current Biology* 20 (2010): 1735–39.

Kight, C. R., and J. P. Swaddle. "How and Why Environmental Noise Impacts Animals: An Integrative Mechanistic Review." *Ecology Letters* 14 (2011) 1052–61.

Kimmerer, Robin Wall. *Gathering Moss: A Natural and Cultural History of Mosses.* Corvallis: Oregon State University, 2003.

Kinietz, W. Vernon. *Indians of the Western Great Lakes, 1615–1760.* Ann Arbor: University of Michigan Press, 1965.

Kroeber, Alfred Louis. *Handbook of the Indians of California.* Washington, D.C.: Government Printing Office, 1925.

Kroodsma, Donald. *The Backyard Birdsong Guide: A Guide to Listening.* San Francisco: Chronicle Books, 2008.

Kunz, Thomas H. et al. "Assessing Impacts of Wind-Energy Development on Nocturnally Active Birds and Bats: A Guidance Document." *The Journal of Wildlife Management* 71, no. 8 (2007): 2449–86.

Larsen, Stephen. *Shaman's Doorway: Opening the Mythic Imagination to Contemporary Consciousness.* Rochester, Vt.: Inner Traditions, 1998.

Latorre, Felipe A., and Dolores L. Latorre. *The Mexican Kickapoo Indians.* Mineola, N.Y.: Dover, 1991. First published Austin: University of Texas Press, 1976.

Longcore, T., and C. Rich. "Ecological Light Pollution." *Frontiers in Ecology and the Environment* 2 (2004): 191–98.

Lorenz, Konrad. *Here Am I—Where are You? The Behavior of the Greylag Goose.* New York: Harcourt, 1991.

Lossing, Benson. *The Hudson: From the Wilderness to the Sea.* Troy, N.Y.: H. B. Nims, 1861.

Mails, Thomas, Dan Evehema, and Katherine Cheshire. *Hote Villa: Hopi Shrine of the Covenant; Microcosm of the World.* New York: Marlowe & Co., 1995.

Michael, Henry N., ed. *Studies in Siberian Shamanism (Arctic Institute of North America Anthropology of the North: Translations from Russian Sources / No. 4).* Toronto: University of Toronto Press, 1963.

Mickleburgh, S. P., A. M. Hutson, and P. A. Racey. "A Review of the Global Conservation Status of Bats." *Oryx* 36 (2002): 18–34.

Oppenheimer, Dr. Stephen. *Eden in the East: The Drowned Continent of Southeast Asia.* London: Phoenix Press, 1999.

Norell, Mark. "The Proof Is in the Plumage." *Natural History Magazine* 110, no. 6 (July/August 2001), 58.

Potter, Ben A., et al. "A Terminal Pleistocene Child Cremation and Residential Structure from Eastern Beringia." *Science* 331 (6020): 1058–62. Supplementary online material: 1–14.

Powell, Peter J. *The Cheyennes, Ma'heo'o's People: A Critical Bibliography.* Bloomington: Indiana University Press, 1980.

Pouyanne, Valerie. *Good Enough for Two! L'art de faire un canot par William Commanda.* DVD. L'Oeil Fou, Inc. 2005. www.loeilfou.ca.

Pritchard, Evan T. *Aunt Helen's Little Herb Book.* Salt Point, N.Y.: Resonance Communications, 1994.

———. *Henry Hudson and the Algonquins of New York: Native American Prophecy and European Discovery, 1609.* Oakland, Calif.: Council Oak Books, 2009.

———. *Introductory Guide to Micmac Indian Words and Phrases.* Beacon, N.Y.: Resonance Communications, 1991.

———. "Magpies with a Message." *Resonance Magazine: A Journal of Art, Music and Ideas* 3, no. 3 (1992), 33.

———. *Native American Stories of the Sacred.* Woodstock, Vt.: Skylight Paths Publishing, 2005.

———. *Native New Yorkers: The Legacy of the Algonquin People of New York.* San Francisco: Council Oak Books, 2002.

———. *No Word for Time: The Way of the Algonquin People.* 2nd edition. San Francisco: Council Oak Books, 2001.

Raftery, Isolde. "Agencies Plan to Reduce Canada Geese Population by Two-Thirds." *New York Times,* July 23, 2010.

Ritz, Thorsten, et al. "Resonance Effects Indicate a Radical-Pair Mechanism for Avian Magnetic Compass." *Nature* 429 (May 13, 2004): 177–80.

Robbins, J. S., et al. "Population Declines in North American Birds That Migrate to the Neotropics." *Proceedings of the National Academy of Sciences* 86 (1989): 7658–62.

Rowland, Beryl. *Birds with Human Souls: A Guide to Bird Symbolism.* Knoxville: University of Tennessee Press, 1978.

Saino, Nicola, et al. "Climate Warming, Ecological Mismatch at Arrival and Population Decline in Migratory Birds." *Proceedings of the Royal Society B* 278 (2011): 835–42.

Sams, Jamie, and David Carson. *Medicine Cards: The Discovery of Power Through the Ways of Animals.* Illustrations by Angela C. Werneke. Santa Fe, N.M.: Bear and Co., 1988.

Sibley, David. *The Sibley Guide to Bird Life and Behavior.* New York: Alfred A. Knopf/Chanticleer Press, 2001.

Skinner, Alanson. "Material Culture of the Menominee." New York Museum of the American Indian, Heye Foundation. *Indian Notes and Monographs* 4 (1921): 30.

Slabbekoorn, H., and E. A. P. Ripmeester. "Birdsong and Anthropogenic Noise: Implications and Applications for Conservation." *Molecular Ecology* 17 (2008): 72–83.

Slotkin, James. "The Menominee Powwow: A Study in Cultural Decay." *Anthropology* 27, no. 4 (1957).

Smith, John. *Works, 1608–1631.* Edited by Edward Arber. English Scholar's Library No. 16. Birmingham, England: 1884.

Spindler, George, and Louise Spindler. *Dreamers without Power: The Menominee.* Prospect Heights, Ill.: Waveland Press, 1971.

Steiger, Brad, and Sherry Hansen. *Mysteries of Animal Intelligence: True Stories of Animals with Amazing Abilities.* New York: Tor Books, 2007.

Swamp, Chief Jake (Tekaronianekon), et al. *Thanksgiving Address: Greetings to the Natural World (Words Before All Else).* Corrales, N. Mex.: Tree of Peace Society/Six Nations Indian Museum and The Tracking Project, 1993. Mohawk by Dan Thompson. English by David Benedict, John Stokes; Available online at www.nativevillage.org/Inspiration-/iroquois_thanksgiving_address.htm.

Swamp, Chief Jake, and Erwin Printup, Jr. *Giving Thanks: A Native American Good Morning Message.* New York: Lee & Low Books, 1997.

Swanton, John R. *The Indians of the Southeastern United States.* New York: Greenwood Press, 1969. First published as *Bureau of American Ethnology Bulletin 137.* Washington, D.C.: Smithsonian Institution, 1946.

Tanner, John. *The Falcon: A Narrative of the Captivity and Adventures of John Tanner.* Introduction by Louise Erdrich. New York: Penguin, 1994. First published New York: G. & C. & H. Carvill, 1830. Original subtitle was "U.S. Interpreter at the Saut-de-Ste. Marie during thirty years residence among the Indians of the North American Interior."

Thom, Dark Rain. *The Shawnee: Kokhumthena's Grandchildren.* Carmel: Guild Press of Indiana, 2001.

Thom, James Alexander, and Dark Rain Thom. *Warrior Women: The Exceptional Life Story of Nonhelema, Shawnee Indian Woman Chief.* New York: Balantine, 2003.

Thumbadoo, Romola Vasantha. *Learning from a Kindergarten Dropout: A Reflection on Elder William Commanda.* Kanata, Ontario: Circle of All Nations, 2010.

Two Bulls. "Sitting Bull's Kindness to Birds." Manuscript. Box 104, folder 20, Campbell Collection.

Utley, Robert M. *The Lance and the Shield: The Life and Times of Sitting Bull.* New York: Ballantine Books, 1993.

Wallace, Paul A. *Indians in Pennsylvania*. 2nd edition. Harrisburg: Pennsylvania Historical and Museum Commission, 2005.

Williams, Ted. "Restoring Owls and Other Biological Boondoggles." *Audubon Magazine,* May 1990.

Willie, Chris. "Mystery of the Missing Migrants." *Audubon Magazine* 92, no. 3 (May 1990): 80–85.

Wissler, Clark. "Societies and Ceremonial Associations in the Oglala Division of the Teton-Dakota." In *Societies of the Plains Indians,* vol 11. The American Museum of Natural History. Edited by Clark Wissler. New York: The Trustees, 1916.

Wittenberg Center for Alternative Resources. "Cry of the Earth Conference: The Legacy of the First Nations." Proceedings of the 1993 United Nations Conference.

Young, Jeff. "Gulf Oil Damage." Segment of *Living on Earth.* Hosted by Steve Curwood. Boston: National Public Radio, air date May 21, 2010. www.loe.org/shows/segments (accessed November 9, 2012).

Youngblood, Robin Tekwelus, and Sandy D'entrement. *Path of the White Wolf: An Introduction to the Shamans's Way.* Ardenvoir, Wash.: Phoenix Publications. 2007.

INDEX

Page numbers in *italics* refer to images.